Samuel Beckett and the Arts

Samuel Beckett and the Arts

Italian Negotiations

Edited by
Davide Crosara and Mario Martino

ANTHEM PRESS

Anthem Press
An imprint of Wimbledon Publishing Company
www.anthempress.com

This edition first published in UK and USA 2024
by ANTHEM PRESS
75–76 Blackfriars Road, London SE1 8HA, UK
or PO Box 9779, London SW19 7ZG, UK
and
244 Madison Ave #116, New York, NY 10016, USA

© 2024 Davide Crosara and Mario Martino editorial matter and selection;
individual chapters © individual contributors

The moral right of the authors has been asserted.

All rights reserved. Without limiting the rights under copyright reserved above,
no part of this publication may be reproduced, stored or introduced into
a retrieval system, or transmitted, in any form or by any means
(electronic, mechanical, photocopying, recording or otherwise),
without the prior written permission of both the copyright
owner and the above publisher of this book.

British Library Cataloguing-in-Publication Data
A catalogue record for this book is available from the British Library.

Library of Congress Cataloging-in-Publication Data
A catalog record for this book has been requested.
2024930958

ISBN-13: 978-1-83998-966-7 (Hbk)
ISBN-10: 1-83998-966-1 (Hbk)

Cover Courtesy Archivio Gastone Novelli

This title is also available as an e-book.

CONTENTS

Notes on Contributors   vii

Introduction   1
Davide Crosara

Part One.   **VISUAL ENCOUNTERS**

Chapter 1.   'The Pantheon at Rome or Certain Beehive Tombs':
Beckett's Posthumous Architecture   11
Mark Byron

Chapter 2.   Some Notes on Beckett and Michelangelo   31
Mariacristina Cavecchi

Chapter 3.   'J'ai eu L'image': Samuel Beckett and Gastone Novelli   51
Davide Crosara

Part Two.   **RADIO AND OPERA**

Chapter 4.   Beckett's *Neither*, an 'Anti-Opera' in Rome   73
Yuri Chung

Chapter 5.   From *Inferno* to Sorrento: Dante, Wartime Radio
and the Italia Prize   91
Pim Verhulst

Part Three.   **POETIC VOICES**

Chapter 6.   Beckett the Troubadour   115
Mario Martino

Chapter 7.   The Empty House: *Watt's* Leopardian Traces   129
William Davies

Part Four.	**ECHOES. TRANSLATIONS, REVERBERATIONS**	
Chapter 8.	Beckett Resonating in Italy: Which Text, Whose Voice? *Rossana Sebellin*	145
Chapter 9.	Beckett after Language *Mena Mitrano*	165

NOTES ON CONTRIBUTORS

Mark Byron is Professor of Modern Literature at the University of Sydney. He is the author of *Ezra Pound's Eriugena* (London: Bloomsbury, 2014) and *Samuel Beckett's Geological Imagination* (Cambridge University Press, 2020), and with Sophia Barnes, *Ezra Pound's and Olga Rudge's The Blue Spill: A Manuscript Critical Edition* (London: Bloomsbury, 2019). Mark is the co-editor with Stefano Rosignoli of the dossier 'Samuel Beckett and the Middle Ages', in the *Journal of Beckett Studies* 25.1 (2016) and is the editor of the essay collection *The New Ezra Pound Studies* (Cambridge University Press, 2019). He is President of the Ezra Pound Society.

Mariacristina Cavecchi is currently Associate Professor in the Department of Languages, Literatures, Cultures and Mediation at the University of Milan, where she teaches History of British Drama and English Literature at graduate level. Her research interests include twentieth- and twenty-first century British drama and theatre, with a particular focus on visual/verbal intersections. She has also written extensively on contemporary appropriations of Shakespeare's plays for theatre and cinema (stage productions, adaptations, rewrites), Shakespeare in contemporary popular culture and Prison Shakespeare. She is the author of *The Art Gallery on Stage. New Vistas on Contemporary British Theatre* (2024), *Cerchi e cicli. Sulle forme della memoria in Ulisse* (2012), *Percorsi nel teatro inglese dell'Ottocento e del primo Novecento* (2012) and *Shakespeare mostro contemporaneo* (1998). She also co-edited *SceKspir al Bekka. Romeo Montecchi dietro le sbarre dell'Istituto Penale Minorile Beccaria* (2020) and *ExpoShakespeare. Il Sommo Gourmet, il cibo e i cannibali* (2016).

Davide Crosara is Adjunct Professor of English at 'Sapienza' Università di Roma. His main fields of interest are Modernism, Romanticism and Beckett Studies. He has published books and essays on Samuel Beckett and Romantic closet drama (*Il buco nel cielo di carta*, 2019), on the relationship between Beckett and Primo Levi (in *Innesti. Primo Levi e i libri altrui*, Peter Lang, 2020) and on the works of other modernist writers (W. B. Yeats and James Joyce). He has also written essays on 'nothingness' in *King Lear* (2009), on writing and history in *Twelfth Night* (2021) and (with Gianluca Cinelli) on plague narratives in Manzoni and Defoe (2022). An essay on late Modernism in *Happy Days* has recently appeared in the Journal *Studium* (2023). He is currently co-editing Samuel Beckett's Italian Modernisms: Tradition, Texts, Performance, Routledge (Due: 2024).

Yuri Chung obtained his PhD from the University of Rome 'La Sapienza' in 2020 writing a dissertation on Modernism and its effects on the libretto. Previously, in his university career, he wrote a thesis in his three-year degree on the relationship between Sir Walter Scott's novel, *The Bride of Lammermoor*, and Donizetti's opera, *Lucia di Lammermoor*. In his master's degree thesis, instead, he focused on the collaboration between Stravinsky and Auden in *The Rake's Progress*. He published the following two essays: 'Napoleon e l'opera lirica' in *Letteratura e storia*, for Lithos in 2021 and 'From *The Beggar's Opera* to *The Threepenny Opera*, a Long-Standing Relationship of Text and Music' in *Marriage between Literature and Music*, for Cambridge Scholars Publishing in 2022.

Pim Verhulst is a postdoctoral researcher at the University of Oxford and a lecturer at the University of Antwerp, as well as a recent recipient of a Marie Curie Skłodowska Postdoctoral Fellowship from the EU. He has published articles in *Samuel Beckett Today/Aujourd'hui*, *Genetic Joyce Studies* and the *Journal of Beckett Studies*, among others, as well as book chapters in *Beckett and BBC Radio* (Palgrave Macmillan, 2017), *Beckett and Technology* (Edinburgh University Press, 2021), *Beckett and Media* (Manchester University Press, 2022) and the *Oxford Handbook of Samuel Beckett* (Oxford University Press, forthcoming). He is also a co-editor of *Beckett and Modernism* (Palgrave Macmillan, 2018) and *Beckett's Afterlives: Adaptation, Remediation, Appropriation* (Manchester University Press, 2023). His two most recent monographs, *The Making of Samuel Beckett's Radio Plays* and *The Making of Samuel Beckett's Television Plays*, are scheduled to appear in the Beckett Digital Manuscript Project series, of which he is an editorial board member.

Mario Martino, after graduating in Rome, obtained his PhD from Florence University in 1994. He is Full Professor of English Literature at La Sapienza, University of Rome. He has previously taught at the Universities of Sheffield and Reading (Great Britain), Messina and Florence. Besides essays on the Elizabethan and seventeenth-century lyric, on the novel and narrative forms of the nineteenth century, and on twentieth century literature, he has published *Il problema del tempo nei sonetti di Shakespeare*, 1984, *Dickens e la crisi della scrittura*, 1996 and *Beckett e il romanzo modernista: Murphy*, 2003. He has translated into Italian *Hard Times* (2004) and *Oliver Twist* (2005), and has edited *Great Expectations*

(1998) and *David Copperfield* (2004). He has also published *Oliver Twist e il cinema* (Palermo 2011) and co-edited *Letteratura e cinema* (Roma 2013), *Visualità e scrittura* (Roma 2017) and *Letteratura e storia* (Roma 2020). He is the director of the series 'Lo Scudo di Achille' (Lithos). Forthcoming book publications include *Samuel Beckett's Italian Modernisms: Tradition, Texts, Performance*, Routledge (coedited. Due: 2024) and *Literature and Science, 1922–2022: Modernist and Postmodernist Perspectives* (co-edited), 2024.

William Davies is a writer and literary critic. His books on Samuel Beckett include *Samuel Beckett and the Second World War* (Bloomsbury, 2020) and *Samuel Beckett's Poetry* (Cambridge University Press, 2022, edited with James Brophy).

Rossana Sebellin is an associate professor in English literature at the University of Rome Tor Vergata, Department of History, Humanities and Society. She received her PhD in 2007 from the University of Urbino Carlo Bo on bilingual writing and self-translation: the case of *Play* and *Not I* by Samuel Beckett. She has published three volumes on Samuel Beckett's drama (*'Prior to Godot'. Eleutheria di Samuel Beckett*, 2006; *L'originalità doppia di Samuel Beckett*, 2008 and *Leggendo Godot*, 2012) and several articles on self-translation, translation, contemporary theatre, intertextuality and early modern drama (*Forms of Hypocrisy in Early Modern England*, Nigri and Tsentourou editors, Routledge, 2018). She has recently published the first Italian translation and critical edition of the anonymous sixteenth-century play *Thomas of Woodstock* (2024).

She is part of national and international research groups on translation (METE), self-translation and Restauration theatre (IRGORD), and a member of the Argo directive board.

Mena Mitrano is Associate Professor of 'Lingue e letterature angloamericane' in the Department of Linguistics and Comparative Cultural Studies, Ca' Foscari University of Venice. Her research interests are in theory and modernism. She explores the link in her new book, *Literary Critique, Modernism and the Transformation of Theory* (Edinburgh University Press, 2022). She is the author of books on great American women writers and thinkers: *Gertrude Stein: Woman without Qualities* (Ashgate, 2005), *In the Archive of Longing: Susan Sontag's Critical Modernism* (Edinburgh University Press, 2016) and *La critica sconfinata. Introduzione al pensiero di Susan Sontag* (Quodlibet, 2022).

INTRODUCTION

Davide Crosara

Beside this window that sometimes looks as if it were painted on the wall, like Tiepolo's ceiling at Würzburg, what a tourist I must have been, I even remember the diaresis
—Malone Dies

Samuel Beckett's interest in Italian culture dated from his juvenile years. It is well known that he graduated from Trinity College in modern languages (French and Italian) and that he took private lessons from his language tutor, Dr Bianca Esposito, a figure who nurtured his interest in Italian literature, was fictionalized as Adriana Ottolenghi in *Dante and the Lobster* and remained in his memories till the last days. The first trip to Italy took place in 1937, starting from Florence and its Renaissance heritage. While these Italian connections are by now an integral part of Beckett's biography, the way in which his early works established a strong connection between the Italian language and Italian arts has been far less noticed.[1] The most clear examples in this regard come from Beckett's early prose works, *More Pricks Than Kicks* and *Dream of Fair to Middling Women*. Belacqua Shuah, the 'hero' of *More Pricks Than Kicks*, is an eager student of Italian and a witty connoisseur of Italian art, with a specific interest in the Renaissance. He clearly acts as Beckett's mouthpiece. Walking and singing through the streets of Dublin, he ironically superimposes Florence to the Free State capital:

> For there Florence would slip into the song, the Piazza della Signoria and the No 1 tram and the Feast of St John. [...]. Then slowly in his mind down the sinister Uffizi to the parapets of Arno, and so on and so forth. This pleasure was dispensed by the Fire Station opposite which seemed to have been copied here and there from the Palazzo Vecchio. In deference to Savonarola? Ha! ha!²

---

[1] A notable exception in the field is Doireann Lalor, '"The Italianate Irishman": The Role of Italian in Beckett's Intratextual Multilingualism', *Samuel Beckett Today/Aujourd'hui* 22 (2010). Lalor explicitly pairs language and the visual arts in Beckett's Italian apprenticeship.
[2] Samuel Beckett, 'A Wet Night', in *More Pricks Than Kicks* (London: John Calder, 1993), 54–55.

Belacqua's Italian imagery vehiculates a subtle attack on Irish provincialism and on British stereotypes about Italy as an exotic, timeless museum. However, Beckett's negotiations with Italian art and language run far deeper. The creative multilingualism of his erudite, post-Joycean intellectuals draws on this imagery in order to outline a parody of modernist cosmopolitanism itself. Beckett, as stated in his *Dante… Bruno. Vico.. Joyce*, was well aware of the dangers of 'the neatness of identifications'.[3] Often presented as fictional reincarnations of Stephen Dedalus, Beckett's early characters tend to disrupt received notions of nationality, race, and origin. They also challenge the continuity between Romanticism and Modernism (the latter seen by Beckett as too often committed to a refashioning of an egotistical Grand Tour), as well as the implicitly romanticized vision of Italy.

It is therefore no surprise that Belacqua, ruminating upon an ideal site for his planned suicide, has to reject Venice: 'So the thing was arranged, the needful measures taken, the date fixed in the spring of the year and a site near selected, Venice in October having been rejected as alas impracticable'.[4] Besides the large use of parodic references, Beckett's early prose derives much of its vitality from the lexicon of Italian art. The writer and the artist share the same task: 'The difficult art of shortening, boys, temper and fresco, in oil and miniature on wood and stones and canvas, tarsia and tinted wood for stories, etching with iron and printing with copper, follow the man with the pitcher, niello, the enamel of the goldsmith and gold and damask having a high time together'.[5] The art of making stories is specifically identified with the craft of an Italian artist. Syneresis, neologisms, and portmanteau words delineate an Italianized English or anglicized Italian. The *Dream* derives 'chiarinoscurissimo' from chiaroscuro (in its turn a compound of chiaro and scuro); the sculptor Benvenuto Cellini gives birth to a verb, 'Cellineggiava'.[6] In *More Pricks Than Kicks*, the Countess of Parabimbi utters enthusiastically: 'Simply Sistine!'.[7] Beckett is, from the very beginning, a writer characterized by a strong visual dimension. This attitude will be confirmed by Beckett's later essays on painting and painters, where his search for a new form enacts a confrontation with contemporary artists such as André Masson,

---

[3] 'The danger is in the neatness of identifications'. Samuel Beckett, *Dante… Bruno. Vico.. Joyce*, in *Disjecta. Miscellaneous Writings and a Dramatic Fragment* (London: John Calder, 1993), 19.
[4] Samuel Beckett, 'Love and Lethe', in *More Pricks Than Kicks* (London: John Calder, 1993), 95–96.
[5] Samuel Beckett, *Dream of Fair to Middling Women*, ed. Eoin O'Brien (London: Faber & Faber, 2020), 78.
[6] Ibid., 122.
[7] Beckett, *More Pricks Than Kicks*, 67.

Tal Coat and the Van Velde brothers. This figurative density will expand with the advent of theatre, finally making of Beckett a stage director and at the same time, as noticed by S. E. Gontarski, an artist preoccupied with, 'like a sculptor, the aesthetic, imagistic shape of his work'.[8] This volume works in this direction, offering a specific line of investigation rarely undertaken by critical studies of the Irish author, namely the examination of Beckett as writer negotiating with Italian arts beyond the mere literary dimension. In the following pages, Beckett's achievement as a novelist and playwright is placed against the backdrop of Italian architecture, painting, sculpture, poetry, music, translation and philosophy. The volume does so by moving past the already known episodes of Beckett's biography and the immediate evidence provided by the juvenile writings mentioned above. The following articles concentrate their attention on Beckett's post-*Godot* production. It is worth noticing that, while the presence of Italy and Italian art is less evident in these mature works, the significance of the *Belpaese* is far from being diminished. The movement (which shows significant affinities with Beckett's approach to the Italian language) is akin to an underground river resurfacing at a long distance from its source. Sometimes the source is hidden, or hard to identify, but its impact on Beckett's endeavour is enormously significant. These articles help to identify the presence and role of Italian arts, and their influence on Beckett's poetry, prose, theatre and intermedial experiments. They also show how Beckett was always well aware of the role of tradition and history, and how he was directly influenced by contemporary events or precise historical circumstances. From this perspective, the title's hint at Stephen Greenblatt's seminal study[9] is not simply a homage or an easy wordplay. The following volume reads Beckett's negotiations with Italian culture as a brilliant, sometimes surprising confrontation with the general movement of history (from Roman history to romance poetry to post-war Europe) and inside this larger frame examines Beckett's dialogue with less-known Italian artists (Novelli), provides new intermedial interpretations of more prominent figures (Michelangelo, Leopardi, and Dante), examines Beckett's reconfiguration of popular genres such as opera and radio, and tests the limits of language by offering insightful meditations on translation, subjectivity and enunciation. In doing so, it highlights underexplored areas of Beckett's work. It also hints at a redefinition of Beckett's call: more than a writer or a playwright, the Irishman appears today as an artist operating across genres

---

[8] Stanley E. Gontarski, *Revisioning Beckett. Samuel Beckett's Decadent Turn* (New York: Bloomsbury, 2018), 159.

[9] See Stephen J. Greenblatt, *Shakespearean Negotiations: The Circulation of Social Energy in Renaissance England* (Oxford: Clarendon Press, 1988).

and languages. Beckett's dialogue with Italian arts entails a reconfiguration of his task: his lifelong enquiry into the limits of the word expands towards an investigation into the limits of the image, the boundaries of language and the fragile prospects offered by a poetry of the ruins. This 'Italian' dimension of Beckett expands and rekindles the unique achievement of a trans-medial and trans-lingual artist always testing the 'impossibilities' of his medium.

This Volume

The following study is divided into four parts and nine chapters. Part One (Byron, Cavecchi, Crosara) analyses Beckett's dialogue with Italy by means of visual elements (architecture, sculpture, painting). Part Two (Chung, Verholst) is centred around Beckett's operatic and radiophonic experiments in an Italian context. Part Three (Martino, Davies) evaluates the influence of Romance and Italian poetry on Beckett's work as a whole, while Part Four (Sebellin, Mitrano) re-examines Beckett's Italian connections through specific considerations on translation and the interpretative tools offered by Italian Theory.

Mark Byron investigates the presence of Roman architecture in Beckett's late prose. Roman buildings – from the Pantheon in *All Strange Away* to the Domus Aurea in *Worstward Ho* – create a 'vocabulary of earth, interment, and geological rifts'. In this context, 'literary archaeology is a feature of Beckett's writing, where etymologies, submerged references, and matters of style and technique can call up figures from the earth'. Beckett's later, more radical writing is made of rifts, tombs and sediments; this prose establishes a geological imagination in which creation and destruction act as both textual and memorial excavations. Evoking the Velabrum or the Cloaca Maxima, Beckett's porous texts make the act of reading itself a process of discovery and interment.

Mariacristina Cavecchi offers a thorough examination of Beckett's long-standing fascination with Michelangelo Buonarroti, with specific references to the latter's influence on Beckett's theatre: 'the Aretine artist may have had a profound influence on Beckett's theatre and guided the playwright in the construction of stage space'. Echoes of Giorgio Vasari's *Life of Michelangelo* can be found in Beckett's works and letters. Moreover, the two artists seem to share the same minimalist method: 'Beckett understood and appropriated in his own way that experience of sculpture, which Michelangelo himself defines as "quella che si fa per forza di levare" ("for sculpture I mean what you make by subtracting").' Cavecchi significantly extends the comparison to other artists who worked in the same direction, Giacometti and Naumann.

Part One of the volume ends with my chapter on Beckett and Gastone Novelli. The Italian painter met Beckett in Paris in 1960. Fascinated by Beckett's use of language, he collaborated with the Irishman on a planned (but never published) *livre d'artiste* derived from *Comment c'est*. Novelli conceived painting as a language and filled his paintings with graphemes. Working on Beckett's prose, 'he cuts and paste the text, stripping it of its original structure. However, the fragments he creates appear as micro-units that remain readable, even if with some difficulty'. Novelli's lithographs provide new insights into Beckett's oeuvre and contribute to illuminate issues – materiality and embodiment – which will play a pivotal role in the post-*How It Is* works.

Part Two is inaugurated by Yuri Chung's sharp examination of the sole operatic work by Beckett, *Neither*, his collaboration with the American composer Morton Feldman. *Neither* premiered on 13 May 1977 at the Teatro dell'Opera in Rome, 'an iconic operatic temple where the first representations of great operas like *Cavalleria rusticana* (1890) and *Tosca* (1900) took place'. The work was immediately identified as an 'anti-opera'. Here, 'with the exception of those sections which are sung, none of the primary requirements that characterize an opera are satisfied. *Neither* has no plot, no scenery, no costumes but solely a soprano that sings in a seemingly wordless manner'. However, Chung highlights how Beckett was well aware of the history of the genre and had an excellent musical knowledge, ranging from Mozart to Debussy and Berg. With *Neither* he creates an anti-Wagnerian work, distancing himself from that bombast, elitist tradition and offering to a puzzled Roman audience an experimental opera attuned with the most relevant modernist musical experimentations.

The chapter by Pim Verhulst investigates the Italian elements in Beckett's radio plays. Most of these works, *All That Fall* and *Rough for Radio II*, in particular, are animated by a productive 'Dantean intertextuality'. The dialogue between Animator and Stenographer in *Rough for Radio II* centred around Dante's use of past tenses in the *Comedy*, shows significant variants in the first draft of *Pochade radiophonique*. The two twin texts and their genetic history expand Beckett's meditation on temporality through Dante: 'Beckett's interest in the *Divina Commedia* is more of a linguistic kind here'. Part of a general European attempt at post-war reconciliation, *Embers*' participation in the Italia Prize in 1957 (the radio drama was awarded the RAI Prize that year, with Beckett giving a rare speech at the award ceremony) and Beckett's 'gruelling Sorrento experience' probably had a direct influence on his last play for radio, *Cascando*.

Part Three brings to the fore the role of Italy in Beckett's poetry. The chapter by Mario Martino surveys 'Beckett's lifelong interest in troubadour poetry, emphasizing how that is also related to Italy'. Since his academic years, Beckett cultivated a passionate interest in the Provençal language, an interest which merged with his juvenile love experiences and which found expression in many of his works. In this context, Martino signals Beckett's continuities and innovations in comparison with the modernist generation (Pound, Yeats, Eliot) which preceded him in the rediscovery of troubadour poetry. Walther von der Vogelweide's verse animates Beckett's first poetic collection, *Echo's Bones and Other Precipitates*, while Sordello and the partially overlapping Belacqua are explicitly evoked in *Molloy*. Martino also brilliantly delves into the *vexata quaestio* of the long hiatus in Beckett's poetical production.

A direct influence of poetry on other genres is also the object of the following chapter, where William Davies retraces the presence of Leopardi in the genetic evolution of Beckett's *Watt*. James Quin, the protagonist of the *Ur-Watt*, 'recalls that in his younger days he engaged in a course of self-education in literature and philosophy, much as Beckett did. It is through this that he came to Leopardi'. Leopardi's *Canti* dominates Quin's existential meditations in the *Ur-Watt*, unsettling 'humanity's metaphysical significance' and providing a political response to the rise of Fascism. Even if the passages related to Quin's existence are elided from *Watt*'s final form, 'the attitude of Leopardi echoes throughout the published text's mockery of the unbounded rationalism adopted by Watt to engage with his experiences of the Knott household'.

Part Four tests the limits of language and representation through the arts of translation and philosophy. Rossana Sebellin examines the status of Beckett's Italian translations, paying particular attention to *Waiting for Godot*. Starting from a specific working hypothesis ('is it time for new translations?'), she highlights how the peculiar bilingual status of Beckett's corpus has generated a situation in which Carlo Fruttero's 'attitude towards Beckett's bilingualism is quite casual if not indifferent: on several occasions he stated he used whatever was sent to Einaudi, regardless of the first language a play was written in. In other cases, though, he claims to have consulted both versions in order to carry out his own translation'. The source text for *Waiting for Godot* is always the French one, 'the English text [...] interwoven with the French text in the Italian translation'. This situation (English insertions in a French background) has heavily influenced Beckett's reception in Italy, generating a confusion that only a more philologically accurate work could clarify.

In the last chapter, Mena Mitrano interprets Beckett's play *Not I* in light of the so-called Italian Theory. A play 'about the impossibility of subjectivity' and 'the fundamentally alienating nature of language', *Not I* invites an investigation into the 'opaque relation between subjectivity and enunciation'. After a keen analysis of relevant categories such as utterance and enunciation (with particular reference to the philosophy of Benveniste and Austin), Mitrano concentrates on Roberto Esposito's notion of '*pensiero vivente* or living thought'. His philosophy retells the story of language through the body. *Not I* is particularly relevant in this context: 'even though it presents itself as a play on speaking, *Not I* stands out because it is about the physical struggle against speech. It suggests how, to use Esposito's words, it is language that "makes the body into a subject"'.

Part One
VISUAL ENCOUNTERS

Chapter 1

'THE PANTHEON AT ROME OR CERTAIN BEEHIVE TOMBS': BECKETT'S POSTHUMOUS ARCHITECTURE

Mark Byron

Abstract

Dante, and particularly the *Commedia*, best represents the ubiquity of Italy in Beckett's oeuvre, providing an intellectual scaffolding and a suite of structuring images in texts ranging from *Dream of Fair to Middling Women* to *Worstward Ho*. Italian words and literary allusions also arise at significant points in Beckett's texts, such as 'lick chops and basta' at the end of *Ill Seen Ill Said*, or the cluster of references to Giacomo Leopardi in the *Watt* manuscript notebooks. One significant Italian allusion is that of the Pantheon in Rome in *All Strange Away* as an architectural model for the confined space in which the two bodies are observed by the narrator. It is not the only reference to Roman or Italian architecture in Beckett's work – the Villa Doria Pamphili is mentioned in the *Watt* notebooks, and the Basilica di San Marco in Venice appears briefly in *Dream*. However, the Pantheon holds a special place in Beckett's architectural vision, not merely due to its exemplary design but as a focal point for Beckett's enduring preoccupation with modes of interment. The figures in *All Strange Away* are entombed in their suffocating space, which is likened to the 'beehive tombs' or Bronze Age *tholoi* of Greece and Western Asia, and which also recall the medieval monastic *clocháns* of southwestern Ireland. The Pantheon is situated between these epochal designations and connects them, casting its singular formal perfections across a history of burial, entombment and memorialization. That this particular building is tied so closely to memory and imagination – and their potential extinctions – bestows it with its own memorial function. It becomes an allusion marking a site of remembrance from which careful excavation will exhume textual relics from the living soil into the life-giving air. This essay will explore how the Pantheon, including its history and structure, anchors this terrain across Beckett's work. It will weigh up how Beckett's architecture of interment pivots on sacred places and their proneness to profanation, and how these sites constitute memorial markers that enable loss to dim into forgetting.

Keywords: Pantheon; architecture; tomb; tumulus; dome; masonry; stone

Italy and Italian culture provide some of the most prominent guides to the thematic and aesthetic formations in Beckett's work. Dante, and particularly his *Commedia*, best represents this Italian undertone, providing an intellectual scaffolding and a suite of structuring images in texts ranging from *Dream of Fair to Middling Women* to *Worstward Ho*. Italian words and literary allusions also arise at significant points in Beckett's texts, such as 'lick chops and basta' at the end of *Ill Seen Ill Said*, or the cluster of references to Giacomo Leopardi in the *Watt* manuscript notebooks. This network of references is usually traced to Beckett's school education and his time at Trinity College, Dublin. Beckett's turn to Rome's classical heritage, particularly its monumental architecture, provides a fertile method by which to explore the intersections of aesthetic creation and earthy containment or burial. References are few, and scattered sparsely throughout his texts, but they carry a strategic valency, opening narrative or dramatic scenes to new ways of observing and understanding the world. Three monumental Roman buildings and civic works embody Beckett's architectural vision, not merely due to exemplary design but as focal points for Beckett's enduring preoccupation with modes of interment: the Pantheon in *All Strange Away* acts as an architectural model for the confined space in which the two bodies are observed by the narrator; the world of mud in *How It Is* draws associations with the Pontine Marshes and the swampy origins of Rome, resolved by the construction of the Cloaca Maxima; and the vocabulary of earth, interment and geological rifts in *Worstward Ho* enter into productive dialogue with the architecture of the Domus Aurea. This essay weighs up how Beckett's architecture of interment pivots on sacred Roman places and their proneness to profanation, and how these sites constitute memorial markers that enable loss to dim into forgetting.

A Rotunda for All Seasons: Beckett's Pantheon

The sustained attention to ancient and classical architecture ranges across Beckett's oeuvre: the Neolithic dolmens, crenellated ruins and Martello towers dotting the Wicklow landscape in *More Pricks Than Kicks*; the image of silence in *The Unnamable* settling like 'sand, on the arena, after the massacres', referring to a gladiatorial battle in the Roman colosseum; the two 'Memnon' statues guarding the tomb of Amenhotep at Thebes, cited in *Malone Dies* and

Fizzle 7; and the 12 standing stones who guard the woman in *Ill Seen Ill Said*, to name only these few examples. Beckett's citation of the Flavian amphitheatre is an unusually specific reference to Roman architecture but it is not the only one. As it creates and decreates the conditions of its narrative world, at one point, *All Strange Away* locates its protagonist Emma within a 'rotunda three foot diameter eighteen inches high supporting a dome semi-circular in section as in the Pantheon in Rome or certain beehive tombs'.[1] Consecrated in the second quarter of the second century CE, the imposing scale and durability of Hadrian's temple are typified by its rotunda: at 43 metres in diameter, it remains the largest unreinforced concrete dome in the world.[2] Its influence on subsequent structures comprises an entire genre in the history of architecture – Filippo Brunelleschi's dome atop Santa Maria del Fiore in Florence and Andrea Palladio's Villa Rotonda outside of Vicenza are two prominent Italian examples from the fifteenth and sixteenth centuries, to which may be added foreign emulations such as the Rotunda at the University of Virginia (built in 1822–26) which houses the library of Thomas Jefferson.

Beyond its neat symmetry and function as a container for figures in a white vast space, why would Beckett cite a structure with such an outsized celebrity and significance, especially in the context of the modest assemblage within which he fits his narrative subjects? The 'rotunda' appears again in *Imagination Dead Imagine*, where the vastness of external space introduces differences of scale – 'that white speck lost in the whiteness'[3] – echoing the structure of *All Strange Away*. This second indirect reference to the Pantheon adds an ironic hue: the monumental set against the diminutive, as though Beckett is sketching a model in prose as so many architects drafted cross sections of the Hadrianic structure across the centuries, and he does so as a narrative thought experiment in interment. Beckett's citation draws attention to the Pantheon's symmetry, with its dome reaching a height equal to its diameter. This is the key feature for Palladio as he explains in his *Four Books on Architecture*: 'Some maintain it is the same round shape as the world: the height from the floor

---

[1] Samuel Beckett, *All Strange Away*, in *Texts for Nothing and Other Shorter Prose, 1950–1976*, ed. Mark Nixon (London: Faber & Faber, 2010), 77.

[2] For a comprehensive discussion of the dome's construction, see Giangiacomo Martines, 'The Conception and Construction of Drum and Dome,' in *The Pantheon: From Antiquity to the Present*, ed. Tod A. Marder and Mark Wilson Jones (Cambridge: Cambridge University Press, 2015), 99–131. The existing Hadrianic structure replaced an earlier building constructed by Agrippa that was destroyed by fire in 80 CE. See Eugenio La Rocca, 'Agrippa's Pantheon and Its Origin,' in *The Pantheon: From Antiquity to the Present*, 49–78.

[3] Samuel Beckett, *Imagination Dead Imagine*, in *Texts for Nothing and Other Shorter Prose, 1950–1976*, ed. Mark Nixon (London: Faber & Faber, 2010), 89.

to the opening in the ceiling, from whence light enters, is the same as its width, that is, the diameter from one wall to the other.'[4] Where Palladio saw symbolic and perhaps metaphysical significance in the building's dimensions, the quandary facing Beckett's protagonists rests in the question of their significance as anonymous expressions of bare life housed in an austere, claustrophobic structure positioned within a vast undifferentiated space. The legendary statuary that once adorned the Pantheon, its bronze doors and portico, and the tombs of Raphael, Annibale Carracci, and Arcangelo Corelli (and in the nineteenth century the two Italian monarchs Vittorio Emmanuele II and Umberto I) present a formidably rich decorative array to complement the building's architecture, again in polar contrast to the bare walls of the miniature rotunda in Beckett's text.[5]

A key feature of the Pantheon is the *oculus*, the round opening at the apex of its dome that opens to the sky, letting in light and rain onto the marble floor. This aperture to the heavens serves a symbolic purpose of direct communication with the gods (or with the Christian God once the structure was consecrated as the Church of St Mary and the Martyrs by Pope Bonifacio IV in 609). This notion of a structural aperture becomes significant in *Worstward Ho*, opening the narrative scene to the possibilities of visual projection. Here, the structural morphology of the roof of the Domus Aurea is telling – the Octagonal Hall of the Domus is also topped by a dome with an *oculus* – where the building's interior functions as a giant centre of perception, whether a symbolic eye looking up to the gods, or a symbolic mind or brain housed within a 'sepulchral skull' and 'cyclopean dome' as Beckett puts it in Fizzle 7. The Pantheon might be viewed as a monumental *camera obscura*, able to project an image of a world through its aperture whilst inviting access to the heavens and the structure's main source of light by the same means.

Beckett's citation of the Pantheon is accompanied by a reference to 'certain beehive tombs', linked thematically as places of interment and thus consistent with the mordant irony of comparison with the rotunda in Beckett's story. The word *rotunda* entered English in the 1680s, first as a description of the Pantheon itself (as the Chiesa di Santa Maria Rotunda), and then as a generic term for a building topped by a dome. The Latin term *rotundus*, in usage from at least the time of Cato the Elder, referred to Greek or Roman circular buildings including *tholoi* in which a circular wall was topped by a flat or

---

[4] Andrea Palladio, *I quattro libri dell'architettura*, vol. 4 (Venezia, 1570), 73; quoted in Martines, 99.

[5] Edmund Thomas, 'The Cult Statues of the Pantheon,' *Journal of Roman Studies* 107 (2017): 146–212.

domed roof, such as the Tholos of Delphi. This is distinct from the *tholoi* or 'beehive tombs' to which Beckett refers, tombs constructed in the Late Bronze Age in the Eastern Mediterranean, including in the Early Minoan period in the third millennium BCE on Crete and called θολωτόςτάφος or 'domed tombs' by the Greeks. These structures bear a resemblance to the early medieval monastic *clocháns* found in south-western Ireland, in that they feature domed roofing, although *tholoi* were often buried within large tumulus mounds covering the structure's doorway (*stomion*) and entryway (*dromos*). These scant references thus draw together a long history of interment, from the Bronze Age, through classical Rome, to early modern and then post-unification Italy. The geographic range of *tholoi* is still bounded by the Pantheon, constructed north of the centre of Imperial Rome and now very much at the heart of the city. Rome is the measure by which life and its afterlife are gauged, as though, to adapt Samuel Johnson, if one does not know Rome then one has not properly lived.

Aquam Ducere: The Cloaca Maxima in the Heart of Rome

For all of Rome's great civic achievements, its perilous terrain often punctuated this history with disaster and hardship, whether earthquake, fire, flood or intractable topography. The Pontine Marshes south of the city comprised an impoverished geography at least as far back as the early Republic when the marshes were sparsely populated, malaria was endemic and Rome's access to grain further south was hampered by impassable terrain. This situation persisted into the twentieth century despite innumerable attempts to build roads and drain the boggy land. The eventual draining of the marshes during the Mussolini regime allowed it to lay a claim as the symbolic inheritor of Roman civic *potentia*. While classical writers such as Livy, Pliny the Elder and Horace mention the Pontine Marshes they provide only the barest descriptions of a forsaken and mosquito-plagued terrain, half-land and half-swamp. With the geoengineering of the area in the 1930s, modernist writers such as James Joyce have been linked with one of Rome's most ambitious and longstanding civic engineering schemes, but again, literary and ecocritical attention is relatively fleeting.[6] While Beckett never mentions the Pontine Marshes

---

[6] See James Fairhall, 'The Bog of Allen, the Tiber River, and the Pontine Marshes: An Ecocritical Reading of "The Dead",' *James Joyce Quarterly* 51.4 (2014): 567–600. On the Fascist project to eradicate malaria in the Pontine Marshes, see Federico Caprotti, 'Malaria and Technological Networks: Medical Geography in the Pontine Marshes, Italy, in the 1930s,' *The Geographical Journal* 172.2 (2006): 145–55.

directly, his interests in unproductive and forsaken geographies is widespread through his texts and is the subject of scholarly attention.

In counterpoint to the 'stony rubbish' afflicting the terrain of T. S. Eliot's *Waste Land*, Beckett finds mud a productive element through which to think both philosophically and phenomenologically, reaching a crescendo in his novel *Comment c'est/How It Is*. The ubiquity of mud presents opportunities to think through the relations of existence for the novel's characters. By locating this substance as the basis for meditation, it relates albeit indirectly to another marsh, this time at the centre of Rome's geography and history: namely the Velabrum, sodden land between the Capitoline and Palatine hills extending to the Tiber and the location for one of Rome's earliest and most important civil engineering projects. The Cloaca Maxima was constructed around 600 BCE, functioning as Rome's primary sewer for much of its history. Its significance as a durable work of civic engineering in the cause of public health is difficult to overstate: 'The Cloaca Maxima not only constitutes the oldest infrastructure of Rome, considered over the centuries for its grandeur, it also holds the record of a virtually unbroken continuity of existence.'[7] The persistence of malaria in the city throughout its history and into the twentieth century had it known as the 'Roman fever', spread by virtue of the *aria cattiva* or 'bad air' settling on the city[8]: Henry James has Daisy Miller die of malaria contracted at a visit to the Colosseum, which was built on the former site of the Neronic artificial lake constructed as part of the Domus Aurea complex a century earlier. Another source of the disease was the south-westerly breeze bringing the stagnant air of the Pontine Marshes to the city. The marshy ground between the Palatine and Capitoline hills abutted some of the earliest settled parts of the city, causing major problems in developing its centre and making transport from the Forum to the Tiber uncertain and potentially dangerous. The location of marshy ground in the historic heart of Rome, dividing its devotional and administrative centre from its major river, impelled a fundamental rethinking of urban planning in ancient Rome, addressing the problem of living with mud as the arbiter of managing the city. Recent archaeological evidence suggests that low-lying areas of the Velabrum were reclaimed to a depth of up to three metres in the seventh century BCE

---

[7] Eugenio Tamburrino, 'Foreword,' in *Aquam Ducere II: Proceedings of the Second International Summer School, Water and the City: Hydraulic Systems in the Roman Age (Feltre, 24–28 August 2015)*, ed. Eugenio Tamburrino (Edizioni DBS: Seren del Grappa, 2018), 177.

[8] For an account of the origins and prevalence of malaria in the ancient Mediterranean, see François Retief and Louise Cilliers, 'Malaria in Graeco-Roman Times,' *Acta Classica* 47 (2004): 127–37.

during the reign of the Tarquinian kings, following which the first major works on the Cloaca Maxima began.[9]

The world of *Comment c'est/How It Is* is imbued in mud: characters crawl through it in search of restitution; it dominates the proscribed field of vision; and even the leaching of punctuation and sentence structure from the narrative has its language start to resemble mud's sedimentary suspension. Mud bears a distinguished Italian literary tradition, appearing at strategic points in Dante's *Inferno* and in Giacomo Leopardi's poetry. Given that it also shapes Rome's urban planning at the most foundational level, mud is an abiding parameter of Italy's literary and social architecture. There is a broad critical consensus that *Comment c'est/How It Is* occupies a pivotal position in Beckett's oeuvre as his last long work, marking a decisive shift to the minimalist and verbally experimental later works on page and stage. How might mud function as an emblem of this shift, turning, for example, from the more explicit images of geological stratification in Beckett's earlier works to some of the generative terms and images arising in his later fiction?

The central motif of mud in Beckett's text foregrounds the challenge of ascribing to it a coherent form. Although *Comment c'est/How It Is* forgoes punctuation (except for apostrophes) including capital letters (save for proper names, the first-person singular and to signify the raised voice), it does abide by a certain structural integrity. The text is divided into three parts, established in the first 'paragraph' of the text as though the entire narrative is captured fractally: 'how it was I quote before Pim with Pim after Pim how it is three parts I say it as I hear it'.[10] The gesture towards quotation at the outset of the narrative is mirrored in the final paragraph of Part 3 – 'good good end at last of part three and last that's how it was end of quotation after Pim how it is'.[11] The effect of this prolonged quotation is to render the text, barring its first three and final five words, at one remove from direct speech, suspended much like the abiding substance of mud comprises a suspension of water and soil or clay. This larger framing quotation also telescopes the many quotations within the narrative, drawing on a wide array of sources including Beckett's own texts. *How It Is* toggles between scales of narrative and paragraph, between the geomorphic and the granular, and between individual utterance and an implicit encyclopaedism of literary and cultural reference. This scalability is directly implicated in the mud upon and within which the narrative persists.

---

[9] Elisabetta Bianchi, 'Projecting and Building the *Cloaca Maxima*,' in *Aquam Ducere II*, 177–209 [179].

[10] Samuel Beckett, *How It Is*, ed. Édouard Magessa O'Reilly (1964; London: Faber, 2009), 3.

[11] Beckett, *How It Is*, 129.

How Beckett absorbs literary references to mud in *How It Is* suggests how the material substance and its symbolic or figurative valencies can be harnessed productively, against the tendency to render architecture in the solid matter of stone and marble. In Canto 7 of *Inferno*, Virgil guides Dante through the fifth circle where the wrathful are submerged in the Stygian marsh, each according to the kind of anger they possess.

> E io, che di mirare stave inteso,
> vidi genti fangose in quell pantano,
> ignude tutte, con sembiante offeso.

> And I, my gaze transfixed, could see
> people with angry faces in that bog,
> naked, their bodies smeared with mud.[12]

Inferno deploys this topographical feature of the muddy bog or swamp as a transitional zone, not only demarcating the kinds of suffering according to a particular sin but also signifying a shift in Dante's understanding of the entire economy of punishment. This use of the swamp as a porous and ambiguous ecology[13] ties in with the history of the Roman Velabrum. Dante is drawing on Virgil's familiarity with this terrain in his own poetry, evident in his Fourth Georgic in which he narrates the story of Orpheus and Eurydice. As Orpheus pursues Eurydice into the Underworld, he comes across a vision of the innocent dead of all ages, enclosed by two rivers:

> around whom lay the clabber, and disfigured reed beds by Cocytus,
>   that kept them
> locked in, among stagnant pools and murky marshes,
> and the Styx' nine coils that kept them prisoner.[14]

This literary economy in which mud signifies due punishment for moral transgression is deeply ingrained in the Western epic imaginary, tracing out a lineage from Gilgamesh and Homer to Edmund Spenser's *Faerie Queene* (the Slough of Despond) and Milton's *Paradise Lost* (the Stygian Marsh in Book 2).

---

[12] *Inferno* VII, ll. 109–111, in Dante, *The Inferno*, translated by Robert Hollander and Jean Hollander (New York: Random House, 2002), 136–37.
[13] Casey Ireland, '*Discors Concordia*: Swamps as Borderlands in Dante's *Inferno*,' *Neophilologus* 104 (2020): 177–88.
[14] Georgics Book 4, ll. 478–80, in Virgil, *Georgics*, ed. and trans. Peter Fallon (Oxford: Oxford University Press, 2004), 91.

Beckett was drawn to Giacomo Leopardi's stoic worldview, in which life is a pensum for the sin of being born. Leopardi's poem 'A se stesso' ('To Himself') captures this sense of dead illusions taking hope and desire with them, with a world of filth or mud – 'fango è il mondo' – being the material remainder with which humans are required to contend until the gift of death is realized.[15] Daniela Caselli detects persistent negative elements of the poem, not only negating 'cari inganni' (cherished deceptions) and 'vane speranze' (vain hopes), but embedded in a dense fabric of grammatical negations, and negative pronouns, adjectives and nouns that ironically provide a space for desire in the act of enunciating its negation.[16] Beckett quotes from this poem in his early monograph *Proust*, detecting in Leopardi's dialectical struggle with the extinction and ignition of desire an early formulation of his own struggle between failure and persistence in literary creation.

The odyssey in and through mud in *How It Is* narrates a battle for knowledge and agency, measured by slow transit and punctuated by violence. This journey becomes a global trek, and, as Hamm puts it in *Endgame*, the earth a 'muckball': 'and so in the mud the dark on the belly in a straight line as near as no matter four hundred miles in other words in eight thousand years if I had not stopped the girdle of the earth meaning the equivalent'.[17] This dramatizes how foundation myths wrestle between urban and agricultural spaces, on the one hand, and wild unregulated spaces, on the other, populated by barbarians and replete with danger. Yet mud and swampy land cannot be externalized completely, and may in fact be a primordial condition and substance from which all culture rises: '[t]he marsh appears to be a distinguishing element of the world's origins, of that chaotic primordial landscape previous to the coming of mankind and, consequently, of culture'.[18] The origins of Rome itself are traced to Romulus and Remus, abandoned in the wild, perhaps even in the Velabrum itself: 'stagnant waters, indeed, keep the children from being abandoned to

---

[15] 'A se stesso' / 'To Himself,' in Giacomo Leopardi, *Canti*, trans. Jonathan Galassi (London: Penguin, 2010), 234–35. For a sustained account of Leopardi's role in Beckett's aesthetics, see Roberta Cauchi-Santoro, *Beyond the Suffering of Being: Desire in Giacomo Leopardi and Samuel Beckett* (Firenze: Firenze University Press, 2016).
[16] Daniela Caselli, 'Beckett and Leopardi,' in *The Beckett Critical Reader: Archives, Theories, and Translations*, ed. S. E. Gontarski (Edinburgh: Edinburgh University Press, 2012), 135–51 [137].
[17] Beckett, *How It Is*, 33.
[18] Federico Borca, '*Palus Omni Modo Vitanda*: A Liminal Space in Ancient Roman Culture,' *The Classical Bulletin* 73.1 (1997): 3–12 [3].

the real current of the river, save the divine twins from death and thus let them accomplish the mission of establishing the culture.'[19]

Progress in the narrative journey is measured with reference to learning – the harsh lessons of repetition and violence as well as a suite of cultural and philosophical references which function as a recognizable pedagogy for the reader[20] – with biblical references scattered among a wide range of literary allusions (including John Dryden, Samuel Taylor Coleridge, Robert Herrick and John Donne) as well as catalogue of self-citation from *Murphy*, *Watt*, *Waiting for Godot*, *The Unnamable* and *Endgame*, as though the entire cultural patrimony was embedded and submerged in the mud through which the narrative subjects plough. The act of reading sifts these allusions from the general mass, draining away the grammar of hesitation, repetition and violence to reveal the literary structure beneath. In this sense, reading *How It Is* bears analogy to the Cloaca Maxima, a restorative work of engineering that drains the marshlands to provide space for the edifice of culture to emerge. This too entails interment: the voice 'that buries all mankind' haunts the text, and the memory of Pim in Part 1 of the narrative is recalled in Part 2 as 'squatting in the deep shade of a tomb,'[21] a measure of the shadow Beckett's posthumous architecture casts across his oeuvre.

Abode of Stones: The Domus Aurea and *Worstward Ho*

Several of the most spectacular Roman archaeological finds have brought to light an object or site lost to history, such as the statue group *Laocoön and His Sons*, excavated in 1506 on the Oppian Hill and promptly installed in the Vatican Museums. Praised for its quality by Pliny the Elder in Book X of his *Natural History*,[22] the sculpture's provenance remains uncertain. Thought to be a product of late Hellenism by a group of sculptors working on the island of Rhodes around 200 BCE, it is also widely regarded as a copy of an earlier work, created

---

[19] Borca, 5. The Velabrum is an exceedingly difficult place in which to perform archaeological digs. The accretions of material layers since the eighth century BCE means the surface now sits up to 17 metres above the natural soil in some places, with the lower levels corresponding to early Republican Rome located below the modern city's water table. See Albert J. Ammerman, 'Looking at Early Rome with Fresh Eyes: Transforming the Landscape,' in *A Companion to the Archaeology of the Roman Republic*, ed. Jane DeRose Evans (Oxford: Blackwell, 2013), 169–80.

[20] On *How It Is* and its institutions of pedagogy, see Anthony Cordingley, *Samuel Beckett's* How It Is: *Philosophy in Translation* (Edinburgh: Edinburgh University Press, 2017).

[21] Beckett, *How It Is*, 53 and 45.

[22] Pliny the Elder, *Natural History, Volume X: Books 36–37*, trans. D. E. Eichholz, Loeb Classical Library 419 (Cambridge, MA: Harvard University Press, 1962), 28–31.

in the mid-first century BCE.[23] The location of its discovery is also ambiguous, reputedly discovered by Felice De Fredis in an ancient subterranean chamber uncovered when digging a field to plant new vines. The statue's discovery soon caused a sensation in Italy and across Europe, spearheading renewed interest in classical sculpture and drawing a connection between the texts of Pliny and Virgil: 'the Rhodians' marble provided a bridge from one ancient text to another ancient text and from both of them to the visible reality of the contemporary world – this, if anything, was a true rebirth of the glory of antiquity'.[24] This event crossed the barriers of time in reversing both the literal and figurative submergence of previous cultural monuments, bringing the distant past into the present and initiating the field of classical archaeology. Pope Julius II summoned Michelangelo to the site immediately upon the discovery, an act which helped bind the production of art to classical principles and inform how the arts and culture were to be understood thenceforward.[25]

The exhumation of the Laocoön sculpture is an outsized example of how the orders of knowledge and understanding may be shifted by archaeological discoveries. Other belated discoveries of Roman antiquities – such as the excavations at Pompeii and Herculaneum in the eighteenth century which began as civic earthworks or the discovery in 2023 of Nero's Theatre on a site close to the Vatican – highlight how antiquity and novelty may coincide, bringing forgotten artefacts and aesthetic techniques into contemporary consciousness. Although at some distance from the Roman world, the rediscovery of the Epic of Gilgamesh in 1849 reordered the literary heritage of the broader Mediterranean region.[26] As the first of its genre, the disinterred Akkadian epic fundamentally reoriented Mesopotamian literature, bringing together the known Sumerian

---

[23] There is a complex and longstanding debate concerning the provenance of the statue, critically evaluated in Rita Volpe and Antonella Parisi, 'Alla ricerca di una scoperta: Felice de Fredis e il luogo di ritrovamento del Laocoonte,' *Bullettino della Commissione Archeologica Comunale di Roma* 110 (2009): 81–110. See also Glenn W. Most, 'Laocoons,' in *A Companion to Vergil's Aeneid and Its Tradition*, ed. Joseph Farrell and Michael C. J. Putnam (Hoboken, NJ: John Wiley, 2010), 325–40, at 329–35.

[24] Most, 336.

[25] See Maren Elisabeth Schwab and Anthony Grafton, *The Art of Discovery: Digging into the Past in Renaissance Europe* (Princeton: Princeton University Press, 2022), especially Chapter 5, 'Disentangling Ancient Sources,' 162–89. The recent theory asserting that the statue was a clever forgery by Michelangelo – see Lynn Catterson, 'Michelangelo's Laocoön?' *Artibus et Historiae* 26.52 (2005): 29–56 – has gained little traction.

[26] For an account of the text's rediscovery and its literary historical significance, see David Damrosch, *The Buried Book: The Loss and Rediscovery of the Great Epic of Gilgamesh* (New York: Henry Holt, 2006). For a comprehensive account of its reception, see Theodore Ziolkowski, *Gilgamesh among Us: Modern Encounters with the Ancient Epic* (Ithaca and London: Cornell University Press, 2012).

Gilgamesh poems and providing a line of provenance to several episodes of the Bible (such as Noah and the Flood in Genesis) as well as to the Homeric poems the *Iliad* and *Odyssey*, and thus indirectly to Virgil's *Aeneid* as the founding epic of Rome. This brief excursion to the origins of Mediterranean literature and back to Rome illustrates not only the potential interconnectedness of texts, narratives and cultural artefacts, but also how acts of recuperation and rediscovery by means of archaeology can recalibrate teleologies of genre, narrative, image and literary subject matter. Taken in a metaphorical sense, this kind of literary archaeology is a feature of Beckett's writing, where etymologies, submerged references and matters of style and technique can call up figures from the earth, demonstrating that the 'ground' of literature is one steeped in filiations both acknowledged and forgotten, and where Rome comprises a pivotal domain of this ancestry.

Archaeology can be thought of as an inhabitation of belatedness, where the past has accreted sufficiently to submerge its objects partially or wholly, requiring excavation of intervening strata to fully reveal its character (or what physically remains of its character). Yet archaeology may also be thought of as a field defined by timeliness, in bringing forth objects and structures that have partially escaped the erosions of time by virtue of their continued existence and whose agency as persisting entities allows them to communicate the past in the present. This paradox of archaeology as an expression of pastness and presentness performs similar work to Beckett's deployments of language in his later prose works, particularly in the way etymologies are gathered and distributed across the text surface, guiding the reader to consider their historic strata, semantic evolution and half-hidden networks of meaning.

Beckett's penultimate prose work *Worstward Ho* brings this process to a point of concentration by sedimenting a vocabulary that refers to the earth, its etymologies drawing back to shifting ground and uncovered rifts. This serves not only to bring focus to the terrain of the story in its more literalized forms, but to cast Beckett's own writing career into a complex stratification: it becomes inevitable to read this text as a reflection on Beckett's past writing as well as the introduction of new methods and styles by which to marshal Beckett's linguistic and tropological repertoire. By deploying figures of ruination and excavation, *Worstward Ho* engages in a radical mode of creativity evident in its narrator's capacity to create and destroy place and character. The rifts and ruins in the texts also serve to recover memory – a process in contemporary archaeology that Bjørnar Olsen describes as 'a slow-motion archaeology, or self-excavation, that exposes the formerly hidden and black-boxed'.[27]

---

[27] Bjørrnar Olsen, *In Defense of Things: Archaeology and the Ontology of Objects* (Lanham, MD: AltaMira Press, 2010), 170.

These discovered strata, sherds, ostraka and processes of memory bind the nomenclature of archaeology with sifting layers of a writing career.

The prose style of *Worstward Ho* functions with a different linguistic intensity to Beckett's other prose texts, even as their residues, themes and images are spectrally visible. The barest vestige of plot or narrative involves the raising up of three 'shades' – a composite figure of man and boy, an old woman, and the seeing head – and the environment they inhabit is progressively created and decreated in terms defined by a wilful narrator. Alternating between superlative and diminutive characterizations of the place in which the figures are posed, the text settles on paradoxical but intelligible combinations of least and most: 'Unnullable least. Say that best worse. With leastening words say least best worse. For want of worser worst. Unlessenable least best worse.'[28] The terms of existence are predicated on being as close to zero, absence, extinction without actually reaching such a state, maintaining an opening for hope, evolution and change. This quality of the text's logic works in step with its etymologies, where a preponderance of words stems from geological processes and geomorphic images: 'till', 'vast', 'rift', 'void', 'gulf' and 'grot'. Even words such as 'lessen' start to take on the hues of tillage and earthwork – via the German verb *lesen* (to read), the Latin *legere* and ultimately the Proto-Indo-European *leg- which means 'to gather, to pick out' (words) – where reading is figured in terms of agricultural harvesting practices.[29]

How might such a vocabulary orient the reader of *Worstward Ho*, and how might it develop Beckett's enduring relationship with Roman archaeology? The etymology of *rift* provides a first clue: entering Middle English in the early fourteenth century from Scandinavian sources (the Old Norse *ripa* means 'to tear apart'), it also signified ploughed farmlands. Although there is no evidence that Beckett's emphasis on this word was meant to recall the discovery of the *Laocoön* statue in the ploughed fields of Felice De Fredis in 1506, the uncanny link between event and word is evidence of the deep etymological links formed across languages and time. This nod to archaeology in *Worstward Ho* befits the way this late text cites and echoes so many of his earlier works, as though they persist in its subterranean strata. Themes of digging and earthworks are abundant: the stonecutters in *Watt*, *Malone Dies* and *First Love*;

---

[28] Samuel Beckett, *Company, Ill Seen Ill Said, Worstward Ho, Stirrings Still*, ed. Dirk Van Hulle (London: Faber & Faber, 2009), 94–95.

[29] Mark Byron, *Samuel Beckett's Geological Imagination* (Cambridge: Cambridge University Press, 2020), 55–56. For an account of the etymology of reading and its links with harvesting, see Ivan Illich, *In the Vineyard of the Text: A Commentary to Hugh's* Didascalicon (Chicago: University of Chicago Press, 1993), 58ff.

the earthen abode of Winnie in *Happy Days*; and the standing stones of *Ill Seen Ill Said*, among others. Residues appear in the text's imagery too: the clenched eye in *Worstward Ho* recalls the eye of *Film* and the 'eye of prey' in *Imagination Dead Imagine*; the narrator's exclamation of 'Meaning!' cites Hamm's dread that he and Clov might begin to 'mean something' in *Endgame*; and the old woman visiting the 'old graveyard' returns the reader to the opening of *First Love* as well as to the old woman visiting the gravestone in *Ill Seen Ill Said*. Beneath this stratum of reference resides a lifetime of Beckett's sources, including King Lear's pronouncement on 'nothing', the 'joy' permeating Romantic poems from Schiller to Keats to Shelley, the 'rifts' recalling the 'deep romantic chasm' of Coleridge's 'Kubla Khan' as well as the rich vein of references to John Webster and Thomas Dekker and to Charles Kingsley in the text's title.

The stratification of *Worstward Ho* provides a text surface that manipulates the functions of language, establishing a new semantics and mode of measurement. Its depths are where Beckett's writing career and the history of literary expression become visible to the careful excavator. This archaeological mode – of the text, and as a reading strategy – returns to the scene of Rome in the words *gulf* and *grot*: 'Say a grot in that void. A gulf. Then in that grot or gulf such dimmest light as never.'[30] The words *gulf* and *void* refer to open spaces or chasms, although in Beckett's usage here they signify dim spaces closed off from light, supported by the Proto-Indo-European root **kuolp-* meaning 'arch' or 'vault', and reaching English via the Italian *golfo*. This return to geological and architectural structure draws in *grot*, a corruption of the Greek κρῠπτός or 'hidden' and κρυπτή or 'vault', and the Latin *crypta* or 'vault, cavern'. In English, the usage of *grot* is unusual – it also has a now-obsolete Anglo-Saxon meaning of fragment or particle (a 'smithereen', as Clov puts it in *Endgame*) – and functions as an abbreviation of *grotto*, entering into modern usage with the discovery of the Domus Aurea in Rome at the end of the fifteenth century, only a few years before the *Laocoön* was unearthed nearby. This event had profound implications for subsequent art history as the initiating point for the *grotesque* style, named after the *grotto* in which Roman frescoes were newly visible. Being accessible via a narrow aperture in the ceiling, the Domus also functioned as a kind of camera obscura and constituted a pivotal space for the development of pictorial perspective. Beckett's grot, with its 'dimmest light as never' makes contact with the history of optics and perspective in a series of chambers from Roman antiquity rediscovered in the Italian Renaissance.

The rediscovery of the Domus Aurea was not by plough but by rift, when a Roman youth fell through a crevice in the Esquiline hillside into a low cavern with

---

[30] *Worstward Ho*, 96.

walls replete with painted figures. The Domus had been built by the Emperor Nero on a vast scale, spanning the Esquiline and Oppian hills on newly vacant land following the great fire of 64 CE. The complex was itself dismantled in large part by subsequent rulers and eventually destroyed in the fire of 104 CE, falling into disuse following an attempt at repair. The enormous halls and chambers were filled with rubble and earth over the next several decades and the complex receded from view and memory, much of the site given over to the construction of the Baths of Titus and eventually falling into complete obscurity and lying undisturbed for nearly 1500 years. Artists including Michelangelo and Raphael lowered themselves into the chambers to observe the *grotteschi* – frescoes painted in what became known as the ornamental or Fourth Style of Pompeii[31] and largely preserved by rapid infill – which then became the basis for polychromatic painting in Italy during the sixteenth century, most notably Raphael's decoration of the Vatican's loggias.[32] The style of the newly visible images befitted expectations of classical decorum, but their subject matter full of strange bestiaries and fantastic inventions, 'interrogated what pictures were – the "ontology" of the image'.[33] The hillside 'rift' that physically opened access to the Domus also provided figurative access to the artistic techniques of Imperial Rome to the practitioners of the Italian Renaissance, forging a link between ancient and early modern eras, and between art and archaeology. These concerns are central to Beckett's aesthetics throughout his oeuvre, reaching a point of concentration in the text that carries the cipher of this rift and grot, *Worstward Ho*.

The challenge to artistic composition presented by the *grotteschi* was registered as early as Vitruvius, who commented on the lack of rational

---

[31] For a detailed analysis of the Pompeiian fourth style see 'Fourth Style Ensembles, AD 45–79,' in John R. Clarke, *The Houses of Roman Italy, 100BC – AD 250: Ritual, Space, and Decoration* (Berkeley, Los Angeles, and London: University of California Press, 1991), 164–265.

[32] For a comprehensive account of the *grotteschi* and the *Nachleben* or influence on Renaissance aesthetics and techniques of perspective, see Michael Squire, ' "Fantasies so Varied and Bizarre": The Domus Aurea, the Renaissance and the "Grotesque",' in *A Companion to the Neronian Age*, ed. Emma Buckley and Martin D. Dinter (Oxford: Blackwell, 2013), 444–64. Giorgio Vasari mentions Raphael as one of the first visitors to the 'grottoes' in his *Lives of the Most Eminent Painters, Sculptor, and Architects* first published in 1550. For an account of Raphael's prioritisation of *grotteschi* in his Vatican decorations, see Nicole Dacos, *The Loggia of Raphael: A Vatican Art Treasure*, trans. Josephine Bacon (New York: Abbeville Press, 2008) and Alessandra Zamperini, *Ornament and the Grotesque: Fantastical Decoration from Antiquity to Art Nouveau*, trans. Peter Spring (London: Thames and Hudson, 2008).

[33] Squire, 451.

composition in depicting such *monstra*. By challenging the boundaries between what exists and what is imaginary, these figurations shadow Beckett's strategies in *Worstward Ho*, where the narrator creates an *imaginarium* populated by the three figures, modelling and refurbishing along the way, consciously making aesthetic decisions as to how to construct this narrative world: 'The real and the unreal, the believable and the incredible, the significant and the nonsensical, the trivial and the important, the reasonable and the meaningless: the grotesque intrigued precisely because it visually broke down these verbally established dialectics.'[34] The text becomes an exercise in testing the grotesque in its original formulation, the aperture through which Renaissance artists descended into the caverns mimicking the aperture of the *camera obscura*, the 'pinhole' through which a world (or more properly its inverted image) is thrown upon a receptive screen. *Worstward Ho* is thus an exemplary exercise in pictorial perspective, with its 'three pins and one pinhole' performing the image-making function that binds the ancient *camera obscura* with modern image projection.

The architecture of *Worstward Ho* reflects the image-projecting quality of its final metaphor of the *camera obscura*. This forges a thematic link with the rediscovery of the Domus Aurea through a ceiling aperture as well as with the Pantheon displaying its *oculus* at the centre of its dome. The capacity to measure perspective against these apertures and the space between observer and object also forges a connection with the machinery of perspective in the Italian Renaissance. Filippo Brunelleschi's invention of the surveying rod put into practice a system of measuring perspective prior to Leon Battista Alberti's formalization in his *Della pittura* of 1436, which was then passed on to such artists as Leonardo Da Vinci and Albrecht Dürer.[35] This 'scopic regime' of linear perspective ushers in modernity in artistic practice according to Erwin Panofsky, where perspective is likened by Alberti to viewing the world through an open window.[36] Alberti's system implies 'a singular monocular eye that is static rather than mobile and roaming in a mobile body'.[37]

---

[34] Squire, 456.
[35] Lyle Massey, 'Framing and Mirroring the World,' in *The Renaissance World*, ed. John Jeffries Martin (London: Routledge, 2007), 51–68.
[36] Erwin Panofsky, *Perspective as Symbolic Form*, trans. Christopher S. Wood (1927; New York: Zone, 1991), 28. For a critical evaluation of the 'scopic regime' of linear perspective in Western art from the early modern period, see Ian Verstegen, 'Perspective, Space and Camera Obscura in the Renaissance,' in *The Palgrave Handbook of Image Studies*, ed. Krešimir Purgar (Cham: Palgrave Macmillan, 2021), 75–92.
[37] Donald Maloney, 'Representation and the Scopic Regime of (Post-)Cartesianism,' in *The Palgrave Handbook of Image Studies*, ed. Krešimir Purgar (Cham: Palgrave Macmillan, 2021), 449–65 [451].

This is the critical point in Beckett's deployment of the visual apparatus of perspective in his prose: to convey a stable mode of viewing grounded in the static observer, but then to trouble its foundation by introducing a roving eye. What is taken for the representation of a fictional world turns attention to the mode by which that world is perceived and shown to possess the possibility of radical re-vision.

Conclusion

Networks of citation and allusion in Beckett's work have long preoccupied scholars, and with extensive access to his manuscripts and other paratextual materials, these networks are shown to be richer and deeper than may be first evident in his published texts. This shift in perception – from the text surface to a submerged field of citation accessible via an aperture of a word or phrase – pertains to Beckett's consideration of Roman architecture. Sparse references to architectural rotunda, the Pantheon, the Colosseum and the swampy earth on which the fabrication of a building is impossible open up new ways of understanding the themes and vocabulary of Beckett's texts. Each of these examples comprises spaces or structures dedicated to interment of one kind or another: whether the literal interment of famous artists and musicians in the Pantheon, the interment of Neronian art and luxury in the buried and rediscovered Domus Aurea, or the challenge of overcoming mud and marshland of the Velabrum in the construction of the city. The modes by which these allusions are revealed reflect the imagery with which they are presented: the oculus of the Pantheon in *All Strange Away* and the grotto of *Worstward Ho* recalling the rediscovered rooms of the Domus Aurea, where each projects a lost world by embodying the technology of the *camera obscura*; and the apparent ubiquity and consistency of mud in *How It Is* reflects the Roman project of marshland drainage from the very earliest stages of the city's development. Interment as a preservative process gives objects of the past a new life in the present, as the *Laocoön* statue so vividly demonstrates. This new life provides a means by which to reconcile the deep past with the present and to transform its meaning, casting it in a new light projected upon the surface of Beckett's texts.

Bibliography

Alighieri, Dante, *The Inferno*, translated by Robert Hollander and Jean Hollander (New York: Random House, 2002).
Ammerman, Albert J., 'Looking at Early Rome with Fresh Eyes: Transforming the Landscape,' in *A Companion to the Archaeology of the Roman Republic*, ed. Jane DeRose Evans (Oxford: Blackwell, 2013), 169–80.

Beckett, Samuel, 'All Strange Away,' in *Texts for Nothing and Other Shorter Prose, 1950–1976*, ed. Mark Nixon (London: Faber & Faber, 2010). 71–84.

———, *Company, Ill Seen Ill Said, Worstward Ho, Stirrings Still*, ed. Dirk Van Hulle (London: Faber & Faber, 2009).

———, *How It Is*, ed. Édouard Magessa O'Reilly (1964; London: Faber, 2009).

———, 'Imagination Dead Imagine,' in *Texts for Nothing and Other Shorter Prose, 1950–1976*, ed. Mark Nixon (London: Faber & Faber, 2010). 85–89.

Bianchi, Elisabetta, 'Projecting and Building the Cloaca Maxima,' in *Aquam Ducere II: Proceedings of the Second International Summer School, Water and the City: Hydraulic Systems in the Roman Age* (Feltre, 24–28 August 2015), ed. Eugenio Tamburrino (Edizioni DBS: Seren del Grappa, 2018), 177–209.

Borca, Federico, '*Palus Omni Modo Vitanda*: A Liminal Space in Ancient Roman Culture,' *The Classical Bulletin* 73.1 (1997): 3–12.

Byron, Mark, *Samuel Beckett's Geological Imagination* (Cambridge: Cambridge University Press, 2020).

Caprotti, Federico, 'Malaria and Technological Networks: Medical Geography in the Pontine Marshes, Italy, in the 1930s,' *The Geographical Journal* 172.2 (2006): 145–55.

Caselli, Daniela, 'Beckett and Leopardi,' in *The Beckett Critical Reader: Archives, Theories, and Translations*, ed. S. E. Gontarski (Edinburgh: Edinburgh University Press, 2012), 135–51.

Catterson, Lynn, 'Michelangelo's Laocoön?' *Artibus et Historiae* 26.52 (2005): 29–56.

Cauchi–Santoro, Roberta, *Beyond the Suffering of Being: Desire in Giacomo Leopardi and Samuel Beckett* (Firenze: Firenze University Press, 2016).

Clarke, John R., *The Houses of Roman Italy, 100BC – AD 250: Ritual, Space, and Decoration* (Berkeley, Los Angeles, and London: University of California Press, 1991).

Cordingley, Anthony, *Samuel Beckett's How It Is: Philosophy in Translation* (Edinburgh: Edinburgh University Press, 2017).

Dacos, Nicole, *The Loggia of Raphael: A Vatican Art Treasure*, trans. Josephine Bacon (New York: Abbeville Press, 2008).

Damrosch, David, *The Buried Book: The Loss and Rediscovery of the Great Epic of Gilgamesh* (New York: Henry Holt, 2006).

Fairhall, James, 'The Bog of Allen, the Tiber River, and the Pontine Marshes: An Ecocritical Reading of "The Dead",' *James Joyce Quarterly* 51.4 (2014): 567–600.

Illich, Ivan, *In the Vineyard of the Text: A Commentary to Hugh's Didascalicon* (Chicago: University of Chicago Press, 1993).

Ireland, Casey, '*Discors Concordia*: Swamps as Borderlands in Dante's *Inferno*,' *Neophilologus* 104 (2020): 177–88.

La Rocca, Eugenio, 'Agrippa's Pantheon and Its Origin,' in *The Pantheon: From Antiquity to the Present*, ed. Tod A. Marder and Mark Wilson Jones (Cambridge: Cambridge University Press, 2015), 49–78.

Leopardi, Giacomo, *Canti*, trans. Jonathan Galassi (London: Penguin, 2010).

Maloney, Donald, 'Representation and the Scopic Regime of (Post-)Cartesianism,' in *The Palgrave Handbook of Image Studies*, ed. Krešimir Purgar (Cham: Palgrave Macmillan, 2021), 449–65.

Martines, Giangiacomo, 'The Conception and Construction of Drum and Dome,' in *The Pantheon: From Antiquity to the Present*, ed. Tod A. Marder and Mark Wilson Jones (Cambridge: Cambridge University Press, 2015), 99–131.

Massey, Lyle, 'Framing and Mirroring the World,' in *The Renaissance World*, ed. John Jeffries Martin (London: Routledge, 2007), 51–68.

Most, Glenn W., 'Laocoons,' in *A Companion to Vergil's Aeneid and Its Tradition*, ed. Joseph Farrell and Michael C. J. Putnam (Hoboken, NJ: John Wiley, 2010), 325–40.

Olsen, Bjørrnar, *In Defense of Things: Archaeology and the Ontology of Objects* (Lanham, MD: AltaMira Press, 2010).

Palladio, Andrea, *I quattro libri dell'architettura*, vol. 4 (Venezia: Domenico de' Franceschi, 1570).

Panofsky, Erwin, *Perspective as Symbolic Form*, trans. Christopher S. Wood (1927; New York: Zone, 1991).

Pliny the Elder, *Natural History*, Volume X: Books 36–37, trans. D. E. Eichholz, Loeb Classical Library 419 (Cambridge, MA: Harvard University Press, 1962).

Retief, François, and Louise Cilliers, 'Malaria in Graeco-Roman Times,' *Acta Classica* 47 (2004): 127–37.

Schwab, Maren Elisabeth, and Anthony Grafton, *The Art of Discovery: Digging into the Past in Renaissance Europe* (Princeton: Princeton University Press, 2022).

Squire, Michael, ' "Fantasies so Varied and Bizarre": The Domus Aurea, the Renaissance, and the "Grotesque," ' in *A Companion to the Neronian Age*, ed. Emma Buckley and Martin D. Dinter (Oxford: Blackwell, 2013), 444–64.

Tamburrino, Eugenio, ed., *Aquam Ducere II: Proceedings of the Second International Summer School, Water and the City: Hydraulic Systems in the Roman Age* (Feltre, 24–28 August 2015) (Edizioni DBS: Seren del Grappa, 2018).

Thomas, Edmund, 'The Cult Statues of the Pantheon,' *Journal of Roman Studies* 107 (2017): 146–212.

Vasari, Giorgio, *Lives of the Most Eminent Painters, Sculptor, and Architects* (1550, 1567; New York: Random House, 2006).

Verstegen, Ian, 'Perspective, Space and Camera Obscura in the Renaissance,' in *The Palgrave Handbook of Image Studies*, ed. Krešimir Purgar (Cham: Palgrave Macmillan, 2021), 75–92.

Virgil, *Georgics*, ed. and trans. Peter Fallon (Oxford: Oxford University Press, 2004).

Volpe, Rita, and Antonella Parisi, 'Alla ricerca di una scoperta: Felice de Fredis e il luogo di ritrovamento del Laocoonte,' *Bullettino della Commissione Archeologica Comunale di Roma* 110 (2009): 81–110.

Zamperini, Alessandra, *Ornament and the Grotesque: Fantastical Decoration from Antiquity to Art Nouveau*, trans. Peter Spring (London: Thames and Hudson, 2008).

Ziolkowski, Theodore, *Gilgamesh Among Us: Modern Encounters with the Ancient Epic* (Ithaca and London: Cornell University Press, 2012).

Chapter 2

SOME NOTES ON BECKETT AND MICHELANGELO

Mariacristina Cavecchi

Abstract

Beckett's deep immersion in the visual images of the Italian Old Masters emerges in the pages of several scholars, although this story has yet to be told in coherent and comprehensive terms. This essay focuses mainly on the Irish playwright's interest in, not to say fascination with, Michelangelo Buonarroti, a giant through whom he may have found his artistic way. From his first published story, *Assumption* to *Catastrophe*, in which Protagonist stands on a plinth like a sculpture, Michelangelo was firmly rooted in Beckett's mind and played a pivotal role in his theatre, a role that is somehow impossible to describe with precision but inescapable.

Keywords: Michelangelo; sculpture; directing; stone; contrapposto; Bruce Nauman; Old Masters; curatorship; Giorgio Vasari.

In the Italian Rooms

The impact of Italian Old Masters on Beckett's plays is a story not yet written in coherent and comprehensive terms, even if Beckett's deep immersion in the visual images of Italian Old Masters emerges in the pages of several scholars. It suffices here to mention James Knowlson, who reports that Beckett's first visit to Florence, in 1927, was 'a breathtaking revelation:' the Pitti Palace, 'the sinister Uffizi' gallery, the Academia with Michelangelo's *David*; the Church of Santa Maria Novella, the Brancacci Chapel of Santa Maria del Carmine with Masaccio's famous frescoes.[1]

---

[1] James Knowlson, *Damned to Fame. The Life of Samuel Beckett* (London: Bloomsbury, 1996), 74–5.

While writing that Beckett generally 'preferred the Dutch and Flemish painters to the Italians', the biographer argues he 'was not insensitive to the wonders of the Florentine Tizianos, Giorgiones, Peruginos, Uccellos and Masaccios'.[2] Insensitive he certainly was not, as is proved by the many references to Italian art scattered throughout his artistic oeuvre and in numerous letters.

Unlike the broken man C in *That Time*, for whom the National Portrait Gallery is merely a place to shelter from the rain and cold, Beckett was famously an assiduous and knowledgeable visitor and also a *connoisseur* of the Italian Old Masters. Sometimes he even rightly doubted what the curators and the official catalogues said about an artist. Notably, experts had to conclude Beckett was right when he observed that Giorgione's *Venus Sleeping* in Dresden's Gemäldegalerie was 'in a mess'. As he suggested to his friend MacGreevy, 'the putto with the arrow and the bright bird sitting at her feet (by Giorgione or Titian?) was painted over with senseless landscape in the 19th century and the whole line of the left leg is destroyed'.[3]

Indeed, the correspondence with MacGreevy reveals Beckett's expertise in Italian art as well as his peculiar sensibility for questions relating to curatorship and exhibition. As early as 1931, he complained about the display of the newly acquired Perugino *Pietà* in the National Gallery of Ireland, 'buried behind a formidable barrage of shining glass, so that one is obliged to take cognisance of it progressively, square inch by square inch'.[4] This image of a difficult view of a painting that is 'rottenly hung in a rotten light behind this thick shop window, so that a total view of it is impossible'[5] will reappear in *That Time* (1974). Here, C speaks of a similar obstacle to a clear view, when he describes portraits in the Portrait Gallery as 'black with dirt and antiquity'[6] and remembers 'a vast oil black with age and dirt [...] black behind the glass where gradually as you peered trying to make it out gradually of all things a face appeared'.[7] Five years later, he would be equally unsatisfied by the 'big Perugino' which was back from Vienna where it had been restored and cleaned, or, in his opinion, 'overcleaned'.[8]

---

[2] Ibid.
[3] Samuel Beckett, Letter to Tom MacGreevy, 16 February 1937, in *The Letters of Samuel Beckett. 1929–1940*, vol. 1, eds. Martha Dow Fehsenfeld and Lois More Overbeck (Cambridge: Cambridge University Press, 2009), 444.
[4] Samuel Beckett, Letter to MacGreevy, 20 December 1931, vol. 1, 100.
[5] Ibid.
[6] Samuel Beckett, 'That Time', in *Samuel Beckett. The Complete Dramatic Works* (London: Faber and Faber, 1986) 385–95 (391).
[7] Ibid., 389.
[8] Beckett, Letter to MacGreevy, 17 July 1936, in *The Letters of Samuel Beckett. 1929–1940*, 358, 359–60 n. 6.

That his eye had been trained as the eye of a curator[9] is proved once again by the letter he wrote in May 1937, after seeing George Furlong's redistribution of the Dutch and Italian collections at the National Gallery of Ireland. On viewing the Italian collection, newly rehung and distributed across the first floor rooms (formerly the Dutch, Irish and Italian rooms), Beckett could not but dissent with the single line hanging ('which is all very well when there is plenty of room & the line set at the right height') as well as with the wallpaper chosen: 'an incredible shade of anchovy' which, he adds mockingly, Furlong, the director of the gallery, 'asserts "goes well" with "Italian pictures"', as a man might have a prejudice in favour of stout with oyster'. It is a display that brings Beckett to forcibly conclude 'it is time someone put him in mind of the purpose of a picture gallery, to provide pictures worth looking at and the possibility of seeing them'.[10] There is no need, here, to comment not only on Beckett's expertise but also on his interest for the impact on spectators of the works of art displayed. This expertise and interest also fuelled his theatre and led him to develop precise opinions and aesthetic tastes in staging, as confirmed by many. Suffice it to mention here the British theatre designer Jocelyn Herbert, who recalls that, when they collaborated for the premiere of *Endgame* in French at the Royal Court Theatre in 1957, their first meeting 'was a bit difficult' because 'Sam didn't like the [dark grey] colour of the set', although she thought 'it seemed quite suitable'.[11]

Interestingly too, Italian Old Masters and their masterpieces seem to come to Beckett's mind in one of the important moments of his life. Notably, when he wrote to his friend Thomas MacGreevy in 1933 to inform him that 'in a moment of gush' he had applied for a job as an assistant at the National Gallery in Trafalgar Square, he again referred to an Italian Old Master, Paolo Uccello, this time, punning on his name as well as Hamlet's line to Guildenstern (*Hamlet*, 2.2.375):

> In a moment of gush I applied for a job as assistant at the National Galley, Trafalgar Square, and got Charles Prentice & Jack Yeats to act as referees. I think I would be happy there for a time among the pigeons and not too far from the French charmers in the Garrick. Apart from my conoysership that can just separate Uccello from a handsaw I could cork the post as well [as] another.[12]

---

[9] Mariacristina Cavecchi, 'From Playwriting to Curatorship. An Investigation into the Status of Beckett's Stage Objects', in *The Exhibit in the Text. The Museological Practices of Literature*, eds. Caroline Patey and Laura Scuriatti (London: Peter Lang, 2009), 161–82.

[10] Letter to MacGreevy, 14 May 1937, vol. 1, 496–97.

[11] Jocelyn Herbert in *Beckett Remembering/Remembering Beckett. Uncollected Interviews with Samuel Beckett and Memories of Those Who Knew Him*, eds. James and Elizabeth Knowlson (London: Bloomsbury, 2006), 165.

[12] Beckett, Letter to MacGreevy, 9 October 1933, vol. 1, 166, 167.

Given the considerable evidence scattered in his work, it is hardly surprising that Beckett's connoisseurship of Italian art emerges in the pages of many scholars, who acknowledge that it impacted both the genesis and the form of his own visual/theatrical imagery, as well as his relationship with the stage. If it is true, as Katharine Worth has written, that, 'the air Beckett's characters breathe is thick with quotation',[13] much of the air in their lungs is thick with Italian art, even though, the fabric of visual intertextuality in Beckett's theatre is a mosaic of fragments, which are difficult to single out. Thus, to give just one example, it is worth mentioning that the much-quoted iconic figure of May in *Footfalls*, which transfigures and turns Antonello da Messina's *Virgin of the Annunciation* with her arms crossed over her chest into a more anguished and despairing figure, more in tune with Eduard Munch's *The Scream*,[14] could also, perhaps, be indebted to Donatello's *Santa Maria Maddalena*.[15] Although Beckett never acknowledged this source of inspiration, May's deep circles under her eyes and the dynamism of her robes are reminiscent of the wooden sculpture of this emaciated Mary Magdalen that Beckett may have seen in the Baptistery in Florence and read about in Vasari's *Lives*.[16]

In the Footsteps of Michelangelo

Perhaps it is no exaggeration to say that among the many Italian Old Masters who seem to have fuelled Beckett's imagination, Michelangelo Buonarroti played a hitherto underestimated role. Indeed, the Aretine artist may have had a profound influence on Beckett's theatre and guided the playwright in the construction of stage space.

It was Martin Esslin who, in his 1962 volume dedicated to studies in French fiction, compared Beckett's way of writing to Michelangelo's artistic practice:

> Like Michelangelo, who chipped away the rock to reveal the delicate beauty that had always been imprisoned within, Beckett works by discarding layer upon layer of conventional narrative material: description, character, psychology,

---

[13] Katharine Worth, *Samuel Beckett's Theatre: A Life Journey* (Oxford: Clarendon Press, 2001), 113.
[14] John Haynes and James Knowlson, *Images of Beckett* (Cambridge: Cambridge University Press, 2003), 83. Notoriously, Billie Whitelaw herself declared that in *Footfalls* she 'felt like a moving, musical Eduard Munch painting.' Billie Whitelaw, *Billie Whitelaw … Who He? An Autobiography* (London: Hodder & Stoughton, 1995), 144.
[15] An image and the technical description of the sculpture, which is now held at the Museo dell'Opera del Duomo in Florence, are visible at the following link: https://duomo.firenze.it/it/scopri/museo-dell-opera-del-duomo/le-sale/sala-della-maddalena/8620/donatello-maddalena-penitente, accessed 12 March 2024.
[16] Giorgio Vasari, *Le vite de' più eccellenti pittori, scultori ed architetti, 1550*, eds. Luciano Bellosi and Aldo Rossi (Torino: Einaudi, 1986), 334.

incident, plot, to lay bare the secret workings of the human mind. But here too he can only work as it were, by measuring out the limits of the sayable so that the unsayable may be guessed, hidden behind the last, impenetrable barrier.[17]

Yet, this comparison has never been truly embraced or coherently developed. The Irish playwright's interest in – not to say fascination with – Michelangelo is a chapter yet to be written, even though Beckett's entire literary career opens and almost closes with references to the Renaissance artist and his sculptural work.

In his first published short story, *Assumption* (1929), the protagonist painter mentions Michelangelo and his tomb when he wants to describe the insolence of women and expresses his initial annoyance at the woman who broke into his room and broke his silence:

> He clenched his hands in a fury against the enormous impertinence of women, their noisy intrusive curious enthusiasm, like the spontaneous expression of admiration bursting from American hearts before Michelangelo's tomb in Santa Croce.[18]

The passage demonstrates the great impression the visit to Santa Croce must have had on the Irish writer, who two years later still recalls the enthusiasm aroused by the sight of Michelangelo's tomb even without going so far as to conclude, as Emily F. Oliver does, that in the short story 'the whispering man' is Michelangelo himself and the woman the Sistine Chapel.[19] Beckett's reference to Michelangelo in relation to his interest in 'the relationship between viewer and object'[20] is something Beckett will pick up on a couple of years later in *A Dream of Fair to Middling Women*, when the narrator describes the way Belacqua stares at the starfield: 'he stands well out in the dark arena, his head looked up uncomfortable at the starfield, like Mr Ruskin in the Sistine, looking for Vega.'[21] In fact, according to Conor Carville, the reference to Ruskin's *Modern Painters* 'sets the tone of a passage that is as much a meditation on

---

[17] Martin Esslin, 'Samuel Beckett' in *The Novelist as Philosopher: Studies in French Fiction 1935–1960*, ed. John Cruickshank (London: Oxford University Press, 1962), 145.

[18] Samuel Beckett, 'Assumption' in Samuel Beckett, *The Complete Short Prose. 1929–1989*, ed. S. E. Gontarski (New York: Grove Press, 1995), 5.

[19] Emily F. Oliver, *'That Flesh-locked Sea of Silence': Language, Gender, and Sexuality in Beckett's Short Fiction* (Digital Commons@Georgia Southern: University Honors Program Thesis) 95, accessed 27 December 2022, https://digitalcommons.georgiasouthern.edu/cgi/viewcontent.cgi?article=1104&context=honors-theses.

[20] Conor Carville, *Samuel Beckett and the Visual Arts* (Cambridge: Cambridge University Press, 2018), 53.

[21] Samuel Beckett, *Dream of Fair to Middling Women*, eds. Eoin O'Brien and Edith Fournier (Arcade Pub. in Association with Riverrun, 1993), 16.

the image as a description of the firmament', which Beckett offers by equating 'ideas of pure perception' with 'material surface'.[22]

Even the elderly woman 'with her stone face' protagonist of *Mal vu mal dit*, the prose-poem written in 1980–81, almost at the end of Beckett's career, confirms a connection between Michelangelo and Beckett's 'using a stone to problematize the space between the perceiving subject and the object perceived viewer', 'between decaying subjectivity and stony permanence'.[23] Thus, the woman who wonders whether the stone tomb she is observing owes its 'rough-hewn air' to atmospheric agents or to some human hand forced to desist refers to the hands of Michelangelo who left the bust of Brutus unfinished at the Bargello:

> Changed the stone that draws her when revisited alone. Or she who changes it when side by side. Now alone it leans. Backward or forward as the case may be. Is it to nature alone it owes its rough-hewn air? Or to some too human hand forced to desist? As Michelangelo's from the regicide's bust. If there may not be no more questions let there at least be no more answers. Granite of no common variety assuredly. Black as jade the jasper that flecks its whiteness. On its what is the wrong word its uptilted face obscure graffiti. Scrawled by the ages for the eye to solicit in vain. Winter evenings on her doorstep she imagines she can see it glitter afar. When from their source in the west-south-west the last rays rake its adverse face. Such ill seen the stone alone where it stands at the far fringe of the pastures.[24]

Beckett returned to Michelangelo's unfinished bust of Brutus in a letter written to MacGreevy when, holding back from buying a volume on Adriaen Brouwer, he compared himself to Michelangelo, who abandoned the project to sculpt the bust of Brutus[25]:

> Zwemmer's have a number [of *Classiker der Kunst*] at reduced prices. I nearly bought a Brouwer in the Künstlermappen series but withheld my hand like Michelangelo from Brutus.[26]

Moreover, Beckett himself wrote to MacGreevy in January 1935 and told him about the 'stuff' in his 'little room' in London and the reproduction,

---

[22] Carville, *Samuel Beckett and the Visual Arts*, 53.
[23] Michael Angelo Rodriguez, '"Everywhere Stone Is Gaining": The Struggle for the Sacred in Samuel Beckett's *Ill Seen Ill Said*', *Samuel Beckett Today / Aujourd'hui*, vol. 14, *After Beckett / D'après Beckett* (2004): 105–16 (108–9).
[24] Samuel Beckett 'Ill Seen Ill Said', in *Samuel Beckett. Company. Ill Seen Ill Said. Worstward Ho. Stirrings Still*, ed. Dirk Van Hulle (London: Faber and Faber, 2009), 67–68.
[25] Beckett, Letter to MacGreevy, 14 February 1935, vol. 1, 252n.
[26] Ibid., 250.

above the mantelpiece, of Michelangelo's *Crepuscolo*, the unfinished sculptural figure on Lorenzo dei Medici's tomb in the Medici Chapel:

> I have got all my stuff together in this little room at last, and shelves up. I wish you could see my four old men over the mantelpiece, the Chartres Aristotle & Père Eternel, the Buonarroti Crepusocolo [*for* Buonarroti Crepuscolo] & the Tête du Christ du Calvaire from the Puits de Moïse at Dijon.[27]

Michelangelo's work was firmly rooted in Beckett's mind.

Why? Anne Atik remembers that during a conversation about Alberti, Vasari and other Italian art theorists, Beckett gave his friend Avigdor Arikha his copy of Giorgio Vasari's *Lives of the Most Eminent Italian Architects, Painters and Sculptors*, a 1568 volume tracing the history of Renaissance art from Giotto to Michelangelo,[28] which he had bought 'eager to learn more about early Italian art'[29] when he went to Italy in summer 1927. Beckett, who 'as a child in Foxrock had nurtured a self-confessed "love" for certain stones' that he used to take home with him from the beach 'in order to protect them from the wearing away of the waves or the vagaries of the weather',[30] might have found some interest in the life of Michelagnolo Buonarroti. He was an artist who was placed in the care of a stone-cutter's wife and who grew up in Settignano, a place three miles from Florence that Vasari describes as 'copioso di sassi e per tutto pieno di cave di macigni, che son lavorati di continovo da scarpellini e scultori, che nascono in quel luogo la maggior parte'[31] ['rich in stone, more especially in quarries of the *macigno* which are constantly worked by stone-cutters and sculptors, for the most part natives of the place'.[32]]. Would it be too far-fetched to assume that Beckett wrote the famous 'seize pierres à sucer' section of *Molloy*[33] having in mind Michelangelo's image of himself sucking 'chisels and hammers' along with the milk of his nurse? An image he could

---

[27] Beckett, Letter to MacGreevy, 29 January 1936, vol. 1, 306.
[28] Anne Atik, *How It Was. A Memoir of Samuel Beckett* (London: Faber and Faber, 2001), 2, 52.
[29] Knowlson, *Damned to Fame*, 74–75.
[30] Ibid., 29.
[31] Giorgio Vasari, *Le Vite dei più eccellenti pittori, scultori e architetti* (Firenze: Le Monnier, 1856), vol. XII, 159.
[32] Giorgio Vasari, *Vasari's Lives of the Artists. Giotto, Masaccio, Fra Filippo Lippi, Botticelli, Leonardo, Raphael, Michelangelo, Titian*, ed. Marylin Aronberg Lavin, trans. Jonathan Foster (Mineola, New York: Dover Publications, 1967), 111.
[33] Samuel Beckett, *Molloy*, in Samuel Beckett, *Molloy. Malone Dies. The Unnamable* (New York, London, Toronto: Alfred A. Knopf, 2015), 78–80.

have found in the *Lives*, where Vasari reports what Michelangelo had once confessed to him:

> Giorgio, if I have anything good in me, it comes from my birth in the pure air of your country of Arezzo, and perhaps also from the fact that, with the milk of my nurse, I sucked in the chisels and hammers wherewith I make my figures.[34]

But beyond the biographical coincidence, there are several reasons why the two artists' aesthetics are intertwined. Indeed, in the chapter Vasari devotes to Michelagnolo Buonarroti, Beckett may have found a common attraction for the stone imagery that he would later make his own and develop in his work.

Although the analysis of the many references to stones, pebbles and slabs scattered throughout Beckett's *oeuvre*, ranging 'from seemingly frivolous episodes to sustained narratives of profound mythological import',[35] and the discussion of their possible different meanings are beyond the scope of this essay, it seems plausible to assume that Buonarroti's work with stones and marble, as described by Vasari, may have profoundly affected Beckett's imagination. Easily, one could perceive an echo of Vasari's description of Michelangelo's childhood, spent in a place resonating with a similar constant noise of stonecutters and sculptors in the image in *Malones Dies* of 'the hammers of the stone cutters ringing all day like bells':

> No, they are no more than hills, they raise themselves gently, faintly blue out of the confused plain. It was there somewhere he was born, in a fine house, of loving parents. Their slopes are covered with ling and furze, its hot yellow bells, better known as gorse. The hammers of the stone cutters ring all day like bells.[36]

Critics have interpreted Beckett's obsession with stones in his plays in different ways; some of them have related it to the imaginary of the statue, although none of them have ever explicitly referred to Michelangelo.

Benjamin Keatinge focuses on the imagery of the statue in Beckett's drama when he analyses 'the synergy of the animate and inanimate'.[37] If the Ovidian myth of petrification, Echo, is behind many plays from *Not I*, *Footfalls* or *That Time*, to *Rockaby*, he argues, the myths of Mnemon and Pygmalion, who represent the opposite process of reanimation and

---

[34] Vasari, *Vasari's Lives of the Artists*, 111.
[35] Rodriguez, *Everywhere Stone Is Gaining*, 105–16 (106).
[36] Samuel Beckett, *Malone Dies*, in Beckett, *Molloy. Malone Dies. The Unnamable*, 326.
[37] Benjamin Keatinge, '"The Hammers of the Stone-Cutters": Samuel Beckett's Stone Imagery', *Irish University Review*, vol. 37, no. 2 (Autumn–Winter, 2007): 322–39 (329).

reawakening, are found in *Catastrophe*, in the reanimation of the Protagonist as he 'raises his head, fixes the audience',[38] defying the Director, a 'human statue liberating itself from its calcified repression'.[39] Verna Foster also associates the imagery of stone with sculpture and focuses on 'the powerful verbal and visual image of stone sculpture' at the end of *Ohio Impromptu* as she compares the two protagonists of 'the sad tale', the Listener and the Reader, who 'sat on as though turned to stone',[40] to Hermione, who is discovered 'standing like a statue' at the end of Shakespeare's *The Winter's Tale* (5.3.21), one of Beckett's sources of inspiration, even though the stone image is used for opposite aims.[41]

Also in *That Time*, where the ruin of selfhood is suggested by recurring allusions to stone, one might find a hint at the artistic work of a sculptor carving marble in the image of the 'seat marble slab' in the Portrait Gallery where the protagonist C sits down and dries off. 'A tombstone? A dolmen? A monument dating from patriarchal Druidic times?' asks Bettina Knapp.[42] The sculpture image passes from play to play, from performance to performance; perhaps it is no coincidence that Benedict Nightingale describes the actor Patrick Magee, 'old white face, long flaring white hair',[43] as 'some unearthly blend' of Michelangelo God in the Sistine Chapel and Ibsen in his wild old age.[44]

It is also significant that what Keatinge observes of Beckett, in whose hands 'the very inexpressive qualities of stone become expressive'[45] resonates with the words of Vasari who, when confronted with Michelangelo's *Pietà*, speaks of Michelangelo's 'miracle' of turning into 'perfection' a stone, which just before was without form or shape:

> Quivi è dolcissima aria di testa, et una concordanza né muscoli delle braccia et in quelli del corpo e delle gambe, i polsi e le vene lavorate, che inverso si maraviglia lo stupore che mano d'artefice abbia potuto sì divinamente e propriamente fare in pochissimo tempo cosa sì mirabile; che certo è un miracolo che un

---

[39] Keatinge, *The Hammers of the Stone-Cutters*, 333.
[38] Samuel Beckett, *Catastrophe*, in Beckett, *The Complete Dramatic Works*, 461.
[40] Samuel Beckett, *Ohio Impromptu*, in Beckett, *The Complete Dramatic Works*, 447, 448.
[41] Verna Foster, 'Beckett's Winter's Tale: Tragicomic Transformation in *Ohio Impromptu*', *Journal of Beckett Studies*, vol. 1, no. 1–2 (January 1992): 67–76.
[42] Bettina Knapp, 'Beckett's *That Time*: 'That double-headed monster... Time', *Études irlandaises*, no. 15–2 (1990): 65–73 (67).
[43] Beckett, *That Time*, 388.
[44] 'Benedict Nightingale in *New Statesman*', 28 May 1976, in *Samuel Beckett: the Critical Heritage*, eds. Lawrence Graver and Raymond Federman (London: Routledge, 2003) 391.
[45] Keatinge, *The Hammers of the Stone-Cutters*, 337.

sasso, da principio senza forma nessuna, si sia mai ridotto a quella perfezione, che la natura a fatica suol formar nella carne.[46]

Michelangelo was a giant, a milestone through which possibly Beckett found his own artistic way. Indeed, not only the idea of stripping away the layers of language and meaning, so familiar from the famous German letter in which Beckett refers to language as 'a veil that must be torn apart in order to get at the things (or the Nothingness) behind them', or his description of the creative process as a 'getting below the surface [...] the infinitesimal murmur [...] a gray struggle, a groping in the dark for a shadow',[47] but also the way he directed by subtraction seems to corroborate the hypothesis that Beckett understood and appropriated in his own way that experience of sculpture, which Michelangelo himself defines as 'quella che si fa per forza di levare' ('for sculpture I mean what you make by subtracting').[48]

It is a practice by way of *levare* that, blended with the tendencies of minimalism and conceptual art to empty the stage, albeit with due distinction, Beckett also seems to share with his friend Alberto Giacometti,[49] as evidenced by their now famous collaboration on the 1961 production of *En attendant Godot* at the Théâtre de l'Odéon in Paris. Their common preoccupation with existential emptiness and the tropes of 'reduction, negation, cancellation and despair'[50] emerge clearly from the anecdote by Italian poet and novelist Giorgio Soavi, who recounts how the tree was created through a process of progressive subtraction that the two artists completely shared:

> Al momento delle prove generali della commedia i due artisti si diedero appuntamento nella platea, deserta, di quel piccolo teatro parigino. Al buio nella sala, fumando accanitamente, Giacometti e Beckett osservavano il tecnico delle

---

[46] Vasari, *Le Vite de' più eccellenti pittori, scultori ed architetti*, 918. Trans. 'There is besides a most exquisite expression in the countenance, and the limbs are affixed to the trunk in a manner that is truly perfect. The veins and pulses, moreover, are indicated with so much exactitude that one cannot but marvel how the hand of the artist should in a short time have produced such a work, or how a stone, which just before was without form or shape, should all at once display such perfection as nature can but rarely produce in the flesh' (Vasari, *Vasari's Lives of the Artists*, 118).

[47] Samuel Beckett to Lawrence Harvey, *Samuel Beckett, Poet and Critic* (Princeton: Princeton University Press, 1970), 247.

[48] Michelangelo Buonarroti, *Letter to messer Benedetto Varchi*, CDLXII, in *Le lettere di Michelangelo Buonarroti pubblicate coi Ricordi ed i contratti artistici*, ed. Gaetano Milanesi (Firenze: Coi Tipi dei Successori Le Monnier, 1875), 522–23.

[49] Andrea Pinotti, 'Soltanto l'essenziale. Beckett e Giacometti', in *Tra le lingue tra i linguaggi. Cent'anni di Samuel Beckett*, eds. Mariacristina Cavecchi and Caroline Patey (Milano: Cisalpino, 2007), 263–80.

[50] H. Porter Abbott, *Beckett Writing Beckett* (Ithaca: Cornell University Press, 1996), 108.

luci preparare la scena. I due non parlavano ma stavano concentrati, ciascuno per la propria parte.

Poi Giacometti disse: toglierei quel ramo. È di troppo. Tu cosa ne pensi?

Beckett proruppe in una specie di lamento di gioia. E confermò: era la sola cosa che ti volevo dire. Di togliere quel ramo. Adesso va benissimo.

No, disse Giacometti che nel frattempo si era rimesso a sedere. Dobbiamo stare attenti. In scena ci deve essere soltanto l'essenziale. Non farmi fretta. Fammi pensare.

Passò altro tempo. Nessuno in sala, o sul palcoscenico, osava fiatare. Quando Giacometti si alzò aveva deciso. Attraversò il teatro, salì con un certo sforzo, dato che trascinava il piede ferito, in palcoscenico, si tolse quel relitto che chiamava impermeabile che finì per terra, tolse anche la giacca, poi salì su un praticabile e guardando da vicino il proprio albero cominciò a togliere un rametto dopo l'altro.

Ogni tanto si fermava e, facendosi schermo con la mano, gridava a Beckett seduto laggiù in fondo al buio della platea: adesso va meglio, no?

È perfetto, diceva Beckett. Adesso va proprio bene. Un momento ancora, diceva Giacometti. Aspetta. Spezzò altri rametti. E così?

Be', così è perfetto.

Aspetta. Ecco.

Quando Giacometti fu soddisfatto, dell'albero era rimasto soltanto l'esile tronco. Dalla platea, dove i due vi si trovarono per fumare insieme, si vedeva una cosa striminzita e storta, una specie di niente della natura che a loro sembrò l'ideale...[51]

---

[51] Giorgio Soavi, *Il quadro che mi manca* (Milano: Garzanti, 1986), 36–38. Trans. 'For the general rehearsal the two artists met in the empty stalls of that small theatre in Paris. In the dark, relentlessly smoking, Giacometti and Beckett were observing the light technician while he was preparing the scene. They did not say a word. They were focused. Then Giacometti said: I would take that bough away. It's too much. What do you think?

Beckett burst out in a kind of joyful moaning. And he confirmed: it was the only thing I wanted to tell you. To take that bough away. Now it is right.

No, said Giacometti, who in the meantime had sat down again. We must be careful. On stage there must only be the essential. Don't rush me. Let me think.

Some time passed by. No one in the stalls or on the stage dared to breathe. When Giacometti stood up, he had decided. He crossed the theatre, dragged himself up the stage with some effort given his wounded foot, took off that rag he used to call a raincoat, which ended up on the floor, took off his jacket, too, then climbed on a practicable and looking at his own tree from close up he started taking away sprig after sprig.

Sometimes he stopped and, shielding his eyes with his hands, he shouted to Beckett, who was sitting in the back of the dark stalls: it is better now, isn't it?

It is perfect, was Beckett's answer. Now it is right indeed.

Wait a moment. Giacometti said. Wait. He broke two other sprigs. And now?

Well, now it is perfect.

Wait. Now.

When Giacometti was satisfied with the tree, what was left was only the thin trunk. From the stalls, where the two artists met to smoke together, they saw a stunted and crooked thing, a kind of nothing of nature that to them appeared as ideal...'

Billie Whitelaw's well-known words about working with Beckett on *Footfalls* support the association between his directing and sculpture by way of *levare*: 'Sometimes I felt as if he were a sculptor and I a piece of clay. At other times I might be a piece of marble that he needed to chip away at.'[52] Beckett was not the kind of director who gave instruction from the stalls; on the contrary, he used to step into the space of the stage and work with the actor's body.

This image of a director moulding the actor's body in the way a sculptor moulds matter recurs in his play commissioned for the 1982 Avignon Festival's Havel Night, *Catastrophe*, a play in which, according to David Lloyd, 'the theatre itself becomes the scene not so much of a performance as of a spectacle', and the Protagonist stands on a plinth 'for all the world like a sculpture'.[53] The Protagonist's 'whitened' hands, legs and 'cranium' have led many commentators to point to 'centuries of an iconography of the martyred Christ or martyred saints'[54] and the numerous paintings of 'secular and anonymous *Ecce Homo* exhibiting the appearance of this human thing as an image of catastrophe'[55] as a persuasive source of inspiration. Also considered are 'the praying, stonelike figures in a Mantegna painting',[56] particularly in his famous *Saint Sebastian* in the Louvre, which shows the monumental figure standing on a pedestal of ruins, and Antonello da Messina's *Saint Sebastian*, which Beckett saw in Dresden in 1937 and which he recalls almost perfectly in a letter to Duthuit in 1948.[57] It is significant that the Protagonist emerges both by subtraction, as he is progressively stripped of his clothes, and by whitening, as his flesh 'is whitened to approximate to stone or white marble'.[58] In this dramaticule, which has been interpreted both as a political metaphor and as a Beckettian parody of the Director-Despot, the Protagonist is also a living sculpture, which was inspired not only by Michelangelo's art of *levare* but also by the various episodes of Michelangelo the sculptor at work with his statues that Beckett had read about in Vasari's *Lives*. Above all, more than a perfect and stable monument, the Protagonist reasserts himself as a living sculpture in tune with that dramatic geometry that traces paths of

---

[52] Whitelaw, *Billie Whitelaw…Who He?*, 144.
[53] David Lloyd, *Beckett's Thing. Painting and Theatre* (Edinburgh: Edinburgh University Press, 2018), 223.
[54] Knowlson, *Damned to Fame*, 826, n. 108.
[55] Lloyd, *Beckett's Thing*, 223.
[56] Samuel Knowlson, *Damned to Fame*, 826, n. 108.
[57] Samuel Beckett, Letter to Georges Duthuit, 27 July 1948, in *The Letters of Samuel Beckett. 1941–1956*, vol. 2, eds. George Craig, Martha Dow Fehsenfeld, Dan Gunn and Lois More Overbeck (Cambridge: Cambridge University Press, 2011).
[58] Knowlson, *Damned to Fame*, 826, n. 108.

movement for actors who are enclosed in a limited space, from *Happy Days*, where Winnie's body sinks like sculpture into a mound of earth, to *Quadrat*, where the movement of each performer is meticulously traced, not forgetting *Not I*, *That Time*, *Footfalls*, *Rockaby* and *A Piece of Monologue*. As P raises his head against the Director's attempt to turn him, a human being, into an inorganic and inanimate object, Beckett eschews the distinction between organic and inorganic at the ontological level. As Knowlson explains, later in his life, the Irish playwright 'came to rationalise' his 'fascination' for mineral and petrification and 'linked his interest with Sigmund Freud's view that human beings have a prebirth nostalgia to return to a mineral state'.[59] But Beckett's passion for stones also reveals a posthuman inclination. As Amanda Dennis argues, his work 'may sketch plans for a [...] *post-human* version of agency, a more collaborative mode of acting, so to speak, that eases the divide between the human, the world of inanimate objects, and the earth'.[60] Thus, in *Catastrophe*, he explores 'the link between bodily limitations and abjection – even incarceration – and the possibility of reconfiguring the structures that enable such conditions',[61] shifting the Protagonist's passivity into a version of agency. This shift also occurs in *Quad*, even if in this case the agency does not depend upon a single gesture. In this TV play, generally interpreted as dramatizing a lack of human agency, the four performers walking their courses, never deviating, suggest an alternative version of agency: 'not the agency of willing and intention we might attribute to a humanist subject (a voluntarism), but an agency that develops from the capacity of a physical body or a collaboration of bodies to fashion space and to organize and determine an environment'.[62]

A Coda

Finally, the sculptural inspiration of Beckett's theatre could be corroborated by the ideal conversation of the American artist Bruce Nauman with the Irish playwright. It is 'a loose exchange'[63] which shows the two artists' common interest in issues related to body and space. Significantly, Beckett's interest

---

[59] Knowlson, *Damned to Fame*, 29.
[60] Amanda Dennis, 'Compulsive Bodies, Creative Bodies: Beckett and Agency in the 21st Century', *Journal of Beckett Studies* 27.1, 2018, 5–21 (8).
[61] Ibid., 17.
[62] Ibid.
[63] Ingrid Schaffner speculates about 'a loose exchange between two matures bodies of work' in her essay 'Circling Oblivion / Bruce Nauman through Samuel Beckett' in *Bruce Nauman*, ed. Robert C. Morgan (Baltimore and London: John Hopkins University Press, 2002) 163–73 (166). The relationship between the two artists was the focus of the 'Samuel Beckett/Bruce Nauman' exhibition at the Kunsthalle in Wien (4/2 – 30/4 2000).

in sculpture became a source of inspiration for Nauman's experimentation with the body and exploration of the *contrapposto*,[64] masterfully exemplified by Michelangelo's *David*, that he would later develop in his videos.

In the black and white video *Walk with Contrapposto* (1969), Nauman sets in motion the pose of *contrapposto* and shows its absurdity by walking in an exaggerated way, with the body twisted so that hips, shoulders and head are turned in different directions, occupying the limited space of a corridor only 20 inches wide. Again, in his late-career revisit of this early work, the *Contrapposto Studies, I through VII* (2015/16) and *Contrapposto Studies, I through vii* (2015/16), Nauman plays 'the role of David'[65] to show that 'the pose we intellectually receive as having set Western sculpture in motion – by breaking with a static frontal presentation – is impossible'.[66] More than that, he recognized in Beckett's characters a model for that living sculpture that he would later impersonate. The absurdity of the contrapposto and the consequent fracturing between the real and the represented are therefore underlined in *Slow Angle Walk (Beckett Walk)* (1968), one of the exercises through which Nauman developed his artistic language by using his body as a piece of material[67] and manipulates it into a 'body sculpture',[68] 'a kind of living sculpture'[69]:

> In front of a fixed camera, placed on its side – so that the filmed image is also on its side – the artist spent about an hour repeating a laborious sequence of bodily movements. [...] Hands together behind his back, the artist starts out

---

[64] The *contrapposto* is the pose of a standing human body resting its weight on a single leg, thus provoking a dynamic torsion that contrasts with the rigidity of the poses of Archaic Greek sculpture, which became a fundamental aspect of Western sculpture since its appearance in Greece in the fifth century BC, as well as one of the main features of Renaissance art. Erica F. Battle, 'Bruce Nauman: Bodies at Work', in *Bruce Nauman, 'Contrapposto Studies'*. Palazzo Grassi – Punta della Dogana. Venezia (23.5.21–27.11.2022), eds. Carlos Basualdo and Caroline Bourgeois (Venezia: Marsilio, 2021) 132–42 (135).

[65] Damon Krukowski, 'Following the Sounds', in *Bruce Nauman*, eds. Basualdo and Bourgeois, 101–6 (106).

[66] Krukowski, 'Following the Sounds', 105.

[67] Bruce Nauman quoted in Willoughby Sharp, 'Two Interviews (1970)', in *Bruce Nauman*, ed. Robert C. Morgan (Baltimore and London: John Hopkins University Press, 2002), 242.

[68] Sharp, *Two Interviews*, 243.

[69] Marco De Michelis, 'Spaces', in *Bruce Nauman: Topological Gardens*, eds Carlos Basualdo and Michael R. Taylor (New Haven and London: Philadelphia Museum of Art in association with Yale University Press, 2009), 65–83 (71).

with one leg at a right angle, swings around 45 degrees and lets his foot come nosily down. Again, he stretches out his leg backwards at a right angle and starts again with the other leg, his body swinging forward like a pendulum.

As he advances towards the camera, and therefore the viewer, it becomes progressively harder to discern his actions. Nauman's body is shown as fragmentary: the head is often cut off with only a feet or leg on view. At times he exits the screen completely with only the sound of his steps indicating his presence. [...] The recording was continuous and lasted an hour, with no break in either the filming or the action (an hour is the running time of the film). While the movement is methodically executed, the action does not exclude chance or a sense of tension, as when the artist loses his balance and falls. The spectator's impression of witnessing an absurd situation is confirmed by the extreme concentration of and conviction manifested by Nauman throughout his performance.[70]

Meaningfully, the video overtly references Samuel Beckett and alludes to the absurd locomotion of Beckett's characters, such as Molloy or Watt, in the peculiar pattern of movement that Nauman adopted. The American artist describes his exercises in movement as 'a tedious and complicated process to gain even a yard'.[71] In similar terms, Molloy gives details of his own walking patterns and the difficulty of using crutches:

I left the shelter of the doorway and began levering myself forward, swinging slowly through the sullen air. There is rapture, or there should be, in the motion crutches give. It is a series of little flights, skimming the ground. You take off, you land, through the thronging sound in wind and limb, who have to fasten one foot to the ground before they dare lift up the other. And even their most joyous hastening is less aerial than my hobble.[72]

Like Molloy, who finds that he can use the curvature of the road to even out the length of his legs, Nauman 'finds a solution to the problem of walking without bending his legs, swinging them through on each step. As he does

---

[70] Programme of the exhibition *Bruce Nauman, 'Contrapposto Studies'* at Palazzo Grassi – Punta della Dogana, Venice (23.5.21–27.11.2022), curated by Carlos Basualdo and Caroline Bourgeois, 11–12.
[71] Nauman in Schaffner, *Circling Oblivion / Bruce Nauman through Samuel Beckett*, 167.
[72] Samuel Beckett, *Molloy* (New York: Grove Press, 1955), 86.

so his direction changes, the pattern adopted resembling, but not precisely replicating, that performed by Watt in Beckett's novel'[73]:

> Watt's way of advancing due east, for example, was to turn his bust as far as possible towards the north and at the same time to fling out his right leg as far as possible towards the south, and then to turn his bust as far as possible towards the south and at the same to fling out his left leg as far as possible towards the north [...] and so on, over and over again, many many times, until he reached his destination and could sit down.[74]

Like Watt, Nauman changes direction on every step to form a pattern around the floor of the studio, thus transforming his body into 'a sculptural entity subject to repetitive actions interacting with the surround space'.[75]

Both Beckett and Nauman deal with limits, and the living statues they create on stage or in the studio acknowledge their limits, their entrapment. What Nauman finds in Beckett's work is the awareness and representation of movement, however difficult or minimal, which Beckett discovered in Michelangelo's statues, such as the *David*, whose pose – 'the head forcefully turned to the left, the disengaged left leg pulling the left hip ever so slightly downward, and the musculature of the right knee slowly bulging to respond to the added weight it is carrying'[76] – suggests 'imminent movement and lifelike action'.[77]

Last but not least, the encounter between Nauman and Beckett, should one wish to explore it further, leads one to consider how both Nauman and Beckett see performance as an integral part of their way of considering sculpture, as both seek 'a way to present, to involve people in the work'.[78] If Nauman claims that 'sculpture was always involved in performance in the sense that it involves the spectator, because the spectator has to walk around it',[79]

---

[73] Ruth Burgon, 'Pacing the Cell: Walking and Productivity in the Work of Bruce Nauman', *Tate Papers* no. 26, Autumn 2016.
[74] Samuel Beckett, *Watt* (New York: Grove Press, 1953), 23.
[75] Programme of the exhibition *Bruce Nauman*, 10.
[76] John T. Paoletti, *Michelangelo's* David (Cambridge: Cambridge University Press, 2015), 176.
[77] Ibid.
[78] Bruce Nauman quoted in Robert C. Morgan, 'Interview with Bruce Nauman', in *Bruce Nauman*, ed. Robert C. Morgan (Baltimore and London: John Hopkins University Press, 2002), 262–69 (266).
[79] Ibid., 266.

Beckett's sculptural figures also require the viewer to actively participate and continuously change perspective. In *Catastrophe*, the movement of the Director, disrupting the fourth wall, 'denies the audience any imaginary identification with a single perspective that could secure it in place before the spectacle'.[80] As Lloyd argues the spectators are implied ' "in the picture", but doubled: at first apparently as subjects of spectatorship', and then in the end, as 'the objects of the Protagonist's gaze that "fixes" ' them, 'with all the force of ambiguity that stage direction musters'.[81] In a similar way, Reader and Listener in *Ohio Impromptu* are not only the subject but also the object of the narrative, as 'the narrative and act of narration seem to run parallel and merge with one another'.[82] It is a perpetual shift between the subject and the object of observation, which Beckett has also developed through Michelangelo, whose statues – the *David* above all – not only give the idea of movement but also presuppose a continuous change in the viewer's perspective.

Definitely not an easy triangle, Michelangelo, Beckett and Nauman have, nevertheless, a story to tell, in which one may discover how their perceptions of movement are strangely connected, and ultimately grasp Michelangelo's extraordinary capacity to endure in the living statues that perform on Beckett's stages or in Nauman's studio.

Bibliography

Abbott, H. Porter. *Beckett Writing Beckett*. Ithaca: Cornell University Press, 1996.
Atik, Anne. *How It Was. A Memoir of Samuel Beckett*. London: Faber and Faber, 2001.
Basualdo, Carlos and Caroline Bourgeois, eds. *Bruce Nauman*. 'Contrapposto Studies'. Venezia: Marsilio, 2021. Published following the exhibition Bruce Nauman, 'Contrapposto Studies' at the Palazzo Grassi – Punta della Dogana, Venice (23.5.21–27.11.2022).
Battle, Erica F. 'Bruce Nauman: Bodies at Work'. In *Bruce Nauman*, 'Contrapposto Studies', edited by Carlos Basualdo and Caroline Bourgeois. Venezia: Marsilio, 2021. 132–42.
Beckett, Samuel. *Company. Ill Seen Ill Said. Worstward Ho. Stirrings Still*, edited by Dirk Van Hulle. London: Faber and Faber, 2009.
———. *Dream of Fair to Middling Women*, edited by Eoin O'Brien and Edith Fournier. New York: Arcade Publishing in association with Riverrun Press, 1993.
———. *Molloy*. New York: Grove Press, 1955.

---

[80] Lloyd, *Beckett's Thing*, 225.
[81] Ibid. See also Craig N. Owens 'Applause and Hiss: Implicating the Audience in Samuel Beckett's *Rockaby* and *Catastrophe*', *The Journal of the Midwest Modern Language Association*, vol. 36, no. 1, Thinking Post-Identity (Spring 2003): 74–81 (79–80).
[82] Laurens Des Vos, 'The Observer Observed. The Promise of the Posthuman: Homeostasis, Autopoiesis and Virtuality in Samuel Beckett', *Journal of Beckett Studies* 27.2 (2018): 245–60 (251).

——. *Molloy. Malone Dies. The Unnamable*. New York, London, Toronto: Alfred A. Knopf, 2015.

——. *The Complete Dramatic Works*. London: Faber and Faber, 1986.

——. *The Complete Short Prose. 1929–1989*, edited by S. E. Gontarski. New York: Grove Press, 1995.

——. *The Letters of Samuel Beckett. 1929–1940*, vol. 1, edited by Martha Dow Fehsenfeld and Lois More Overbeck. Cambridge: Cambridge University Press, 2009.

——. *The Letters of Samuel Beckett. 1941–1956*, vol. 2, edited by George Craig, Martha Dow Fehsenfeld, Dan Gunn and Lois More Overbeck. Cambridge: Cambridge University Press, 2011.

——. *Watt*. New York: Grove Press, 1953.

Buonarroti, Michelangelo. 'Letter to messer Benedetto Varchi, CDLXII'. In *Le lettere di Michelangelo Buonarroti pubblicate coi Ricordi ed i contratti artistici*, edited by Gaetano Milanesi. Firenze: Coi Tipi dei Successori Le Monnier, 1875. 522–23.

Burgon, Ruth. 'Pacing the Cell: Walking and Productivity in the Work of Bruce Nauman'. Tate Papers no. 26, Autumn 2016.

Carville, Conor. *Samuel Beckett and the Visual Arts*. Cambridge: Cambridge University Press, 2018.

Cavecchi, Mariacristina. 'From Playwriting to Curatorship. An Investigation into the Status of Beckett's Stage Objects'. In *The Exhibit in the Text. The Museological Practices of Literature*, edited by Caroline Patey and Laura Scuriatti. London: Peter Lang, 2009. 161–82.

De Michelis, Marco. 'Spaces'. In *Bruce Nauman: Topological Gardens*, edited by Carlos Basualdo and Michael R. Taylor. New Haven and London: Philadelphia Museum of Art in association with Yale University Press, 2009. 65–83.

Des Vos, Laurens. 'The Observer Observed. The Promise of the Posthuman: Homeostasis, Autopoiesis and Virtuality in Samuel Beckett'. *Journal of Beckett Studies*, vol. 27, no. 2 (2018): 245–60.

Dennis, Amanda. 'Compulsive Bodies, Creative Bodies: Beckett and Agency in the 21st Century'. *Journal of Beckett Studies*, vol. 27, no. 1 (2018): 5–21.

Esslin, Martin. 'Samuel Beckett'. In *The Novelist as Philosopher: Studies in French Fiction 1935–1960*, edited by John Cruickshank. London: Oxford University Press, 1962. 145.

Foster, Verna. 'Beckett's Winter's Tale: Tragicomic Transformation in Ohio Impromptu'. *Journal of Beckett Studies*, vol. 1, no. 1–2 (January 1992): 67–76.

Graver, Lawrence and Raymond Federman, eds. *Samuel Beckett: The Critical Heritage*. London: Routledge, 2003.

Haynes, John and James Knowlson. *Images of Beckett*. Cambridge: Cambridge University Press, 2003.

Keatinge, Benjamin. '"The Hammers of the Stone-Cutters": Samuel Beckett's Stone Imagery'. *Irish University Review*, vol. 37, no. 2 (Autumn–Winter 2007): 322–39.

Knapp, Bettina. 'Beckett's That Time: "That double-headed monster... Time."' *Études irlandaises*, no. 15-2 (1990): 65–73.

Knowlson, James. *Damned to Fame. The Life of Samuel Beckett*. London: Bloomsbury, 1996.

—— and Elizabeth Knowlson, eds. *Beckett Remembering/Remembering Beckett. Uncollected Interviews with Samuel Beckett and Memories of Those Who Knew Him*. London: Bloomsbury, 2006.

Krukowski, Damon. 'Following the Sounds'. In *Bruce Nauman, 'Contrapposto Studies'*, edited by Carlos Basualdo and Caroline Bourgeois. Venezia: Marsilio, 2021. 101–6.

Lloyd, David. *Beckett's Thing. Painting and Theatre.* Edinburgh: Edinburgh University Press, 2018.

Oliver, Emily F. 'That Flesh-locked Sea of Silence: Language, Gender, and Sexuality in Beckett's Short Fiction'. Digital Commons@Georgia Southern: University Honors Program Thesis 95. Accessed 27 December 2022, https://digitalcommons.georgiasouthern.edu/cgi/viewcontent.cgi?article=1104&context=honors-theses

Owens, Craig N. 'Applause and Hiss: Implicating the Audience in Samuel Beckett's Rockaby and Catastrophe'. *The Journal of the Midwest Modern Language Association*, vol. 36, no. 1, Thinking Post-Identity (Spring 2003): 74–81.

Paoletti, John T. *Michelangelo's David.* Cambridge: Cambridge University Press, 2015.

Pinotti, Andrea. 'Soltanto l'essenziale. Beckett e Giacometti'. In *Tra le lingue tra i linguaggi. Cent'anni di Samuel Beckett,* edited by Mariacristina Cavecchi and Caroline Patey. Milano: Cisalpino, 2007. 263–80.

Rodriguez, Michael Angelo. '"Everywhere Stone Is Gaining": The Struggle for the Sacred in Samuel Beckett's Ill Seen Ill Said'. *Samuel Beckett Today / Aujourd'hui*, vol. 14, After Beckett / D'après Beckett (2004): 105–16.

Schaffner, Ingrid. 'Circling Oblivion / Bruce Nauman through Samuel Beckett'. In *Bruce Nauman,* edited by Robert C. Morgan. Baltimore and London: The Johns Hopkins University Press, 2002. 163–73.

Sharp, Willoughby. 'Two Interviews (1970)'. In *Bruce Nauman,* edited by Robert C. Morgan. Baltimore and London: Johns Hopkins University Press, 2002. 233–61.

Soavi, Giorgio. *Il quadro che mi manca.* Milano: Garzanti, 1986.

Vasari, Giorgio. *Le Vite dei più eccellenti pittori, scultori e architetti.* Firenze: Le Monnier, 1856.

―― *Le vite de' più eccellenti pittori, scultori ed architetti, 1550,* edited by Luciano Bellosi and Aldo Rossi. Torino: Einaudi, 1986.

―― *Vasari's Lives of the Artists. Giotto, Masaccio, Fra Filippo Lippi, Botticelli, Leonardo, Raphael, Michelangelo, Titian,* edited by Marylin Aronberg Lavin, trans. Jonathan Foster. Mineola, New York: Dover Publications, 1967.

Whitelaw, Billie. *Billie Whitelaw...Who He? An Autobiography.* London: Hodder & Stoughton, 1995.

Worth, Katharine. *Samuel Beckett's Theatre: A Life Journey.* Oxford: Clarendon Press, 2001.

Chapter 3

'J'AI EU L'IMAGE': SAMUEL BECKETT AND GASTONE NOVELLI

Davide Crosara

Abstract

The Italian painter Gastone Novelli (1925–1968) met Samuel Beckett in Paris in 1960. The encounter was the culmination of Novelli's long-lasting interest in Beckett's work. The two artists established a collaboration that had a significant impact on their works. Novelli realized a series of lithographs designed to accompany *L'image* (1959), Beckett's pre-publication excerpt from *Comment c'est* (1961). This partnership (the two met on several occasions, exchanged letters and commented on each other's work) had important consequences on both Beckett's and Novelli's artistic journeys, well beyond the idea (which was never put into print) of *L'image* as a 'livre d'artiste'. On the one hand, it entered – and probably changed – the genetic history of *Comment c'est*. On the other, it reoriented Novelli's idea of painting as language towards the more radical concept of a painting made of – and not accompanied by – words. While retrieving the aural, Joycean quality of Beckett's prose, Novelli established an interesting connection between Beckett's prose, French Nouveau Roman and Italian Neoavanguardia.

Keywords: Letters; images; intermediality; materiality; embodiment

Beckett's relationship with the visual arts, his observations on painting and his collaborative efforts with artists have been widely explored.[1] However,

---

[1] Beckett's dialogue with the arts (music, painting, poetry, digital media) has found growing critical attention, from Lois Oppenheim's seminal, comprehensive study (Oppenheim, 1999) to more recent contributions (Gontarski, ed., 2014, Lloyd, 2018). The field has progressively moved from a general inquiry into Beckett's work to issues related to intermediality and embodiment (Maude, 2009, Tajiri, 2007), posthumanism and technology (Boulter, 2019, Kirushina, Adar, Nixon eds, 2021), and intersections with popular culture (Pattie and Stewart, eds, 2019).

while the less examined role played by Italian art in his work has gained critical attention in recent years,[2] his aesthetic partnership with Gastone Novelli (1925–1968) has yet to be investigated.

The Birth of Novelli's Artistic Vision

Novelli was born in Vienna in 1925, the son of Margherita Mayer von Ketschendorf, a woman belonging to the old Hapsburg nobility, and Ivan Novelli, military attaché at the Italian Embassy in Austria. The family moved to Rome, where Novelli graduated in sociology and political sciences from Sapienza University. His choice of a field of study not directly connected to the visual arts is particularly relevant to Novelli's cultural outlook. He was not a painter by trade, and even when he became one, he kept a sustained interest in political, social and anthropological issues. Another key element in his life is his involvement in the Second World War. When the war broke out, Novelli joined the Resistance. He became a member of a Partisan Brigade operating in Rome. In 1943, he was arrested and tortured by the Nazis. He refused to collaborate with the occupying forces and was given a life sentence. He was liberated on 4 June 1944, when the Allies entered Rome. His experiences during the war had a profound influence on his aesthetic and ethical perspective. As many artists of his generation, Novelli felt the need to rethink artistic form in a post-Auschwitz world. Poignantly, he became a painter only after the war, when he decided to move to Brazil.

He lived in Sao Paulo from 1948 to 1950 and from 1951 to 1954. Here, he started working in the fields of graphic design and setting up activities which would eventually lead him to painting. The 'discovery' of painting was accompanied by a profound interest in language. Novelli decided to embark on a journey along the Amazon River. Here, he met some native populations of southern Brazil. He lived for several months among the Indios and was profoundly fascinated by the 'Guaranì' language. He spoke about his interest in this language in an interview (a conversation with Riccardo Nastasi and Verena Schütze, 1964) in which he also referred to his collaboration with Beckett. He states, 'I became interested in how it is possible to assemble several expressions with few phonetic means, how that language [the Guaranì] operates exactly as a catalogue'.[3] When these people need to add words to the catalogue, they do this with slight variations on the same linguistic pattern.

---

[2] See Mariacristina's Cavecchi's article on this volume.
[3] Gastone Novelli, Conversation with R. Nastasi and V. Schütze, in Gastone Novelli, *Scritti '43-'68*, edited by P. Bonani (Roma, Nero, 2019), 157. All translations from the Italian are mine.

The Guaranì language is structured around 'families of words'. Novelli gives specific examples of this mechanism:

> Sometimes a family of words provides slight variations of the sign, as is the case of 'going'. All the words in the family mean 'going somewhere', but they differ if they need to specify if one 'is going slowly or quickly, hunting or fishing'. Another family of words does not provide graphic, but only phonetic variations. In the family of words connected to 'going home or coming home' for example, the words are exactly the same. The only variation is provided by the speaker's tone. The last changes in order to indicate the arrival of an enemy or a friend. Or, if one wants to express the idea of someone that is gone (i.e. dead), she/he needs to use a sad tone. Even the identity of the person arriving is indicated by the tone of the voice.[4]

Novelli found in Guaranì a language that was, in his opinion, extremely individualized: this linguistic feature constituted an antidote to ordinary, codified linguistic habits; he saw it as an invaluable source of creativity. During the Brazilian years, far from the civilization that begot the camps, Novelli reimagined the relationship between images and words; he envisaged no hierarchical difference between the visual and aural fields. It is in Brazil that he most likely began to think of painting as a language. In his opinion, an artist can either invent a language – in 1964 he used Joyce's *Finnegans Wake* as an example of this – or he can devise 'a magical text by means of an ordinary language'.[5] He thought of the latter as a language inhabiting a newly created universe. Where the first form responds to Novelli's search for magical, ritual elements in his art, the second reflects Beckett's approach and work. Novelli was probably fascinated by Beckett's use of repetition with slight variations, by the closed spaces, enclosed universes and modular structure of his post-*Trilogy* short proses. His interest in Beckett and his collaboration with other writers with whom he felt a natural kinship or consonance (Georges Bataille, Claude Simon, Giorgio Manganelli, among others) accompanied his artistic life.

Novelli's use of words in his art was progressive. He took his first steps as a painter very close to Concrete art (he was certainly influenced by Max Bill) (Figure 3.1).

He soon turned to Informalism (Art Informel), although he retained some abstract and geometrical elements in these works. His interest continued to nurture the necessity to advocate for freedom of referentiality; Informalism

---

[4] All the quotations in this section are referred to G. Novelli, *Scritti* '43-'68, cit., 157–58.
[5] Ibid., 160.

Figure 3.1 *Superficie grande (Broad Surface)*, 1959. Courtesy of Archivio Gastone Novelli.

does this through a deconstruction of both sign and meaning that is evident in Novelli's works of the 1950s, as exemplified in Figures 3.2 and 3.3.

Novelli's Use of Language and Graphemes

It is at this point that language begins to enter Novelli's art. The first typographical signs (graphemes or words) are discernible in these paintings, while the surface of the painting progressively turns into a wall. This innovation in Novelli's artistic vision was probably influenced by his collaboration with the Brazilian group O.D.A. (Oficina de Arte), a movement that advocated for the popularization of art (the group manifesto began with the line, 'art is not a privilege') and its circulation beyond the museum, together with the use of poor materials. However, it found its turning point in Novelli's first *livre d'artiste*, *Scritto Sul Muro* (*Written on the Wall*), a book published in 1958 which contains 26 lithographs, each one dedicated to a letter of the Italian alphabet. Novelli's introduction to the book offers a succession of standard typographic characters and half-deleted words or phrases in bold type. Novelli imagines 'an alphabet written on 26 wall fragments, or 26 wall fragments with things written on them. […] An alphabet that has yet to be invented'. [The artist has to]

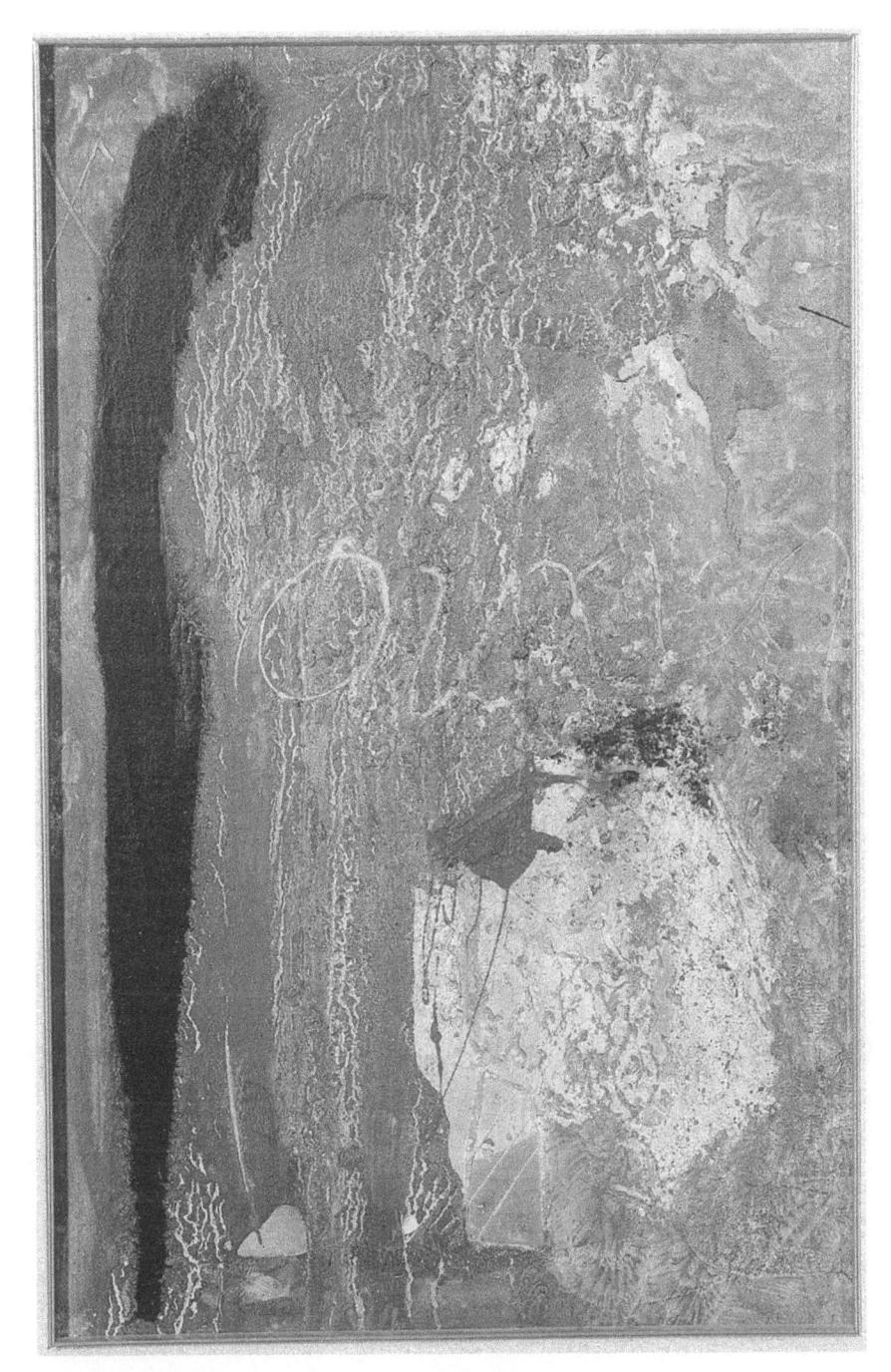

Figure 3.2 *Il giardino dei ricordi* (*Garden of Memories*, 1957). Courtesy of Archivio Gastone Novelli.

Figure 3.3 *Pescasecoli (Fishing through Centuries)*, 1957. Courtesy of Archivio Gastone Novelli.

'persevere in the effort of knowing nothing'.[6] The conclusion of Novelli's introduction significantly recalls Beckett's *Trilogy*, specifically *The Unnamable*:

> I will go on writing words, making spots and scratching them with my nails, until nails broke and refuse to grow back.[7]

---

[6] G. Novelli, Introduction to *Scritto sul muro*, in *Scritti '43-'68*, 122–23.
[7] Ibid.

You must say words, as long as there are any, until they find me, until they say me, strange pain, strange sin, you must go on, perhaps it's done already.[8]

Novelli's conception of words as stains or scratches on a surface (the wall, the canvas) also seems to anticipate Beckett's post-*Unnamable* short proses, namely the so-called *skullscapes*.

Novelli was certainly aware of Beckett's reception in French culture between the late 1950s and the early 1960s. *L'innomable* became a textbook (as *The Trilogy* as a whole, as well as Beckett's iconic plays) for the New Novelists. Beckett's novel is quoted by Claude Simon, one of Novelli's closest friend, in his essay *Novelli ou le problème du langage* (*Novelli and the Problem of Language*):

> Sa peinture «raconte», comme par exemple celle de Jérôme Bosch, mais avec la différence que chez Novelli il n'y a jamais rien d'anecdotique, que rien n'est jamais imité mais plutôt signifié. D'une part, le magma confus de nos sensations, de nos émotions, de l'autre les mots, les sons ou les couleurs. De la rencontre des uns et des autres, de leur adaptation ou de leur non-adaptation les uns aux autres, de leur conflit ou de leur interaction, résulte ce par quoi l'homme se définit : le langage, irréductible compromis entre l'innommable et le nommé, l'informe et le formulé.
>
> Aujourd'hui, étant donné que notre époque et les événements qui ont bouleversé le monde ont remis en question entièrement l'ordre social et les notions établies, ce problème se pose à nous de façon plus insistante que jamais. Ce n'est certainement pas par hasard que sont apparues, peu après la guerre, des œuvres aux titres significatifs comme Le Degré zéro de l'écriture de Roland Barthes et L'Innommable de Samuel Beckett, tandis que dans les mêmes années s'élaborait la peinture de Dubuffet, de Bissier, de Novelli...[9]
>
> To try, while being perfectly aware of the futility of the attempt. To draw the unnameable and at the same time to know that doing so is an illusion, that it can never be immobilized, enclosed, fixed.[10]

Simon notes that Novelli's art is a painting about painting and that language is always a 'compromise between the namable and the unnamable, the unformed and the formulated'. He pairs Beckett's novel with the coeval *Writing*

---

[8] Samuel Beckett, *The Unnamable*, preface by S. Connor (London: Faber and Faber, 2010), 134.
[9] C. Simon, *Novelli ou le problème du langage* (1962), in G. Novelli, *Voyage en Grèce* (Lyon: Trente-trois morceaux, 2015), 91–99 (92).
[10] C. Simon, *Gastone Novelli and the Problem of Language*, translation by Richard Howard, in *Gastone Novelli. Paintings*, Exhibition Catalogue, New York, Alan Gallery, 26 November-15 December 1962, 9.

Degree Zero by Roland Barthes (1953). His implicit question is whether, and to what extent, Novelli's art is a 'Painting Degree Zero'.

Simon is also one of the first to highlight the recursive presence of chessboards or grids in Novelli's paintings of the early 1960s. He also connects these paintings to the art of Paul Klee, a painter who has certainly influenced Novelli (the Italian artist was also the first to translate Klee's writings into Italian) and who was deeply admired by Beckett. Simon's words testify also to the growing interconnection between words and images in Novelli's works. In analysing an important painting by Novelli, *Museum Hall II* (1960, see Figure 3.4) he observes:

> If we look at this grid a long time we discover that it constitutes a kind of 'explanation', an ordered commentary on the right-hand portion of the painting where, in the chaos of grisaille, half-effaced, blurred, diluted under the plaster and repainted areas, bits of forms and indistinct inscriptions appear. This 'explanation' is itself equally incomprehensible.[11]

Figure 3.4 Il *Sala del Museo* (*Museum Hall* II, 1960). Courtesy of Archivio Gastone Novelli.

---

[11] C. Simon, Gastone *Novelli and the Problem of Language*, in Gastone Novelli. *Paintings*, exhibition catalogue, New York, Alan Gallery, 26 November–15 December 1962, pp.4-5. The original version of the essay, initially unpublished, appeared as *Novelli ou le problème du langage*, in « Les Temps modernes», n° 628–629, nov. 2004-fév. 2005.

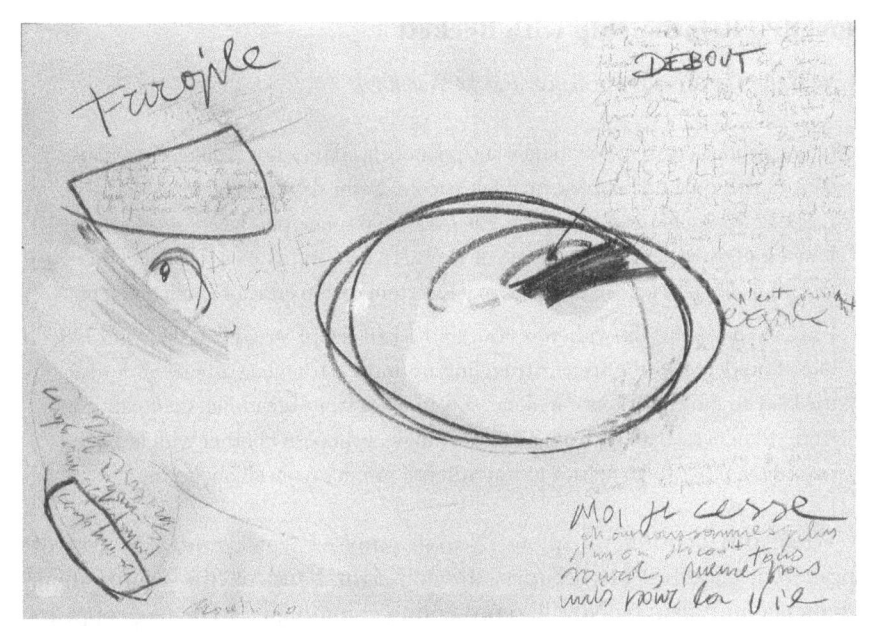

Figure 3.5 Untitled ['Fragile, Debout'], 1960. Mixed media on paper, 69 × 99.6 cm Signed 'Novelli 60' On the recto 'Fragile, Debout' On the verso 'for Barbara from Sam with love Paris May 1962' London, British Museum. Courtesy of Archivio Gastone Novelli

Novelli's paintings become labyrinths where the viewer has to find possible relations between signs and images, echoing the arbitrary relationship between signifier and signified investigated by Michel Foucault (Novelli was fascinated by structuralist linguistics: he created a painting centred around excerpts from Claude Lévy-Strauss' *Wild Thought*).[12] More importantly, Novelli's technique aims at offering to the viewer a kind of stratification, a surface where layers of colour partially hide letters. The latter, almost suffocated by paint, strive to emerge under violent brush strokes. Novelli adopted this technique in the first works he drew from Beckett. *Fragile, Debout*[13] is a drawing inspired by Beckett's *Textes pour rien / Texts for Nothing* (see Figure 3.5).

---

[12] The painting is *Il vocabolario*, 1964.
[13] The work, which Novelli gave to Beckett, was probably donated by the latter to Barbara Bray. It is currently held by the British Museum.

Novelli's Relationship with Beckett

Novelli quotes an excerpt from *Text for Nothing I*:

> Ouste, debout, et je sens l'effort qu'il fait, pour obéir, comme une vieille carne tombée dans la rue, qu'il ne fait plus, qu'il fait encore, avant de renoncer. Je dis à la tête, Laisse le tranquille, reste tranquille, elle cesse de respirer, puis halète de plus belle. Je suis loin de toutes ces histoires, je ne devrais pas m'en occuper, je n'ai besoin de rien, ni d'aller plus loin, ni de rester où je suis, tout cela m'est vraiment indifférent.[14]

> I say to the body, Up with you now, and I can feel it struggling, like and old hack foundered in the street, struggling no more, struggling again, till it gives up. I say to the head, Leave it alone, stay quiet, it stops breathing, then pants on worse than ever. I am far from all that wrangle, I shouldn't bother with it, I need nothing, neither to go on nor to stay where I am, it's truly all one to me.[15]

While this quasi-literal quote (Novelli employs 'égal' (equal) instead of 'indifférent' (indifferent) occupies the top-right hand of the composition, a sentence in Italian by Novelli representing commonplace language appears in the top-left corner. The direction of the composition is clockwise: it starts from the bottom left ('be my glass' in red, circled in black, in English), then moves top-left ('Che cosa credi che is possa vivere sempre con la testa tra le nuvole le mani in tasca e cambiando continuamente opinione su tutto e su tutti?'), then top-right (Beckett's text), and finally bottom-right, where we find a combination of misquoted Beckettian expressions. This itinerary underscores the complex relationship between the artist and his sources, but it also highlights the danger that any artistic style faces, that of becoming cliché. Further, it anticipates a direction that Novelli will pursue until the end of his life: the compresence of intermediality and bilingualism (or multilingualism, as is the case here). This is a lesson that Novelli probably absorbed from Beckett. The former was fascinated by the Beckettian idea that art was a constant struggle to find a voice, the artist lost into a plurality of languages and media.

It comes as no surprise to see Novelli playing on the phonetic ambivalence 'début/debout' (beginning and standing), an auditory doubling which can also be found in Beckett's *Comment c'est*. This phonetic game is complicated by the other word in the dedication, which indicates that Novelli's first work dedicated to Beckett could be seen as a fragile beginning. The question is whether the text can stand the painting's search for meaning, incarnated by the disquieting passage

---

[14] S. Beckett, *Nouvelles et Textes pour rien* (Paris: Minuit, 1958), 116. The quote is from *Text* n.1.
[15] S. Beckett, *Texts for Nothing*, *Text* 1, in S. Gontarski (ed.) *The Complete Short Prose* 1929–1989. (New York: Grove Press, 1995), 100.

from one shape to the other. This comparison could be expanded further, by also investigating it in light of Beckett's complex bilingualism and his troubled switching of forms in the twin texts *Comment c'est/How It Is*. The title itself is interesting: the English appears as a kind of commentary on the impossibility of translating the duality of the French: the homophony with 'commencer' ('to begin') is notoriously lost in the English version.

A dark circle and dark colours engulf the text in the painting *Homage to Beckett* (1958, see Figure 3.6). The letters on the top left corner are barely discernible.

Figure 3.6 *Homage to Beckett* (1958). Courtesy of Archivio Gastone Novelli.

Two years before 'Fragile, Debout', the struggle between words and images was already a key element in Novelli's artistic journey. The words seem scratched or carved on the surface. At the same time, semi-human or semi-animal shapes are denied intelligibility by the dominant heavy black or white brushstrokes. The painting represents a form attempting to deny itself, a task that fascinated Beckett himself, when he recognized the same attitude in his beloved painter Bram van Velde. The words he used to comment on the latter's work would also make an excellent commentary on Novelli's painting:

> Le frisson primaire de la peinture en prenant conscience de ses limites porte vers les confins de ces limites, le secondaire dans le sens de la profondeur, vers la chose qui cache la chose. L'object de la représentation résiste toujours à la représentation...[16]
>
> I mean only that the instinctive shudder of painting from its limits is a shudder toward the confines of those limits, and the reflective all in depth, from without to within. I mean only that the object of representation is at all times in resistance to representation.[17]

Novelli's interest in Beckett is layered. The two paintings *Untitled (Fragile Debut)* and *Homage to Beckett* reflect Novelli's knowledge of Beckett's *Textes pour rien / Texts for Nothing*, which laid the foundation for the 'novel' *Comment c'est / How It Is*. However, his interest in Beckett's work started when he read *Molloy*. He says about this,

> The starting point was his novel *Molloy*. I copied it, I drew a series of drawings from it. He then saw them, founding them very interesting, and at that point I told him that I would have liked to work on his texts. Our collaboration began in this way: I copied his text first, then I copied my copy, then I copied this second copy deriving from it a third copy and so on, several times, each time adding or removing something, in larger and larger types, till it became impossible to further modify the composition. It thus took a conclusive shape. My litographs were born that way, not very big but packed with things; here the text still exists, but scattered and torn into pieces. And that's how Beckett himself began to look at his own work in a different light. This was *Comment c'est*, or at least a part of it, which later Beckett published.[18]

---

[16] S. Beckett, *Peintres de l'Empêchement*, in *Disjecta. Miscellaneous Writings and a Dramatic Fragment* (London: John Calder, 2000), 135 (emphasis mine).

[17] S. Beckett, 'The New Object', in *Modernism/Modernity* 18 (2011), 878–880 (879). The English version of the essay has not always been attributed to Beckett. See on the subject Peter Fifield's introduction in the same issue of *Modernism/Modernity* (873–877).

[18] G. Novelli, *Scritti '43–'68*, 161.

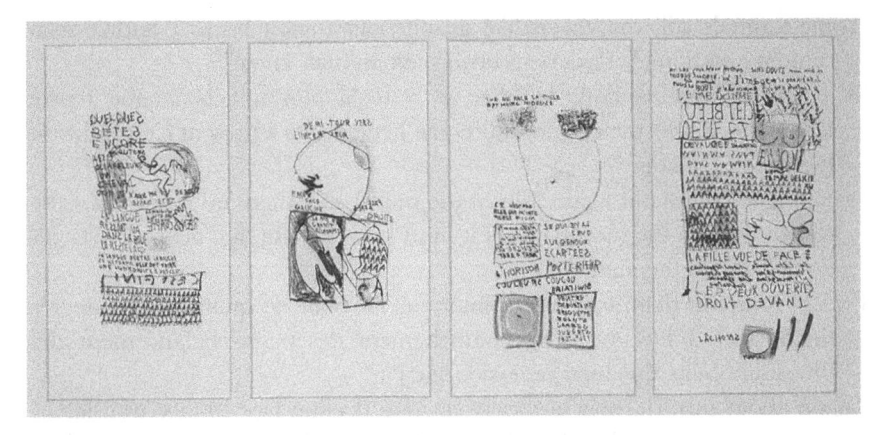

Figure 3.7 Gastone Novelli, *Comment c'est*, 1961. Courtesy of Archivio Gastone Novelli.

As testified by Beckett's correspondence, Novelli sent him drawings inspired by *L'image*, the fragment from which *Comment c'est* originated. In the same letter, Beckett describes painting as deeply correlated with 'montage'.[19] Novelli will interpret *L'image* exactly as a setting up of words and images.

The Birth of *L'image*

Novelli's interest led to their collaboration for *L'image*, the first published extract from *Comment c'est*.[20] Conceived between 1960 and 1961, this project envisaged a *livre d'artiste*, which was to include Beckett's *L'image*[21] set against four lithographs by Novelli (see Figure 3.7).

The lines quoted from Beckett are the following:

Fig. 1: 'quelques bêtes encore les moutons qu'on dirait du granit qui affleure un cheval que je n'avais pas vu debout immobile échine courbée tête basse les bêtes savent'.

---

[19] Samuel Beckett to Gastone Novelli, 8 December 1960. The letter is unpublished. Courtesy of Beckett Collection, Beckett International Foundation, University of Reading.
[20] The 'roman' *Comment c'est* was composed between 1958 and 1961, the year of its publication with Minuit. It has a long and troubled genetic history, made of several rewritings and revisions. The English translation, an equally hard task, appeared in 1964 as *How It Is*. For a general overview of the subject, see S. G. Ackerley/S. E. Gontarski, *The Grove Companion to Samuel Beckett* (New York: Grove Press, 2004), 105.
[21] *L'image*, the first extract from *Comment c'est*, appeared in 'X' on November 1959.

"some animals still the sheep like granite outcrops a horse I hadn't seen standing motionless back bent head sunk animals know"[22]

'la langue ressort va dans la boue je reste là plus soif la langue rentre la bouche se referme elle doit faire une ligne droite à present c'est fini c'est fait j'ai eu L'image'[23]

"my tongue comes out again lolls in the mud I stay there no more thirst the tongue goes in the mouth closes it must be a straight line now it's over it's done I've had the image"[24]

Fig. 2: 'nouveau demi-tour vers l'intérieur au bout de quatre-vingts degrés fugitif face à face transferts rattachement des mains balancement des bras immobilité du chien ce fessier que j'ai'[25]

"again about turn introrse at ninety degrees fleeting face to face transfer of things mingling of hands swinging of arms stillness of dog the rump I have"[26]

Fig. 3: 'Vue de face la fille est moins hideuse c'est pas elle qui m'intéresse moi pâle cheveux en brosse grosse face rouge avec boutons ventre débordant braguette béante jambes cagneuses en fuseau fléchissant aux genoux écartées pour plus d'assise pieds ouverts cette trente degrés demi-sourire béat à l' horizon postérieur figure de la vie qui se lève tweed verts bottines jaunes toutes ces couleurs coucou ou similaire à la boutonnière'[27]

"seen full face the girl is less hideous it's not with her I am concerned me pale staring hair red pudding face with pimples protruding belly gaping fly spindle legs sagging knocking at the knees wide astraddle for greater stability feet splayed one hundred and thirty degrees fatuous half-smile to posterior horizon figuring the morn of life green tweeds yellow boots all those colours cowslip or suchlike in the buttonhole"[28]

Fig. 4: 'et les jambes et les yeux les bleus fermés sans doute eh bien non puisque soudain c'est L'image la dernière soudain là sous la boue je le dis comme je l'entends je me vois'[29]

"and the legs and the eyes the blue closed no doubt no since suddenly another image the last there in the mud I say it as I hear it I see me"[30]

---

[22] S. Beckett, *How It Is* (London: Faber and Faber, 2009), 25.
[23] S. Beckett, *Comment c'est* (Paris: Minuit, 1961), 48.
[24] *How It Is*, 25.
[25] *Comment c'est*, 46.
[26] *How It Is*, 24.
[27] *Comment c'est*, 46.
[28] *How It Is*, 24.
[29] *Comment c'est*, 44.
[30] *How It Is*, 23.

'Je me donne dans les seize ans et il fait pour surcroît de bonheur un temps délicieux ciel bleu oeuf et chevauchée de petits nuages je me tourne le dos et la fille aussi que je tiens qui me tient par la main ce cul que j'ai'[31] [Then 3 partially repeated].

"I look to me about sixteen and to crown all glorious weather egg-blue sky and scamper of little clouds I have my back turned to me and the girl too whom I hold who holds me by the hand the arse I have"[32]

The text is fragmented and dispersed around images that occupy the page in a similar fashion. Neither has any apparent orderly succession. In his Critical-Genetic Edition of *Comment C'est/How It Is* and *L'image*, E. M. O'Reilly chooses the term 'fragments' to indicate Beckett's versets: 'The term fragment does apply to *Comment c'est* and *How It Is*. Just as word groups do occasionally form discernible sentences, paragraphs can be recognized among the fragments. However, the thrust of fragmentation goes contrary to notions of paragraph. These fragments frequently do not coincide with semantic units and do not rely on the lexical tools of syntactic cohesion.'[33]

Novelli works in a similar manner: he cuts and pastes the text, stripping it of its original structure. However, the fragments he creates appear as micro-units that remain readable, even if with some difficulty. Novelli applies here a kind of cut-up or automatic writing technique that testifies his dialogue with American abstract expressionism and anticipates his involvement in Italian Neoavanguardia. This technique not only anticipates the one adopted by Beckett in 1969 for *Lessness*, it also reproduces *How It Is*'s pauses and silences visually. Many words are erased or unreadable, sources are hidden, and images appear as doodles or sketches still awaiting a final form. Novelli's approach to composition produces successive accretions (being in this respect closer to Joyce's or to the early Beckett) but it also meets Beckett's post-*Unnamable* narrative experiments.

Novelli's version of *L'image* also underscores thematic aspects of the novel that are crucial to Beckett. The human figure is deformed as it is in Beckett's pages: Novelli responds to Beckett's crooked, half-human beings, by adding to their depiction a more explicitly grotesque element. The female figures and the words that accompany them (see lit. n.3) capture Beckett's frequent use of a bitter irony in relation to the narrator's love story and to human bonds

---

[31] *Comment c'est*, 44.
[32] *How It Is*, 23.
[33] E. M. O'Reilly (ed.) *Samuel Beckett Comment C'est/How It Is and / et L'Image. A Critical-Genetic Edition Une Édition Critico-Génétique* (New York and London: Routledge, 2016) English Introduction, X.

in general. As noted by Ruby Cohn, *Comment c'est/How It Is* presents tragicomic aspects as well. Cohn observes that 'quite farcical are the ungainly teenager and his ugly girlfriend, accompanied by her genital-absorbed dog'.[34]

Conversely, an element that Novelli seems to neutralize or almost completely eliminate from Beckett's text is its lyricism: harsh and difficult to recite as they are, Beckett's versets or fragments, which include interesting variations of accents from French to English, are also characterized by rare but extraordinarily lyrical moments. The lyrical component is replaced in Novelli by figures, letters, and lines that evoke childhood sketches. This feature of his work is certainly influenced by his prolific relationship with avant-garde figures such as Tzara and Duchamp (he was often labelled as a 'new-Dada' artist), but it is also related to his enquiry into the primeval, elemental origins of language: Novelli's signs can also be read as prehistorical graffiti.

In the paintings immediately following *L'image*, words and letters interact with numbers, lines, doodles, organic and inorganic figures, and shapes alluding to this search for an archetypical language. This passage, which is also marked by the titles of Novelli's paintings (*Alphabet, The Great Language*), is also born as Novelli's response to Beckett's notion of a 'geology of the imagination'.[35] From *The 'Whoroscope' Notebook*[36] onwards Beckett identifies layers and sediments with strata of consciousness by copying in a notebook a geological table. This landscape of the mind is identified in *How It Is* with the mud, 'an amorphous plane between the rock below and air above'.[37] The artist 'peels off' layer after layer in an attempt to recognize the basic elements, the primal motion of the imaginative act: 'how it is' leads inevitably to 'how it was'. This process can also lead, as a young Beckett hypothesized in his *German Letter*, to discover the 'nothingness' possibly lying behind language. With different means but with a similar intent, Novelli digs back to the sign before it becomes meaning, dismembering the articulatory system of language. In his painting *The King of Words* (*Il re delle parole*, 1961) he writes about the need to 'turn over words, so confident of themselves, and reduce them to silence'. James Knowlson points out that Beckett loved stones and Novelli collected many

---

[34] R. Cohn, *A Beckett Canon* (Ann Arbor: The University of Michigan Press, 2005), 259.
[35] See Mark Byron, *Samuel Beckett's Geological Imagination* (Cambridge: Cambridge University Press, 2020).
[36] The notebook, used by Beckett from 1932 to 1937, contains a large variety of entries, sketches and quotations. It derives its name from the reference to the poem *Whoroscope* on the inside cover. It is currently part of the Beckett Collection, Beckett International Foundation, University of Reading.
[37] S. G. Ackerley/S. E. Gontarski, *The Grove Companion to Samuel Beckett*, 220.

Figure 3.8 *Le onde mentali (Mind Waves)*, 1962.

of them during his *Journey to Greece* (1964), where he composed one of his last *livres d'artiste*. Novelli's geological imagination began to appear after his work on *Comment c'est*, as it is evident from his painting *Le onde mentali* (*Mind Waves*, see Figure 3.8).

Materiality and Embodiment

The last shared thematic issue uniting Beckett and Novelli is the deployment of a notion of materiality which will become increasingly pervasive in Beckett's work after *How It Is*. Drawing inspiration from Dante and reversing the structure of the *Commedia*, Beckett fills the English version of *Comment c'est* with a growing tension towards embodiment. In the novel, soul and memory acquire a peculiar weight and are subdued to the laws of gravity. The body, alternating utterance and suffocation, literally measures time and motion. The mud acts as a membrane, determining the tone and the direction of the narrative in terms of both space and memory. Novelli's signs and figures act accordingly: they trace a trajectory on the canvas, an itinerary that is far from being accidental; some art critics have observed that the spectator's eye is challenged to drawing a direction and a narrative from the web of words and images, as happens in the case of a fresco. In Novelli's lithographs for *Comment c'est*, human and animal figures are both embedded among words, they are caught trying to cope with the limits of both space and frame. They seem to share the devouring, if unaccomplished, entropy that constitutes a leitmotiv of *How It Is* and of Beckett's late prose and theatre in general; they address Beckett's 'loss of species'. Where Beckett's 'loss of species' suggests a loss of speech, Novelli's stretch into nothingness is less radical, retaining a more evident level of avant-garde playfulness and anti-system refutation.

Two further elements in the lithographs seem to suggest an even more profound dialogue between Beckett and Novelli. The first one is the presence of breasts, an image of joy and fertility (and of linguistic joyfulness) that progressively acquires sado-masochistic undertones. In lithograph 2, the breast bears some resemblance to a face, with an opening recalling a mouth diametrically opposite to the nipple. In lithograph 4, the breasts in the foreground (there are two and are less identifiable) are encapsulated among words and menaced by a deformed, grimacing figure below, whose nails seem to leave vertical scars at the bottom of the page. Novelli seems to anticipate Pim's education[38] in part two of Beckett's *How It Is*.[39]

The second element is the recursive, quasi-obsessive presence of the letter 'A' in the lithographs. This presence will characterize many of Novelli's later works. Blocs of 'A' are found, for example, at the bottom of lithograph 1, significantly following a reversed 'c'est fini'. They occupy all the central parts of lithograph 4, absorbing the figures. This device is clearly connected to Novelli's linguistic research: the 'A' sound is the origin of the alphabet, the first word of the child, but also a cry, a conjunction of joy and pain. It seems to anticipate the engraving of capital letters on Pim's back in *How It Is*. One of Beckett's first titles for the novel was *Tout bas*, 'barely audible', alluding to these first sounds.

Both Novelli's and Beckett's *ars combinatoria* entail an element of sadism: the letter 'A' and the breasts constitute two sequences (1–2–4 and 2–3–4) in Novelli's lithographs. In this way, he replicates Beckett's sequences of 'versets' in *How It Is* with both visual and aural means.

Beckett and Novelli investigate the utopia of direct writing and painting, of saying things as you hear them, of the coincidence of 'première and dernière image', incorporating this search into a perceptive intermedial dynamic. But any utopia, as they both know very well, is both promising and dangerous. As observed by Alfred Simon, Novelli's sequence of 'A' sometimes recalls fences or barbed wires:

---

[38] Beckett was an attentive reader of Sade. He also planned a translation of his works.

[39] In 1962, Novelli also illustrated Georges Bataille's *History of the Eye*, another well-known re-reading of Sade.

sometimes using the handle of his brush, or a pencil, or a wider scraper, he would inscribe those superimposed lines of uneven letters, wavering like a scream, repeating themselves, never the same: 76 bearing witness AAAAAAAAAAAAAAAAAAAAAAAAAAAAAA AAAAAAAAAAAAAA AAAAAAAAAAAAAAAAAAAAAAAAAAAAAAAAAAAAAAAAAAAAAA.[40]

We are not far from the disquieting, post-Auschwitz resonances of Beckett's numbers and Roman capitals carved on the skin.

Bibliography

Ackerley, Chris J. and Stanley E. Gontarski, *The Grove Companion to Samuel Beckett*. New York: Grove Press, 2007.
Beckett, Samuel, *Comment c'est*. Paris: Minuit, 1961.
Beckett, Samuel, *How It Is*. London: Faber & Faber, 2009.
Beckett, Samuel, The Image, translated by Edith Fournier. In Stanley E. Gontarski (ed.) *The Complete Short Prose 1929–1989*. New York: Grove Press, 1995, 165–168.
Beckett Samuel, *L'Image*. Paris: Minuit, 1988.
Beckett Samuel, Letter to Gastone Novelli, 8 December 1960 'Novelli, Gastone' folder, JEK A/2/217, Beckett Archives, University of Reading Special Collections.
Beckett, Samuel, The New Object. In Peter Fifield, Bryan Anthony Radley, Lawrence Scott Rainey (eds.) *Modernism/modernity 18*. Baltimore: Johns Hopkins University Press, 2011, 878–880.
Beckett, Samuel, *Nouvelles et Textes pour rien*. Paris: Minuit, 1958.
Beckett, Samuel, *Peintres de l'Empêchement, in Disjecta. Miscellaneous Writings and a Dramatic Fragment*. London: John Calder, 2000.
Beckett, Samuel, Texts for Nothing. In Stanley E. Gontarski (ed.) *The Complete Short Prose 1929–1989*. New York: Grove Press, 1995, 100–154.
Beckett, Samuel, *The Unnamable, preface by S.Connor*. London: Faber & Faber, 2010.
Byron, Mark, *Samuel Beckett's Geological Imagination*. Cambridge: Cambridge University Press, 2020.
Cohn, Ruby. *A Beckett Canon*. Ann Arbor: The University of Michigan Press, 2001.
Fifield, Peter, Introduction to S. Beckett, 'The New Object'. In Peter Fifield, Bryan Anthony Radley, Lawrence Scott Rainey (eds.) *Modernism/modernity 18*. Baltimore: Johns Hopkins University Press, 2011, 873–877.
Novelli, Gastone, *Scritti '43–'68*, edited by Paola Bonani. Roma: Nero, 2019.
O'Reilly, Edouard Magessa (ed.) *Samuel Beckett Comment C'est How It Is and / et L'Image. A Critical-Genetic Edition Une Édition Critico-Génétique*. New York and London: Routledge, 2016.
Simon, Claude, Gastone Novelli and the Problem of Language, translation by Richard Howard, in Gastone Novelli. Paintings, Exhibition Catalogue, New York, Alan Gallery, 26 November–15 December 1962.
Simon, Claude, *The Jardin des Plantes: A Novel*. Evanston, Illinois: Northwestern University Press, 2001.
Simon, Claude, Novelli ou le problème du langage (1962). In G. Novelli, Voyage en Grèce. Lyon: Trente-trois morceaux, 2015, 91–99.

---

[40] Claude Simon, *The Jardin des Plantes. A Novel* (Northwestern University Press, 2001), 187.

Part Two
RADIO AND OPERA

Chapter 4

BECKETT'S *NEITHER*, AN 'ANTI-OPERA' IN ROME

Yuri Chung

Abstract

In 1976, while Samuel Beckett was rehearsing *Footfalls* and *That Time* in Berlin, an American avant-garde composer, Morton Feldman, made him a surprise visit. Beckett was utterly astonished when Feldman asked him to write a libretto for his new opera that had been commissioned by the Teatro dell'Opera in Rome. The Irish playwright told Feldman that he did not like opera and suggested him to use one of his own existing texts, as the French composer Marcel Mihalovici had done. However, Feldman immediately replied that those works did not need music in them. Furthermore, Feldman had never composed an opera and thus had no idea of what he wanted from him. He just knew that Beckett was the only person who could offer him the 'quintessence' of what he was searching for. After Feldman showed him a score of one of his own pieces, Beckett wrote what he considered the main theme of his life on it: 'To and fro in shadow, from outer shadow to inner shadow. To and fro, between unattainable self and unattainable non-self.' At the end of the month, while Feldman had already started composing the music, Beckett sent him unexpectedly a card with a handwritten text called *Neither*, containing 86 words in 10 lines. The opera *Neither* premiered at the Teatro dell'Opera on 13 May 1977 receiving a very negative reception. The opera had no plot, no scenery, and apparently no 'Beckett' but solely a soprano that sang in a seemingly wordless manner.

Keywords: Libretto; non-self; re-elaboration; repetitiveness; voice

> *Desidero anche ringraziare Samuel Beckett per aver scritto per me questo testo squisito.*[1]
>
> – Morton Feldman (1977)

> *Though I say not / What I may not / Let you hear, / Yet the swaying / Dance is saying, / Love me dear! / Every touch of fingers / Tells me what I know, / Says for you, / It's true, it's true, / You love me so!*[2]
>
> – Samuel Beckett, *Happy Days* (1961)

At the end of the play *Happy Days* (1961), while being swallowed up slowly by the sand in the desert, the female protagonist Winnie sings softly a waltz. It is an English translation of the love duet 'Lippen schweigen' from Franz Lehár's *The Merry Widow* (1905). Lehár was a prominent composer in Vienna at the start of the twentieth century, who specialized in operetta. Beckett was known to appreciate this popular genre. In his youth, he was particularly fond of Gilbert and Sullivan's light operas, a genre similar to the operetta, playing them often at the piano and singing madly 'variations' of their songs.[3] According to his biographer, James Knowlson, Beckett instead was not so passionate about opera.[4] In his essay of 1930, 'Proust', we get an insight on Beckett's view regarding music and, above all, opera:

> [...] music is the Idea itself, unaware of the world of phenomena, existing ideally outside the universe, apprehended not in Space but in Time only [...] This essential quality of music is distorted by the listener who, being an impure subject, insists on giving a figure to that which is ideal and invisible, on incarnating the Idea in what he conceives to be an appropriate paradigm. Thus, by definition, opera is a hideous corruption of this most immaterial of all the arts: the words of a libretto are to the musical phrase that they particularise what the Vendome Column, for example, is to the ideal perpendicular. From this point of view opera is less complete than vaudeville, which at least inaugurates the comedy of an exhaustive enumeration.[5]

---

[1] Gioacchino Lanza Tomasi et al., *La Stagione Lirica 1976–77: Programma* (Rome: Teatro dell'Opera, 1977), 509.
[2] Samuel Beckett, *Happy Days* (New York: Grove Press, 2013), 69.
[3] James Knowlson, *Samuel Beckett: Damned to Fame* (New York: Simon & Schuster, 1996), 45.
[4] Ibid., 235.
[5] Samuel Beckett, *Proust* (New York: Grove Press, 1978), 71.

Vaudeville was a French music genre which originated in the fifteenth century. It consisted of works which tackled light-hearted issues, generally comic and erotic ones, with the use of popular songs. Like the genres of operetta and light opera, it was an alternative to opera in general. Its aim was to entertain the listener with frivolous, farcical and heartening events. If Beckett seemed to appreciate these works, the same could not be said about the 'hideous corruption of this most immaterial of all the arts', that is opera.

Consequently, the encounter on 20 September 1976 with Morton Feldman must have appeared a hoax of destiny to him. The American composer met him in Berlin at the Schiller Theater during the rehearsals of *Footfalls* (1976) and *That Time* (1976). He then invited Beckett to lunch with an unexpected idea in his mind. Even though Feldman had never composed an opera before but only instrumental music, he asked the renowned Irish playwright to write him a libretto for his new opera that had been commissioned by the Teatro dell'Opera in Rome. A surprised Beckett obviously told Feldman that he did not like opera.

In Beckett's life, opera was clearly absent among his passions even though he was a skilful musician who lived in Paris and had James Joyce, a true melomaniac, as his mentor. Therefore, the fact that Feldman had asked him to write a libretto for an opera commissioned by the Teatro dell'Opera was quite a curious choice. The Roman theatre had been an iconic operatic temple where the first representations of great operas like *Cavalleria rusticana* (1890) and *Tosca* (1900) took place. Then, in the years that followed, the theatre rarely attracted worldwide attention, staging hardly any memorable performance. In 1976, Gioacchino Lanza Tomasi, a renowned musicologist, became the artistic director of the Teatro dell'Opera. His first thought was to refresh the theatre's monotonous repertory with new contemporary works. The first step he took in this direction was to end the 1976–77 season with a series of experimental works, four to be exact, all in the same day. These would then be represented other five times. Three of them would be ballets, Stravinsky's *Feu d'Artifice* (1908), Calder's *Work in Progress* (1968) and Satie's *Mercure* (1924). The fourth work would be the opera *Neither*. Among these compositions, the presence of *Work in Progress* was a clear challenge to the regular spectators of the theatre because it was not the first time it was performed there. As Lanza Tomasi recalls:

> And, lastly, we go from these prior events to the present day, with *Work in Progress* by Calder, sublime *divertissement* on happiness, which I remember in 1968 was drowned by philistine hisses. And since then, the audience of this opera house, which is very hard to please, had to bear to its dregs the various

Cavalleria, the *Chénier* and the *Adriana*. As we approach the performance, memories of the famous turmoil that occurred in these surrealist evenings come to mind, where somebody would even break his arm.[6]

So, nine years before, the premiere of *Work in Progress* was an utter fiasco because the audience was devoted solely to the classical repertory. Nonetheless, Lanza Tomasi decided to move forward undaunted in his convictions. The choice of commissioning an opera to Feldman was the result of a series of interesting coincidences. At the end of August 1976, Feldman was a guest at the Venice Biennale. In the lagoon city, the International Festival of Contemporary Music was taking place. During the series of events called 'Musica aperta', Feldman's new composition, *Routine Investigations*, was first performed on 26 August. The conductor of this performance was Marcello Panni, the concertmaster of the Teatro dell'Opera in Rome. Lanza Tomasi was also present at the event and so the three decided to dine together. It was on this occasion that Lanza Tomasi commissioned an opera to Feldman.

Instead of looking for a seasoned librettist for his opera, Feldman wanted Beckett. The fact that two complete newbies in the field, even though famous in their artistic domains, were to work on an original opera was quite a bizarre idea. It was certainly inconceivable to Beckett. For this reason, he suggested Feldman to use one of his own existing texts, as his friend the French composer Marcel Mihalovici had done adapting *Krapp's Last Tape* (1958) to a chamber opera in 1961. Beckett was not particularly delighted to have his words set to music. As Feldman recounted:

> He [Beckett] was very embarrassed – he said to me, after a while: 'Mr. Feldman, I don't like opera.' I said to him, 'I don't blame you!' Then he said to me 'I don't like my words being set to music,' and I said, 'I'm in complete agreement. In fact it's very seldom that I've used words. I've written a lot of pieces with voice, and they're wordless.' Then he looked at me again and said, 'But what do you want?' And I said 'I have no idea!' He also asked me why I didn't use existing material. […] I said that I had read them all, that they were pregnable, they didn't need music. I said that I was looking for the quintessence, something that just hovered.[7]

---

[6] My translation; original: 'E infine da questi antefatti ad oggi, con *Work in Progress* di Calder, sublime *divertissement* sulla natura felice, che ricordo nel 1968 al Teatro dell'Opera subissato da fischi filistei. E da allora il pubblico di questa sala, difficile fra le difficili, si è sorbito sino alla feccia le *Cavalleria*, gli *Chénier* e le *Adriana*, tanto che nell'approssimarsi dello spettacolo tornano alla memoria i celebri parapiglia delle serate surrealiste, dove qualcuno ne usciva anche con un braccio rotto.' G. Lanza Tomasi et al., *La Stagione Lirica 1976–77*, 486.

[7] Howard Skempton, 'Beckett as Librettist', *Music and Musicians* (1977): 5.

After Feldman showed a score composed on a section of Beckett's *Film* (1965), the Irish playwright eventually wrote on it what he considered to be the main theme of his life: 'To and fro in shadow, from outer shadow to inner shadow. To and fro, between unattainable self and unattainable non-self.'[8] Beckett would then add: 'It would need a bit of work, wouldn't it? Well, if I get any further ideas on it, I'll send them on to you.'[9] By the end of the month, Beckett sent a card to Feldman with a handwritten text called *Neither*, which inevitably became the title of the work. The opera premiered at the Teatro dell'Opera in Rome on 10 June 1977.[10]

The work turned out to be a solo-voice opera with orchestra. The unique singer was the young and inexpert American soprano Martha Hanneman. She rose to prominence at the Buffalo festival exactly one year before, where she performed with great vocal skills in George Crumb's *Madrigals*. Feldman, who lived in Buffalo, decided to hire her because the solo role in *Neither* required 'a pure young voice and an acute musical sense […] and Martha seems to fill the bill'.[11] So in the premiere, besides Hanneman's solo, Marcello Panni would conduct the orchestra and the avant-garde painter, Michelangelo Pistoletto, would be responsible for the stage production. Immediately after the first representation, the work was defined by some critics as an anti-opera. Why?

Before tackling this assertion, it would be better first to define the term 'opera'. In *The Concise Oxford Dictionary of Opera*, it is defined as 'a drama to be sung with instrumental accompaniment by one or more singers in costume; recitative or spoken dialogue may separate set musical numbers'.[12] According to the musicologist, Fabrizio Della Seta, it is 'a theatrical performance in which the action is manifested mainly through the music and the expressive singing of the characters. Opera is a complex genre, based on the collaboration between the literary text, the scenery and the music, which has also the essential function of characterising dramatically the work'.[13] So it is clear that opera has some

---

[8] John Dwyer, 'In the Shadows with Feldman and Beckett', *Buffalo Evening News: Lively Arts*, November 27, 1976.

[9] Ibid.

[10] In Dwyer's article, it is written that the premiere would take place on 15 May with seven further performances ensuing. In the Italian newspapers, instead, we are told that it was to take place on 13 May but was then postponed to 10 June. Anyway, the official archives of the Teatro dell'Opera confirm that the premiere took place on 10 June and that five performances followed. 'Neither 1976–77', accessed December 13, 2022, https://archiviostorico.operaroma.it/edizione_opera/neither-1976-77.

[11] Dwyer, 'In the Shadows with Feldman and Beckett'.

[12] Harold Rosenthal and John Warrack, *The Concise Oxford Dictionary of Opera* (Oxford: Oxford University Press, 1987), 360.

[13] My translation; Fabrizio Della Seta, *Le parole del teatro musicale* (Rome: Carocci, 2010), 81.

fundamental characteristics which are the presence of a plot, a text and costumes. It is mostly sung and follows what are called 'operatic conventions' in which singers are assigned their roles according to the voice type. Furthermore, there is a tacit agreement with the spectator that everything that occurs on stage must not be questioned.

Ironically, in *Neither*, with the exception of those sections which are sung, none of the primary requirements that characterize an opera are satisfied. *Neither* has no plot, no scenery, no costumes but solely a soprano that sings in a seemingly wordless manner creating an 'emotional/aesthetic tension'.[14] This can be explained by the text, the so-called *libretto*, that Beckett sent to Feldman. In contrast to normal librettos, the text is not sung but only works as a form of guide to the listener, helping to reinforce the atmosphere of indefiniteness. Overall, the text contains 86 words in 10 lines. These are the lyrics:

NEITHER

to and fro in shadow from inner to outer shadow

from impenetrable self to impenetrable unself
by way of neither

as between two lit refuges whose doors once
gently close, once turned away from
gently part again

beckoned back and forth and turned away

heedless of the way, intent on the one gleam
or the other

unheard footfalls only sound

till at last halt for good, absent for good
from self and other

then no sound

then gently light unfading on that unheeded
neither

unspeakable home[15]

---

[14] Art Lange, 'Liner notes', in *Neither* (Therwil: HatArt CD, 1997).
[15] Beckett, 'neither', in *Journal of Beckett Studies*, no. 4 (1979): vii.

Giving a quick look at the text, you can notice immediately that it has no capital letters and hardly any punctuation, except for just three commas. The laws of grammar, a human invention, seem unimportant in the universe that Beckett wants to portray in *Neither*. When Feldman received this text, he had already started composing the music. Probably he didn't really expect Beckett to send him an additional text. As Feldman stated in an interview: 'That's why the piece begins textless. I was waiting for the text. I discovered what an overture is: waiting for the text!'[16] To make people wait seems a typical characteristic of Beckett. Inevitably, Feldman looked at the text quizzically and found it extremely peculiar. He stated: 'First of all, like a conventional composer, I started to scan the first sentence: *To and fro in shadow from inner to outer shadow*; it seemed to me as one long period of time. And I noticed that it fell into a grid.'[17] Feldman's grid is supposed to represent a number of bars where half of the line of the text is contained in each, or better, the essential meaning of the text, not forgetting that *Neither*, during the performance, is textless. The female voice instead will float stably in fixed points following the dictates of the *libretto* but with a differing musical context.[18] This is how Feldman described the creative process of this work:

> I wanted to treat each sentence as a world. And there was much to think about, because I noticed that, as the work went on, it became much more tragic. It became unbearable, while here [at the beginning] it's tolerable. It wasn't until page 30 that I had a glimpse of what To and fro is in the text. What he's talking about is the impossibility of fathoming either the 'self' or the 'unself.' You're back and forth, back and forth. Well, I said to myself, I certainly know more than anybody else in my generation what the 'self' is in terms of personal music. I had to invent the 'unself'. I saw the 'unself' as a very detached, impersonal, perfect type of machinery.[19]

Therefore, Feldman tried to create differing worlds which were tied together by the persistent, obsessive idea of the 'self' and 'unself'. Besides, there was this feeling of repetition in the meaning of the whole that gave tragic power to the music. As Feldman stated, *Neither* 'is really the same thought said in

---

[16] Skempton, 'Beckett as Librettist', 5.
[17] Ibid.
[18] Ibid.
[19] Ibid., 6.

another way. And yet the continuity acts as if something else is happening'.[20] In this, Feldman expresses Beckett's words by adapting his idiosyncratic style to the meaning of the text, depicting the same atmosphere he perceived but through the musical medium.[21] The two did not meet during the preparatory work and, therefore, their first encounter represented their only meeting. As Feldman stated:

> But I must tell you something about my meeting with Beckett and the conversation, because it's both humorous and very interesting in relation to my treatment, and because I wanted slavishly to adhere to *his* feelings as well as mine. Yet there was no compromise because we were in complete agreement about many, many things.[22]

If we examine Feldman's career, it would be evident that Feldman had not chosen randomly Beckett as his librettist. *Neither* was Morton Feldman's first and only opera. The fact that the Rome Opera House had commissioned an opera to a novice in this field demonstrated the fame he enjoyed at the time. He was associated with the New York School, an experimental avant-garde movement whose members included the composer John Cage and painters like Robert Rauschenberg and Jasper Johns. In the musical domain, Feldman was considered the precursor of indeterminacy. Also defined by Cage as 'chance music',[23] indeterminacy gave the interpreter the freedom to make personal choices during the performance of the work or leave it to chance. In an interview with the music critic, Mario Bortolotto, published in the magazine 'Lo Spettatore musicale' in January 1969, Feldman explained it instead in the following way:

> When you use the term indeterminate, there is a reference to the fact that there is no analogy with other music: in other words, you use other music as a criterion

---

[20] Alexander Ruch, 'Morton Feldman's Neither', May 17, 2001, accessed March 4, 2022, https://web.archive.org/web/20070528204221/http://www.themodernword.com/beckett/beckett_feldman_neither.html.

[21] Lange, 'Liner notes'.

[22] Skempton, 'Beckett as Librettist', 5.

[23] Despite Cage's greater popular reputation as the evangelist of indeterminacy, the composer credited Feldman as the originator of chance music, or, as Cage described it later, '[music] indeterminate with respect to its performance'. John Cage and Morton Feldman, 'Radio Happening 1', in *Radio Happenings*, October 1967; Ryan Dohoney, *Morton Feldman: Friendship and Mourning in the New York Avant-Garde* (London: Bloomsbury Publishing, 2022), 24.

to classify this new music. My music is not composed in opposition to other music, and so I do not consider it indeterminate. I know what I'm doing. The predetermined composer does not know what I'm doing. For him, I'm indeterminate.[24]

During the period in which he was composing *Neither*, Feldman was trying new experiments giving value again to the rhythm and highlighting the importance of quiet sounds. Opera was another of these experiments and his literary counterpart could only be a similar experimenter, Samuel Beckett. Consequently, there was no real need of further communication between the two. From an initial collaboration, the work was to become a 're-elaboration' made by Feldman.

The ensuing adaptation created by Feldman can certainly be considered a monodrama. It has just one presence, a voice of a soprano, that recalls a wailing ghost. The voice expresses the essential existential words written by Beckett in a typically modern dissonant musical frame. The singing tessitura is quite high, probably to increase the difficulty and reproduce a true natural anguish, on the part of the singer, deriving from the continuous vocal feats. Moreover, the combination of the voice and the music, their open atonality, does not give the impression of a state of harmony but, on the contrary, offers a feeling of alienation, of misplacement inside the world portrayed. The voice, which seems to symbolize the tormented human soul and its awareness of this fact, sings an internal, practically impersonal monologue, a meditation on everyday life issues. It offers glimpses of an illusory solution that will finally convey into repetitiveness, because no true solution to the existential problems can be really achieved. The perceptible hopelessness deriving from the inevitable repetition of the various situations will increase the existing tension in the work creating a dynamic effect from an apparently static situation. The only final solution can be death. Death will be the final silence, 'the unspeakable home', the familiar instrument which Feldman often uses in his own compositions.

Besides Feldman, the director Michelangelo Pistoletto, responsible for the visual part of the performance with Armando Pasti, had to cope with

---

[24] My translation; original: 'Quando tu usi il termine indeterminato, vi è riferimento al fatto che non vi è analogia con le altre musiche: in altre parole, usi le altre musiche come criterio per classificare questa nuova musica. La mia musica non è composta in opposizione alle altre musiche, e così non lo considero indeterminata. So quel che faccio. Il compositore predeterminato non sa ciò che io faccio. Per lui, io sono indeterminato.' G. Lanza Tomasi et al., *La Stagione Lirica 1976–77*, 507.

Beckett's text and search for an interpretative key to the whole work. He wrote on 22 April 1977:

> Now my participation to the opera *Neither* falls within the category of those solitary encounters where each person keeps their own distance. But, nonetheless, I would like to see the audience involved in this fusion of music, voice, form and light. I would like them to perceive the subtle vibrations and the throbbing of the moods beneath their own skin which is the same as everyone's. These are moods of the subconscious which give form to the surface; a surface that spreads out on the banality of everyday life.
>
> The sound, the voice, the poetry, the form stretches out like a thin mist that vibrates in a space half natural and half artificial.
>
> A blanket that divides this from that, it is not this and it is not that, like a sound wave which is between two notes; that is *Neither*.[25]

The representation of *Neither* was practically the work of two soloists, Feldman and Pistoletto, with the shadow of Beckett behind them. Both artists had to interpret Beckett. If Feldman tried to interpret Beckett according to his music ideals, Beckett's presence was made visible through the compromises Feldman had to make. As the reviewer of *Village Voice*, Tom Johnson, wrote in 1978:

> Like most of Feldman's compositions, *Neither* is concerned primarily with dense atonal harmonies and unusual blends of instrumental color. Here, however, the composer works with a wider variety of instruments and a larger span of time than usual. If most of his pieces are easel paintings, this one is a wall-sized mural, and it is so loaded with activity that there is no room for the silences that play such an important part in other Feldman works. [...] The instruments are played in conventional ways, but they come together in unconventional combinations, and there is much more repetition than in most Feldman works.[26]

---

[25] My translation; original: 'Ora la mia partecipazione all'opera *Neither* rientra nel circolo degli incontri solitari dove ognuno mantiene le proprie distanze. Ma, ciononostante, io vorrei che il pubblico fosse coinvolto dalla fusione della musica con la voce, con la forma e la luce, vorrei che avvertisse le sottili vibrazioni e il pulsare degli umori al di sotto della propria pelle che è quella di tutti. Umori del subconscio che danno forma alla superficie; superficie che si stende sulla quotidianità banale della vita. Il suono, la voce, la poesia, la forma si allargano come una nebbia sottile che vibra in uno spazio metà naturale e metà artificiale. Una coltre che divide questo da quello, non è questo e non è quello come un'onda sonora che sta tra due note; cioè Neither.' G. Lanza Tomasi et al., *La Stagione Lirica 1976–77*, 511.

[26] Tom Johnson, 'Morton Feldman writes an 'Opera'', *Village Voice*, December 11, 1978.

The presence of Beckett was not only spiritual but visible, in capital letters, in the official playbill of the event: 'NEITHER, for a text by SAMUEL BECKETT'.[27] The 1977 programme would also display a big photo of Beckett, with the text of *Neither* and words of gratitude for his 'exquisite text'[28] by Feldman. In the same programme, the artistic director, Lanza Tomasi would also describe an active collaboration between the composer and the 'librettist', not forgetting Pistoletto:

> Feldman approached Beckett for a text and a work was born which explored the imperceptible, the threshold of consciousness, the subconscious, the ego, the beginning of memory, of the social factor and of reason. Sound and word, this is the score of Feldman-Beckett. All one has to do is to listen to them, rediscover and rearrange them in spaces spread beyond time.[29] And then again the blanket, the animated sheet of Pistoletto, that distils the boundary between the nothingness and the memory of forms.[30]

Furthermore, the artistic director of the Roman theatre would continue to emphasize the presumed collaboration between the three minds of the performance:

> Lastly *Neither*, not a ballet but a gnoseological opera, an initiation opera, tackled by three different experiences. Feldman, Beckett, Pistoletto, three artists intent on studying in the sound, in the words, in the forms the prolegomena of knowledge.[31]

Inevitably, all the Italian journals talked about Beckett's involvement in this work but instead of the ambiguous 'for the text by Samuel Beckett'

---

[27] My translation; original: 'NEITHER, per un testo di SAMUEL BECKETT'; 'Neither 1976–77', accessed December 13, 2022, https://archiviostorico.operaroma.it/edizione_opera/neither-1976-77.

[28] See citation 1.

[29] Brigitte Schiffer, 'Neither', *Music and Musicians*, August 1977, 49; Translated from G. Lanza Tomasi et al., *La Stagione Lirica 1976–77*, 486; *Rassegna Stampa – Teatro dell'Opera, Volume Quinto* (Rome: Teatro dell'Opera, 1977), 850.

[30] My translation; original: 'E poi ancora il lenzuolo, coltre animata di Pistoletto, che distilla il confine fra il nulla e la memoria di forme.' G. Lanza Tomasi et al., *La Stagione Lirica 1976–77*, 486.

[31] My translation; original: 'Infine *Neither*, non un balletto ma un'opera gnoseologica, un'opera iniziazione, affrontata da tre diverse esperienze. Feldman, Beckett, Pistoletto, tre artisti intenti a studiare nel suono, nelle parole, nelle forme i prolegomeni della conoscenza.' G. Lanza Tomasi et al., *La Stagione Lirica 1976–77*, 487.

present on the official playbill, they would write 'on texts by Samuel Beckett'[32] which later, with the approach of the performance, would become one text. By 3 June, *Neither* would be associated with the trio 'Feldman–Beckett–Pistoletto' and the important notice that it is a real opera.[33] The day before the premiere, the collaboration between Feldman and Beckett would be described as the encounter of the composer who belonged to the most advanced movements of the new American music with the Pontifex Maximus of the avant-garde theatre.[34] On 10 June, the day of the premiere, an active Beckett would be recalled by Feldman in an interview with Mya Tannebaum[35] while talking about the creative process of the work. Even Pistoletto would describe his artistic relationship made of contrasts with Beckett.[36] All of this with no trace of Beckett in person in the Italian peninsula. At night-time, it was finally the time for the premiere. The music critic and composer, Brigitte Schiffer, wrote the following report concerning the performance:

> In the music the impression of timelessness is brought about by a pseudo-repetitiveness with only minimal changes and by a deliberate sameness of colour, dynamics, articulation and register. In the text the ambiguity of the self and the unself, of perception and imperception and the breaking down of communication is further underlined by the immobility of a singer (Martha Hanneman), who, clad in a very wide white robe, with lights attached to her forearms, sings only one single note, a range that is only occasionally extended to three chromatic notes sung in succession and in falsetto, so that the text can never be understood, and this incomprehensibility becomes an additional means of alienation in a work full of doubt and anxiety. On an empty stage and in front of a blank background, which from dark becomes gradually lighter, the immobile singer with an 'immobile' voice is accompanied by an 'immobile' orchestra – immobile in so far as there is no progression, no dialectic and no direction, just sound.[37]

Unfortunately, the audience was not as immobile as the performers. The sole presence of Beckett in letters could not save the opera. It turned out

---

[32] *Rassegna Stampa*, 799–803.
[33] 'Omaggi a Picasso e Balla al Teatro dell'Opera', *Il Messaggero*, June 3, 1977; *Rassegna Stampa*, 805.
[34] 'Musica e pittura in quattro tempi', *Paese Sera*, June 9, 1977; *Rassegna Stampa*, 813.
[35] 'Feldman: l'incontro con Beckett', *Corriere della Sera*, June 10, 1977; *Rassegna Stampa*, 816.
[36] 'Un palcoscenico tutto bianco', *Repubblica*, June 10, 1977; *Rassegna Stampa*, 818.
[37] Schiffer, 'Neither', 50.

to be a complete fiasco even though the management of the theatre was not of the same opinion:

> The audience has nevertheless understood, even though in the wrong way, the provocation proposed by Beckett's 'nonsense' on the 'nonsense' of Feldman's iterative music. Despite the complaints and the protests, which at times were of bad taste, the work was regularly brought to its conclusion by the orchestra conducted by the maestro Marcello Panni.
> It seems to me – said the general manager, Luca di Schiena – that the Roman audience has in some way matured. On another occasion, the protest would have exploded within ten minutes of the performance. The audience, instead, has accepted the proposal, certainly not easy to follow, for over twenty minutes. Maybe the 'piece' was too long, but its goal lay precisely in the provocation.[38]

Undoubtedly, the words of Luca di Schiena might appear excessively positive, but it must not be forgotten, as stated previously, that the Teatro dell'Opera had an audience that was strongly attached to the Italian operatic tradition. So, it was not a random choice to end the season with four experimental works. Probably, it was just a way to make the audience get accustomed gradually to the contemporary works, even at the cost of an utter failure. But, in any case, it was no coincidence that the audience started to show their impatience during the performance of *Neither*. If the other three pieces were ballets, *Neither*, which some journalists believed also to be a ballet, was supposed to be an opera. This did not seem the case as Brigitte Schiffer reports:

> The Italian audience, feeling cheated because an opera without drama, aria and prima donna is hardly an 'opera' (certainly not a *drama per musica*) and not even a piece of music-theatre, this audience was not ready to submit itself to the spell of a music so nude, so stark, so pure. Laughing and booing was their

---

[38] My translation; original: 'Il pubblico ha comunque recepito, anche se in maniera negativa, la provocazione proposta dal "nonsense" della musica iterativa di Feldman. Nonostante le contestazioni e le proteste, che qualche volta sono state anche di cattivo gusto, il pezzo è stato portato regolarmente a conclusione dall'orchestra guidata dal maestro Marcello Panni. "Mi sembra – ha detto il sovrintendente, Luca Di Schiena – che il pubblico romano sia in qualche modo maturato. In altra occasione, la protesta sarebbe deflagrata dopo dieci minuti di esecuzione. Invece, il pubblico ha accettato la proposta, certamente non facile, per oltre venti minuti. Forse il "pezzo" era troppo lungo, ma la sua destinazione risiedeva proprio nella provocazione.' 'Fischi e imbeccate all'Opera di Roma', *La Notte*, June 11, 1977; *Rassegna Stampa*, 820.

spontaneous reaction – a reaction due not only to conventional habits and tastes, but also to the nervous tension created by nearly one hour of timeless immobility and which demanded an immediate release.[39]

In short, spectators would not see it as an opera. It must have appeared to them more like an anti-opera. Was this the real aim of Feldman and the producers or was it Beckett's? As stated previously, the absence of Beckett during the staging of *Neither* was well documented. It would be easy to state that all the people who worked on the opera had used the name of Beckett for their own personal gain and that in reality there was no Beckett in it. However, there's one evidence that dismantles this theory, that is the handwritten card Beckett sent with the original text of *Neither*. If Beckett didn't want to have anything to do with Feldman, he would never have sent him a card. So, another question might now arise. Did Beckett really write on purpose a text which would defy opera through its operatic conventions? It would be easy to state that Beckett had no interest in opera and consequently rejected it but examining closely his official biography we can say that this is not really so. At the beginning of this essay, it was shown that Beckett enjoyed greatly those works which belonged to the world of operetta and its ilk. The operetta was the successor of an operatic genre called the opera buffa. Among these operas, we can count Mozart's *Le nozze di Figaro* (1786). Beckett went to see a performance of it in Dresden in 1937 and took the following notes:

> Theatre radiant. Small public. Admirable orchestra, conducted by Bohm. Exquisite inszenierung [production]. Wonderful costumes. Figaro excellent. Susanna and Chérubin lovely and excellent, especially latter. Barbarina also. Gräfin Almaviva the tragic relief. Her high point the Recitative and Aria in Act III. Last act Watteau enough to be not in the least Watteau. A more puerile world than Watteau's, where the interest even in sexual congress has lapsed. They are all Chérubin.[40]

It is interesting to see how Beckett recorded in detail the performance. Obviously, from the text, you can see that he highly praised the performance. He then stated: 'the first opera that I was sorry to have over'.[41] So, Beckett seemed to enjoy some operas. Perusing Beckett's operatic tastes, he had a

---

[39] Schiffer, 'Neither', 50.
[40] Samuel Beckett, 'German Diaries', in *Notebook 4*, February 3, 1937; Knowlson, *Samuel Beckett: Damned to Fame*, 235.
[41] Samuel Beckett to Tom MacGreevy, February 16, 1937, Trinity College Dublin Library; Ibid.

well-known dislike for Wagner. Maybe because it is with the Wagnerian reform that opera became elitist. Wagner craved for opera to become immortal and so introduced the idea of *Gesamkuntswerk*, a work that comprises all the arts. Unlike traditional opera, Wagner's operatic plots were solely consecrated to mythical characters with the total absence of comic figures. Most probably, Wagnerism must have appeared to Beckett as something excessive and absolutely megalomaniac. As recorded by a painter and friend of Beckett, Avigdor Arikha: 'He disliked Wagner and also Mahler – actually antithetical to his sense of "less is more".'[42] The man who believed in the principle of 'less is more' could not obviously adhere to this overly intellectual approach which kept at a distance the spectator which he yearned for the most, the ordinary person.

Wagnerism had also caused a great split in the operatic world. The comic opera which dealt with middle-class issues gained the name of operetta. This was the name used in France and German-speaking countries. The term 'light opera' would be used instead in Great Britain. Beckett sided with this more popular genre and opposed the classist Wagnerian opera. Consequently, all those composers who pursued the path to immortality such as Wagner were not appreciated by the Irish playwright. Composers like Gustav Mahler[43] and Richard Strauss[44] were on Beckett's blacklist.

When considering instead composers who attempted to adapt opera to the existing world without frills, Beckett's view would change. This explains Beckett's appreciation of Debussy's music. Beckett was an able pianist and loved to play Debussy's preludes.[45] He did not only esteem his piano works but also his only opera, *Pelléas et Melisande* (1902). As Knowlson writes, Beckett could be seen 'even enjoying Debussy's *Pelléas et Melisande*, probably because of its understated nature'.[46] Initially, Debussy had been fascinated by Wagnerian music but in the long run, he decided to emancipate himself from it. If Wagner was more totalitarian, Debussy followed a more impressionist

---

[42] Avigdor Arikha, fax to James Knowlson, April 8, 1994; Knowlson, *Samuel Beckett: Damned to Fame*, 443.
[43] Gustav Mahler was famous for his large-scale compositions which would require orchestras with more than 120 musicians. He was also considered a successor of Wagner.
[44] Strauss was considered one of Wagner's successors and his music had the tendency to embrace all styles. Morten Kristensen uses the term *Stilkunst* 'to describe Richard Strauss's use of multiple styles both between and within works [...]'. He defines it as an attempt 'to describe this bewildering coexistence of diverse and competing styles'. Morten Kristensen, 'Richard Strauss, *Die Moderne* and the Concept of *Stilkunst*', *The Musical Quarterly 86*, no. 4 (2002), 695.
[45] Knowlson, *Samuel Beckett: Damned to Fame*, 78.
[46] Ibid., 186.

approach. In the end, *Pelléas et Mélisande* appeared a more minimal, less intense, 'understated' version of Wagner's *Tristan und Isolde* (1865).

Apart from comic operas and Debussy, Beckett also held in high regard Alban Berg's *Wozzeck* (1925). This opera, which belonged to the expressionist and atonal current, was considered by Beckett as a masterpiece of the modernist era.[47] In contrast to his mentor, Arnold Schönberg, Berg's music was more emotional and instinctive. In this mentor–pupil relationship, Beckett seemed to favour the latter.[48] Berg had to emancipate himself artistically from his cumbersome maestro, Schönberg, to achieve success. Debussy had to do the same with his youthful inspirer Wagner and, similarly, Beckett with his mentor, James Joyce. In a certain way, Beckett did the same with the operatic world that had changed after the Wagnerian revolution. He distanced himself from this overly intellectual, elitist and ambitious dimension that searched for immortality and turned instead to the more popular, emancipated and more human world that took the form of the operetta. This did not mean that Beckett would disdain experimental works as his interest in Debussy and Berg shows. Therefore, according to his tastes, it follows that he enjoyed operas of inclusion in which the composer would not admire himself in the mirror but would express in essence the changing world that was affecting the individual.

Among these works, can be counted Philip Glass's first opera, *Einstein on the Beach* (1976). It was first represented just one year before *Neither*, on 25 July 1976, at the Avignon Festival. That same summer, it was also staged in various major European theatres which included Hamburg, Paris and Venice in September 1976. The work lasted around four hours and it was immediately labelled as a non-opera because it had no ties with the operatic tradition, no plot and the music would not play its original role of completing the text.[49] Most probably, it was the wave of success of *Einstein on the Beach* which might have inspired Lanza Tomasi to commission an opera to Feldman. Furthermore, also Feldman's choice of Beckett might not have been solely artistic.

---

[47] Ibid.

[48] The main difference between Schönberg and Berg was the fact that the former was more theoretical than the latter. His rational, overly intellectual and revolutionary dodecaphonic system would create a distance with the listener compared to the more approachable music of Berg. In truth, Beckett seemed to appreciate Schönberg. As Avigdor Arikha recalls about his experience with Beckett: 'We had a period during which we listened to quite a bit of dodecaphonic music — Schoenberg, Berg, Webern (before 1959).' Knowlson, *Samuel Beckett: Damned to Fame*, 442.

[49] Alessandro Rigolli, '*Einstein on the Beach* di Philip Glass e Bob Wilson: Caratteri di una Non-Opera', *Rivista Italiana di Musicologia 36*, no. 2 (2001): 370.

Glass defined himself in an interview as 'one of Beckett's children'.[50] He explained how he learned in the 1960s to associate music with theatre thanks to Beckett. The latter was the master of the non-narrative, the art of telling a story without telling one, and through this mechanism Glass conceived his musical process. It started when he had to compose the incidental music for a performance of Beckett's *Play* (1963) in Paris in 1965:

> – a love-triangle one-act that Beckett's stage notes nudge toward incomprehensibility ('Rapid tempo throughout. [...] Voices faint, largely unintelligible') – Glass writes that Beckett's text 'provided no clue as to what the emotional shape of the music might be.[...] I was thereby liberated from the necessity of shaping the music to fit the action, or even to *not* fit the action.'[51]

As regards the composer, Beckett would allow him the freedom to express his own music but following a particular path. For example, when Glass was writing music to go with 'Company', the composer received only a single line of instruction from Beckett, which would also have a lasting impact: 'The music should go into the interstices of the text, as it were.'[52] This short message of Beckett obviously reminds us of the card given to Feldman which became *Neither*. It was the way with which Beckett would express himself with them. As a heritage, their music would include a new Beckettian feature, repetitiveness.

Now, returning to our preliminary question, can *Neither* be considered an anti-opera? Or is it a monodrama or an 'art song'[53] as some have defined it? It is all of these. It certainly represents an anti-opera, in the sense that it is an opposition to the opera which has evolved after the Wagnerian revolution, that opera which has distanced itself from the people it should have represented. It is also an opposition to the traditional opera of the nineteenth century, by the fact that it ignores the specific and perfectly ordered conventional structure of an opera. However, this does not mean that it does not belong to the operatic

---

[50] *Philip Glass, one of Beckett's children*, accessed December 24, 2022, https://www.youtube.com/watch?v=CpiRNWIfOAw&list=RDLVCpiRNWIfOAw&index=5.
[51] Seth Colter Walls, 'What Philip Glass Learned from Samuel Beckett', *The New Yorker*, April 22, 2015, accessed December 24, 9.50, https://www.newyorker.com/books/page-turner/what-philip-glass-learned-from-samuel-beckett.
[52] Ibid.
[53] Tom Johnson wrote in a review of *Neither* in 1978 that 'Many of us who have followed the highly abstract output of Morton Feldman over the years were surprised to learn that he had composed an opera, and it is perhaps still questionable whether he really has. *Neither* [...] might be better described as an hour long art song'. T. Johnson, 'Morton Feldman writes an "Opera"'.

category. *Neither* is an experiment, an evolution of opera. It mirrors the period in which it was composed, that Cold War era with its MAD, acronym for Mutual Assured Destruction. It belongs to a period in which no Wagnerian hero can be born, and no Faust can dream of a philanthropic world. It is the period in which the United States and the USSR are investing their resources on nuclear armaments, the so-called nuclear arms race. It is the period in which 'neither' of the two superpowers seem to have the possibility to win, where uncertainty is overly present everywhere. *Neither* reflects all this instability. In 1997, Art Lange ended his Liner Notes to the CD recording of *Neither* with this phrase: 'The eternal present exists in the space between the familiar and the unfamiliar. Which is real? Neither.'[54]

Bibliography

Beckett, Samuel. *Happy Days*. New York: Grove Press, 2013.

———. 'neither'. *Journal of Beckett Studies*, no. 4 (1979): vii.

———. *Proust*. New York: Grove Press, 1978.

Bellingardi, Luigi, et al. *Rassegna Stampa – Teatro dell'Opera, Volume Quinto*. Rome: Teatro dell'Opera, 1977, 790–851.

Colter Walls, Seth. 'What Philip Glass Learned from Samuel Beckett'. *The New Yorker*, April 22, 2015. Accessed December 24, 2022, https://www.newyorker.com/books/page-turner/what-philip-glass-learned-from-samuel-beckett.

Della Seta, Fabrizio. *Le parole del teatro musicale*. Rome: Carocci, 2010.

Dohoney, Ryan. *Morton Feldman: Friendship and Mourning in the New York Avant-Garde*. London: Bloomsbury Publishing, 2022.

Dwyer, John. 'In the Shadows with Feldman and Beckett'. *Buffalo Evening News: Lively Arts*, November 27, 1976.

Johnson, Tom. 'Morton Feldman Writes an 'Opera''. *Village Voice*, December 11, 1978.

Knowlson, James. *Samuel Beckett: Damned to Fame*. New York: Simon & Schuster, 1996.

Kristensen, Morten. 'Richard Strauss, *Die Moderne* and the Concept of *Stilkunst*'. *The Musical Quarterly* 86, no. 4 (2002): 689–749.

Lange, Art. 'Liner notes'. In *Neither*. Therwil: HatArt CD, 1997.

Lanza Tomasi, Gioacchino et al. *La Stagione Lirica 1976–77: Programma*. Rome: Teatro dell'Opera, 1977, 503–11.

Rigolli, Alessandro. "Einstein on the Beach' di Philip Glass e Bob Wilson: Caratteri di una Non-Opera'. *Rivista Italiana di Musicologia* 36, no. 2 (2001): 351–73.

Rosenthal, Harold and John Warrack. *The Concise Oxford Dictionary of Opera*. Oxford: Oxford University Press, 1987.

Ruch, Alexander. 'Morton Feldman's Neither'. May 17, 2001. Accessed March 4, 2022. https://web.archive.org/web/20070528204221/http://www.themodernword.com/beckett/beckett_feldman_neither.html.

Schiffer, Brigitte. 'Neither'. *Music and Musicians*, August 1977, 49–50.

Skempton, Howard. 'Beckett as Librettist'. *Music and Musicians*, 1977, 5–6.

---

[54] Lange, 'Liner notes'.

Chapter 5

FROM *INFERNO* TO SORRENTO: DANTE, WARTIME RADIO AND THE ITALIA PRIZE

Pim Verhulst

Abstract

This article traces the Italian influences in Beckett's radio plays, beginning with Dante's *Divine Comedy* and its intertextual significance for *All That Fall*, *Embers* and *Rough for Radio II* in particular. In the next step, these texts are further analysed, together with *Words and Music*, against the historical backdrop of the Second World War, when radio broadcasting contributed significantly to the rise of Fascism in Europe. Finally, I will read *Cascando* through a biographical lens, in light of Beckett's 1959 trip to Sorrento, where he attended the Italia Prize awards ceremony accompanied by BBC producer Donald McWhinnie. In doing so, on the one hand, the chapter shows how Beckett used Dante to gradually develop a generic radiophonic space that is marked by a lack of sight and dissociated from any specific geography or nationality. On the other hand, it illustrates how this seeming universality is, at the same time, infused with different cultural contexts that merge almost beyond the point of recognizability. These frameworks are not limited to Ireland, which permeates the early radio plays especially, or France, Beckett's permanent home that put him at further remove from his native country in linguistic terms. Germany, which he visited throughout his career, and by extension Italy, where he spent the least time, should not be neglected as crucial in-between spaces that help to navigate the seeming no man's land of Beckett's later radio plays.

Keywords: Broadcasting; radio drama; Italia Prize (Prix Italia); Dante; Fascism

The influence of Italian culture on Beckett's writing has typically been considered from the following angles: his formal study of the language and its literature at Trinity College Dublin from 1923 to 1927, the private lessons he started taking with Bianca Esposito in 1926, his trip to Florence during the summer of 1927 and his lifelong engagement with the *Divine Comedy*. This chapter seeks to expand that focus by concentrating on Beckett's radio plays, beginning with Dante and his intertextual significance for *All That Fall*, *Embers* and *Rough for Radio II*. In the next step, I will dwell some more on the latter two, expanded with *Words and Music*, to situate these works in the historical context of the Second World War, when broadcasting contributed to the spread of Fascism in Europe. Last but not least, I will read *Cascando* through a biographical lens in the light of Beckett's 1959 trip to Sorrento, where he attended the Italia Prize awards ceremony in the company of BBC producer Donald McWhinnie. In doing so, on the one hand, I will show how Beckett used Dante to gradually develop a generic radiophonic space, characterized by a lack of sight and dissociated from any well-defined geography. On the other hand, I aim to illustrate how this seeming universality is, at the same time, infused by different cultural contexts that merge almost beyond the point of recognizability. These national frameworks are not restricted to Ireland, which permeates the earlier radio plays especially, or France, Beckett's permanent home that put him at a further remove from his native country in linguistic terms. Germany, which he visited at various points in his career, and by extension Italy, where he spent the least time, should not be neglected as important in-between spaces that help navigate the seeming no man's land of Beckett's later radio plays.

Intertextuality: Dante's *Divine Comedy*

When he embarked on the relatively young medium of radio in the mid-1950s, at the invitation of the BBC after the success of *Waiting for Godot* in Paris and on London's West End stage, Beckett had very little experience of writing for it. As far as we know, there had only been 'a sketch for Paris Mondial', the French government's official shortwave radio station at the time, which Beckett mentioned in a letter to his agent George Reavey in 1940 but which never materialized,[1] and *The Capital of the Ruins*, a more documentary or journalistic report about the Red Cross hospital at the bombed town of Saint-Lô in France, which was made for Irish radio (RTÉ) in 1946 but never broadcast. With texts of radio plays rarely appearing in print, the medium being so ephemeral,

---

[1] Samuel Beckett, *The Letters of Samuel Beckett, Volume I: 1929–1940*, ed. Martha Dow Fehsenfeld and Lois More Overbeck (Cambridge: Cambridge University Press, 2009), 680.

there was no canon to speak of that Beckett could derive inspiration from. The next logical step for him was to draw on radiogenic works in the more traditional genres he was familiar with. For example, in Dante's *Divine Comedy*, especially the *Inferno* and its emphasis on blindness, Beckett found a match for his own description of radio as 'voices [...] coming out of the dark' in a letter to his American publisher Barney Rosset of 27 August 1957.[2]

In Beckett's first radio play, *All That Fall*, Dante is mentioned explicitly when Mr Rooney asks his wife: 'Shall we go on backwards now a little? [...] Or you forwards and I backwards. The perfect pair. Like Dante's damned, with their faces arsy-versy. Our tears will water our bottoms.'[3] Beckett specified the reference in his so-called 'Eté 56' notebook, crossing it out as soon as it had been incorporated into the manuscript, contained in a second notebook:

Dante's damned – indovini
Inf 20 Watering their bottoms
with their tears. (BDMP12, EN, 03r)[4]

He may well have looked up the passage in one of his Dante copies. Judging from the term *indovini*, it must have been an Italian one, likely 'the Florentia edition in the ignoble Salani collection' from *Dream of Fair to Middling Women*,[5] which Daniela Caselli has managed to narrow down to the Salani edition of 1921, or one of its reprints, edited by Enrico Bianchi.[6] As Everett Frost and Jane Maxwell have noted, it was the copy that Beckett used for his 'first and systematic reading (in Italian) of *The Divine Comedy* under Bianca Esposito's tutelage, in the Spring and Autumn of 1926',[7] when his diligent '[p]reparation consisted of reading the assigned cantos in Italian and making an English synopsis of them'.[8] Beckett may well have revisited

---

[2] Samuel Beckett, *The Letters of Samuel Beckett, Volume III: 1957–1965*, ed. George Craig, Martha Dow Fehsenfeld, Dan Gunn and Lois More Overbeck (Cambridge: Cambridge University Press, 2014), 63.
[3] Samuel Beckett, *All That Fall and Other Plays for Radio and Screen*, pref. Everett Frost (London: Faber and Faber, 2009) 24.
[4] This shorthand refers to the English notebook containing loose jottings for *All That Fall* (forthcoming) in module no. 12 of the Beckett Digital Manuscript Project (www.beckettarchive.org).
[5] Samuel Beckett, *Dream of Fair to Middling Women*, ed. Eoin O'Brien (Dublin: Black Cat Press, 1992), 51.
[6] Daniela Caselli, '"The Florentia Edition in the Ignoble Salani Collection": A Textual Comparison', *Journal of Beckett Studies* 9, no. 2 (2000): 1–20 (1).
[7] Everett Frost and Jane Maxwell, 'TCD MS 10963: Dante, *The Divine Comedy*, Part I', *Samuel Beckett Today/Aujourd'hui* 16 (2006): 39–49 (39).
[8] Ibid., 41.

these early notes or recalled them, seeing as the word 'indovini' appears twice on their pages – once on the cone-shaped 'Plan of Dante's Inferno' (TCD-MS-10963, 01r) and then again on the outline of the 'Distribution of Sins' (31r), both 'copied or traced from the Salani edition'.[9]

Beckett's notes include the appearance of 'Dante's damned' in Canto XX of *Inferno*, about whom he wrote the following: 'As he looks more closely he perceives that each one's head is turned round, the back of the head and the chest thus facing in the same direction. [...] Virgil rebukes Dante for shedding tears of compassion for these victims, who in the world above were "indovini", foretellers' (TCD-MS-10963, 50r–51r).[10] Dante himself does not use the term indovini but *ndivine*, which suggests that Beckett took it from Bianchi's commentary instead. As Caselli clarifies, 'many of Beckett's summaries of the Cantos are translations of the footnotes which "beslubber" the Salani edition'.[11] In fact, the term occurs in Bianchi's concise summary of 'CANTO VENTESIMO', not in his footnotes:

> Nella quarta bolgia dell'ottavo cerchio sono gli *indovini*, che camminano all'indietro col capo volto verso le reni. Tra i molti, antichi e moderni, Dante vede Manto; e Virgilio gli narra com'essa fondo Mantova.[12]

In Bianchi's synopsis, the 'indovini' are described as lowering their heads towards 'le reni', which literally means the kidneys but more generally refers to the lower back or rump. In the corresponding passage from the text – 'quando la nostra imagine da presso / vidi sì torta, che il pianto degli occhi / le *natiche* bagnava per lo fesso'[13] – Dante also uses an obsolete word for kidneys or loins. Related to the modern Italian word *natica/natiche* or buttock(s), it does not have exactly the same meaning in Dante's literary language based on the dialect of Tuscany. Like Bianchi in his synopsis, the reverend Henry Francis Cary's English translation of the *Divina Commedia*, which Beckett also read and took excerpts from, avoids using the word *fesso* or an equivalent: 'That on the hinder parts fall'n from the face / The tears

---

[9] Ibid., 40–47.

[10] Pim Verhulst, *The Making of Samuel Beckett's Radio Plays* (Brussels and London: University Press Antwerp and Bloomsbury, forthcoming).

[11] Daniela Caselli, 'The Promise of Dante in the Beckett Manuscripts', *Samuel Beckett Today/Aujourd'hui* 16 (2006): 237–57 (242).

[12] Dante Alighieri, *Divina Commedia*, ed. Enrico Bianchi (Florence: Salani, 1933), 156; emphasis added.

[13] Ibid., 157; emphasis added.

down-streaming roll'd.'[14] Yet it was exactly the crudity of this body part in Dante that seems to have captured Beckett's creative imagination. Apart from using both 'bottoms' and 'arsy' in *All That Fall*, he also drew a figure in a similarly contorted posture, tears streaming from the eyes down its back towards a well-defined butt crack, on the final page of the Whoroscope notebook (MS-UoR-3000, 147r), which contains more Dante notes primarily taken from the *Inferno* (01r–02r, 60r–61r, 67v–69r, 81r). If Beckett's phrase in the manuscript of *All That Fall* – 'their heads screwed round back to front' (BDMP12, EM, 29r) – was still in keeping with the spirit of his summaries, its later substitution with the compact and liberally phrased 'arsy-versy', also clearly taking a distance from Bianchi and Carey, emphatically marks his transition from a student to a writer some 30 years later, when he came to realize the full potential of this image for his radio drama.

The punishment it describes is inflicted on the damned souls in the eighth circle of *Inferno*, also known as *Malebolge*. This region is made up of 10 *bolgia* or stone ditches, each home to a different type of sinner guilty of fraud. The indovini are sorcerers, astrologers and visionaries who, foretelling the future with forbidden means, were forced by God to look behind them eternally, which is a form of blinding. The reference thus lays the conceptual groundwork for *All That Fall* as a radio play. Dante constantly reminds us that, similar to the performative space of radio, the *Inferno* is a 'blind world' where ears are more reliable than eyes: 'Here in the dark (where only hearing told)' (Canto IV).[15] This is put into practice by Virgil, of whom the poem relates: 'Intently, as though listening hard, he stopped. / Eyesight unaided – in that blackened air, / through foggy, dense swirls – could not carry far' (Canto IX).[16] The *Inferno* is an 'eyeless prison', as Cavalcante calls it in Canto X,[17] shrouded 'in such dark as that, / no eye could penetrate the depths'

---

[14] Dante Alighieri, *The Vision; or Hell, Purgatory, and Paradise*, trans. Henry Francis Cary (London and New York: Frederick Warne and Co., 1889), 60. As Dirk Van Hulle and Mark Nixon have revealed, Beckett still owned two (unmarked) copies of the Cary translation at the end of his life. Dirk Van Hulle and Mark Nixon, *Samuel Beckett's Library* (Cambridge: Cambridge University Press, 2013), 105. These are both available in the Beckett Digital Library. See https://www.beckettarchive.org/library/DAN-VIS.html and https://www.beckettarchive.org/library/DAN-DIV-4.html.
[15] Dante Alighieri, *The Divine Comedy*, trans. Robin Kirkpatrick (London: Penguin, 2012), 16.
[16] Ibid., 38.
[17] Ibid., 43.

(Canto XXIV).[18] Unlike the venerated author of the *Aeneid*, however, personally selected by Beatrice to escort Dante into *Paradiso*, Maddy Rooney is not as reliable a guide for her blind husband in the impaired visibility of radio. First called 'Alfred' (BDMP12, EM, 04r) and 'Hugh' (10r) in the manuscript of *All That Fall*, Beckett changed the character's name to 'Dan' in the typescript, thus putting him in the same position as Dante in the *Divine Comedy*. The similarity with the indovini and their dwelling becomes even more apparent when Dan asks Maddy: 'Are you in a condition to lead me? [*Pause.*] We shall fall into *the ditch*.'[19] This connection between the medium's so-called blindness, the visual punishment of the indovini and the sightlessness of *Inferno* is a remarkably versatile example of Dantean intertextuality in Beckett's work that formed the backdrop for most of his other radio plays.

The *Divine Comedy* is not referenced in *Embers*, apart from Henry's aside that 'conversation' with Ada is 'what hell will be like, small chat to the babbling of Lethe'.[20] It invokes Dante's amnesia at the end of Canto XXXI in *Purgatorio*, after being cleansed in the river of his sins before entering the *Paradiso*, where he is reunited with his beloved Beatrice. The reference is bitterly ironic, devoid of any romance, in Beckett's second radio play. Henry bluntly admits to his wife, who is dead and speaks from beyond the grave, with little hope of a happy reunion in the afterlife: 'I have forgotten almost everything connected with you.'[21] Dante assumes centre stage again in *Rough for Radio II*, Beckett's next radio play, once more in relation to the mind.[22] When Animator boasts 'What a memory – mine!', a dialogue with Stenographer about Dante ensues:

A: Have you ever read the Purgatory, Miss, of the divine Florentine?
S: Alas no, Sir. I have merely flipped through the Inferno.
A: [*Incredulous.*] Not read the Purgatory?
S: Alas no, Sir.
A: There all sigh, I was, I was. It's like a knell. Strange, is it not?
S: In what sense, Sir?
A: Why, one would rather have expected, I shall be. No?
S: [*With tender condescension.*] The creatures! [*Pause.*] It is getting on for three, Sir.[23]

---

[18] Ibid., 107.
[19] Beckett, *All That Fall*, 21; my emphasis.
[20] Ibid., 38.
[21] Ibid., 45.
[22] Generally situated in the early 1960s, the radio play was probably written in 1958. See Pim Verhulst, '"Just howls from time to time": Dating *Pochade radiophonique*', *Samuel Beckett Today/Aujourd'hui* 27 (2015), 143–58.
[23] Beckett, *All That Fall*, 62.

As with *All That Fall*, this passage has fascinating variants in the drafts that cast a different light on the published text. In the manuscript, Animator just referred to the poet as 'Dante' (BDMP12, FN, 06r), which Beckett augmented to 'divin Dante' in the first typescript (FT1, 04r) and then further rephrased as 'divin Florentin' in the second typescript (FT2, 05r). The fact that Beckett replaced Dante's name with an epithet suggests that Animator is unable to remember the poet's actual name and tries to cover up his failure with a rhyme. We cannot even exclude a memory lapse on Beckett's part – unless the confusion is intentional. In the early 1930s, he came across a similar phrase when reading Jules Renard's *Journal*, the entry for 22 February 1890 stating: 'Insupportable comme un homme qui vous parle du divin Virgile.'[24] The passage ends with the saying 'Honore ton père et ta mère, et Virgile', which Beckett adapts to 'honour your father, your mother and Göthe' in the story 'Echo's Bones'.[25] Taking into account Renard's original reference to Virgil, who acts as Dante's guide through the *Inferno* and the *Purgatorio*, as well as Beckett's carefully revised phrase in *Rough for Radio II* across several drafts and preserved in his English self-translation, 'the divine Florentine'[26] seems more than just a coincidence. Yet Beckett's interest in the *Divina Commedia* is more of a linguistic kind here, as suggested by Animator's comment about the past tenses in the exchange quoted above.

James Joyce had alerted Beckett's attention to this trait sometime in the 1920s or 1930s. On 4 November 1982, some 50 years later and roughly 25 years after the genesis of the radio play, Anne Atik, the wife of artist Avigdor Arikha, noted about Beckett in her diary that he '[a]gain quoted Joyce's remark on all of them speaking in the past, beautiful vowels, "fui, fu, fummo"'.[27] *Radio II* is not the only text where this remark occurs, nor was it the first. In the early 1950s, Beckett had already used it in 'Texte pour rien VI' – in relation to the traitors encased in the lake of ice from Canto XXXII, their 'eyelids caked with frozen tears'[28] – with one important addition: 'I was, I was, they say in Purgatory, *in Hell too*, admirable singulars, admirable assurance.'[29] Thus, 'hellish hope',[30] as Molloy puts it dismissively, or being 'doomed to hope unending', as the narrator of *Murphy* diagnoses Neary,[31] makes way for the 'tranquility' of

---

[24] Van Hulle and Nixon, *Beckett's Library*, 108.
[25] Ibid., 232n55.
[26] Beckett, *All That Fall*, 62.
[27] Anne Atik, *How It Was: A Memoir of Samuel Beckett* (London: Faber and Faber, 2001), 114.
[28] Samuel Beckett, *Texts for Nothing and Other Shorter Prose, 1950–1976*, ed. Mark Nixon (London: Faber and Faber, 2010), 27.
[29] Ibid., 26; emphasis added.
[30] Samuel Beckett, *Molloy*, ed. Shane Weller (London: Faber and Faber, 2009), 139.
[31] Samuel Beckett, *Murphy*, ed. J. C. C. Mays (London: Faber and Faber, 2009), 125.

knowing 'there are no more emotions in store'.[32] The characters in Beckett's radio play are given no such assurance, the Animator encouragingly saying to Stenographer at the end – with a touch of Macbeth's last soliloquy:[33] 'Don't cry, Miss, dry your pretty eyes and smile at me. Tomorrow, who knows, we may be free.'[34] As several critics have noted, different from Dante, who clearly distinguishes *Inferno* from *Purgatorio* on theological grounds, Beckett distorts the difference and blurs the two,[35] turning the *Purgatorio* into a 'negative space'.[36] The first draft of *Pochade radiophonique* was slightly different.

There, Stenographer answers Animator's question by saying that she has only read the *Inferno*, not the *Purgatorio* or the *Paradiso*, which is never even brought up in the published text: 'Non, Monsieur. J'ai lu l'Enfer, mais ni le Purgatoire, ni le Paradis' (BDMP12, FN, 06r). Animator is now taken aback by her not having read *Paradiso* instead of *Purgatorio* – '(incrédule) Pas le Paradis?' – at which point she reminds him that it is almost three o'clock (06r–07r). Perhaps with Virgil's *Georgics* in mind – 'Sed fugit interea, fugit irreparabile tempus, singula dum capti circumvectamur amore' – the Animator laments that whenever he brings up the *Paradiso*, Stenographer tells him that time is flying: 'Chaque fois que je veux parler du Paradis tu me rappelle la fuite du temps' (07r). At this point in the manuscript notebook, Beckett did not yet know how to end his radio play, as is indicated by the dangling note 'etc.' underneath the last line of text (13r), followed by a loose jotting on the next recto (14r). For the typescript, he cut the reference to *Paradiso*, shifted focus to *Inferno* and *Purgatorio*, added Animator's digression on Dante's past tenses, and concluded with an uncertain future instead, expressed with a precarious modal verb followed by dead silence.

History: Fascism and the Radio

Beckett could have benefited from the rich tradition of radio drama in 1930s Germany had he visited the country a few years earlier. The short-lived Weimar Republic that rose in the wake of the First World War was a hotbed

---

[32] Beckett, *Texts for Nothing*, 26.
[33] See Dirk Van Hulle and Pim Verhulst, '"Learn by heart": Beckett's Schoolboy Copy of *Macbeth*', *Journal of Beckett Studies* 31, no. 1 (2022): 135–50.
[34] Beckett, *All That Fall*, 69.
[35] Michael Robinson, 'From *Purgatory* to *Inferno*: Beckett and Dante Revisited', *Journal of Beckett Studies* 5 (1979): 69–82.
[36] John L. Murphy, 'Beckett's Purgatories', in *Beckett, Joyce and the Art of the Negative*, ed. Colleen Jaurretche (Amsterdam: Rodopi, 2005), 109–24.

of radio experiments. Writers (Fritz Walter Bischoff, Theodor Csokor, Kurt Fischer), composers (Walter Goehr, Walter Gronostay, Paul Hindemith, Kurt Weill), producers and directors (Hans Bodenstedt, Hans Flesch, Walter Ruttmann), theorists (Rudolf Arnheim, Walter Benjamin, Bertolt Brecht) as well as a plethora of artistic forms that bordered on musical genres like oratorio or opera (*Funkrevue, Geräuschhörspiel, Hörbilder, Hörfolge, Hörspielpartituren, Hörspielsinfonie, literarische Hörspiel, musikalische Hörspiel, Opernquerschnitt, Worthörspiel, Wortspiel*) made German broadcasting unique in Europe at that time.[37] Beckett had read Arnheim's book *Film* (1933) in English translation before his trip,[38] which contained a short section on broadcasting, but it is highly unlikely that he also perused Arnheim's book *Radio* (1936), so at the time he must have been largely oblivious of the medium's rich history in Germany. Brecht, who in 1929 had collaborated with Weill and Hindemith on the radio play *Der Lindberghflug*, in 1930 warned against the dangers of radio being a one-directional technology, arguing that it would not be a genuine means of 'communication' – but one of 'distribution' – until it became a two-way system.[39] His essay turned out to be prophetic. The rise of Fascism and Hitler's Nazi party brought an end to this burgeoning period in 1932, at which point broadcasting became more centralized and conservative, used almost exclusively to spread propaganda, also through art.[40] When Beckett disembarked at Hamburg in October 1936, these cultural politics were in full swing. However, as his diaries and letters of the period reveal, he would occasionally tune in to the wireless.

Mark Nixon has recounted how Beckett's 'minute observations of the reality on the streets, accounts of conversations and of radio speeches invoke an air of menace and constriction' that permeated everyday life in Germany.[41] One particularly insipid broadcast, mentioned in the entry for 28 October 1936, was an '[i]nterminable harangue by Goering on Vierjahresplan [Four Year Plan] relayed from Berlin. Sehr volkstümlich. Kolonien, Rohstoffe, Fettwaren [Very traditional. Colonies, raw materials, fats]'. Around that time,

---

[37] John Gabriel, 'From Acoustic Scenery to Sonic Dramaturgy: Music in Radio-Specific Drama of Weimar Republic Germany', in *Word, Sound and Music in Radio Drama*, ed. Jarmila Mildorf and Pim Verhulst (Leiden and Boston: Brill, 2023), 19–44.

[38] Gaby Hartel, 'Emerging Out of a Silent Void: Some Reverberations of Rudolf Arnheim's Radio Theory in Beckett's Radio Pieces', *Journal of Beckett Studies* 19, no. 2 (2010): 218–27.

[39] Bertolt Brecht, 'The Radio as a Communications Apparatus', in *Bertolt Brecht on Film and Radio*, ed. and trans. Marc Silberman (London: Bloomsbury, 2015), 41–46.

[40] See Mark E. Cory, 'Soundplay: The Polyphonous Tradition of German Radio Art', in *Wireless Imagination: Sound, Radio, and the Avant-Garde*, ed. Douglas Kahn and Gregory Whitehead (Cambridge: MIT Press, 1992), 331–71.

[41] Mark Nixon, *Samuel Beckett's German Diaries 1936–1937* (London: Bloomsbury, 2011), 84.

Beckett also recorded Hitler's declaration that 'Nationalsozialist ist man nicht vom Tage der Geburt an [One is not born a National Socialist]',[42] made in a radio speech commemorating the 10th anniversary of the Gau Berlin. And, on 30 January 1937, Beckett listened

> like a fool to 2 hours of Hitler & an hour of Goering (opening of Reichstag, Goering reelected President, laws controlling 4 years plan extended for another 4[)], the usual from A. H. with announcement of a 20 yr. plan for development of Berlin, 'reply' to Eden consisting mainly in repeated assertion that Germany's policy is not one of isolation; then Goering announces foundation of 3 yearly 'cultural' prices [sic] of 100,000 ? RM & prohibition imposed on any Germans to accept Nobel Prize![43]

Beckett continued to follow these developments back on French soil, writing to Reavey on 27 September: 'I heard Adolf the Peacemaker on the wireless last night. And thought I heard the air escaping – a slow puncture.'[44] As *The New York Times* reported at the time, Hitler had just hosted 'a "historic manifestation" to the nation on the subject of Czechoslovakia in Berlin's biggest auditorium [the Sportpalast] and the whole German people [were] ordered to listen to a broadcast of his address'.[45] The impending annexation of Sudetenland by Nazi Germany received attention on French airwaves because the fate of Europe was hanging in the balance and France had an obligation towards Czechoslovakia to provide mutual military assistance in case of an attack. Nevertheless, the French government was quick to announce it would not enter into a war over the issue and British Prime Minister Neville Chamberlain soon made a radio broadcast to the same effect. This led to the signing of the Munich Agreement on 30 September 1938, officially surrendering Sudetenland to the German Reich and setting in motion a further expansion towards Eastern Europe. A year later, however, the events had escalated to such a degree that peace was no longer a viable option and European powers were forced to take action. On 3 September 1939, Chamberlain officially declared war on Germany in a famous BBC radio speech that Beckett also heard, at his mother's house in Greystones, Dublin.[46]

---

[42] Ibid., 87.
[43] Ibid., 85.
[44] Beckett, *Letters: Volume I*, 642.
[45] Ibid., 643n2. See https://www.nytimes.com/1938/09/26/archives/all-reich-rallied-historic-manifestation-tonight-will-reply-to-a.html.
[46] James Knowlson, *Damned to Fame: The Life of Samuel Beckett* (London: Bloomsbury, 1996), 297.

What must have seemed distant machinations in the Nazi radio broadcasts of recent years, heard in Germany, France and Dublin, were on Beckett's Paris doorstep in 1940. He and Suzanne decided to flee, first to Vichy in the south, where the Joyce family were staying, then further west to the coast town of Arcachon, spending the summer with Marcel Duchamp and Mary Reynolds before returning to the capital. It is well known that Beckett got involved in the Gloria SMH Resistance network at this point, helping it to smuggle military and naval information on the Nazis out of the country to the British.[47] Yet it bears reminding that radio also had a part to play in these subversive activities. As Laura Salisbury has revealed: 'One of the persistent difficulties of Gloria SMH was the fact that it had no funds and no wireless set of its own' so that Gabrielle Picabia, one of the founders of the network, resorted to 'working with Polish and Belgian, alongside British, operatives to get messages sent'.[48] When the Germans closed in on their cell, during the summer of 1942, Beckett and Suzanne had to flee Paris yet again, now to the remote village of Rousillon, deep in the south, from where they continued to support the Resistance. With no letters surviving for this period, precious little is known about how Beckett spent his days, aside from working in the field, reading whatever books he could lay his hands on and writing in the *Watt* notebooks he had brought along. In her recent novel *A Country Road a Tree* (2016), Jo Baker's fascinating work of biofiction that attempts to recreate Beckett's life during this period by building on Knowlson's biography and cultural histories, she also has him gathering around the radio set on an almost daily basis. He listens to music and keeps his ears pricked for any coded messages, but he also stays in touch with the latest news about political developments in Europe.[49]

These historical circumstances left traces in Beckett's radio plays. *All That Fall* stays quite close to home, but Henry in *Embers* offhandedly says to his dead father that, since his body never turned up, 'there was nothing to prove you hadn't run away from us all and alive and well under a false name in the Argentine', which 'held up probate an unconscionable time'.[50] This specific place name was still the rather more general 'South America' in the earliest two drafts (BDMP12, ET1–2, 01r), first revised to 'Venezuela' on the third typescript (ET3, 01r), then to 'Argentina' on the Faber and Grove proofs, before being changed one last time to 'Pérou' in the French

---

[47] Ibid., 297–318.
[48] Laura Salisbury, 'Gloria SMH and Beckett's Linguistic Encryptions', *The Edinburgh Companion to Samuel Beckett and the Arts*, ed. S. E. Gontarski (Edinburgh: Edinburgh University Press, 2014), 153–69 (167n6).
[49] Jo Baker, *A Country Road, A Tree*, (New York: Vintage Books, 2016).
[50] Beckett, *All That Fall*, 36.

translation (*Cendres*) that Beckett made with Robert Pinget.[51] These variants point to countries implicated in Nazi escape routes or so-called 'ratlines' after the Second World War, Argentina's Juan Domingo Perón regime being notorious for inviting, hiding and protecting fugitive German criminals. Knowlson discovered that 'Dick', the torturer's name in *Rough for Radio II*, was the Resistance alias of Alfred Péron, who perished in Switzerland en route home after his release from the Mauthausen concentration camp.[52] Closely related to the unfolding events of the Algerian War in the late 1950s and the early 1960s,[53] when Beckett helped Minuit publisher Jérôme Lindon to stash illegally printed books that were critical of the French regime, it is one of several radio plays that feature a tyrant figure whose authority is undermined. Much like the tortured Fox in *Radio II* seems to have more leverage over his interrogators than they have over him, Croak is bested by his two minions at the end of *Words and Music*, letting his club fall to the ground and limply retreating to the sound of shuffling carpet slippers. In fact, When Beckett and his cousin John first discussed their collaboration on the radio play, it consisted of 'two tyrants' ('deux tyrans') who commanded their 'underlings' or 'players' ('exécutants') to 'speak or play' ('parler ou jouer'), as Pinget recorded in his diary for 19 January 1961.[54] While the pair was later reduced to just one character, it is tempting to relate the two colluding tyrants to Hitler and Jozef Stalin or Hitler and Benito Mussolini.

During Beckett's prolonged sojourn in Germany, it entered into a formal alliance with Fascist Italy, a country that had undergone a similar, though not completely identical, evolution with regard to the medium. Even though it is 'difficult to speak of any specific influence of Italian Futurism', as John Gabriel points out, there is 'evidence that German radio sonic dramaturgy directly influenced Futurist approaches to radio'.[55] So, in addition to their politics, also the two nations' cultural-artistic histories intertwined. The earliest Italian radio experiments were closely bound up with the Futurist art movement, through Luigi Russolo's so-called 'noise music' or Filippo Tommaso Marinetti and Pino Masnata's 1933 manifesto 'La Radia'. Their pamphlet objected to the realist misuse of radio for the broadcasting of

---

[51] Samuel Beckett, *La dernière bande suivi de Cendres* (Paris: Les Éditions de Minuit, 2007), 39.
[52] Knowlson, *Damned to Fame*, 341–2.
[53] Anthony Uhlmann, 'Witholding Assent: Beckett in Light of the Stoic Ethics', in *Beckett and Ethics*, ed. Russell Smith (London: Continuum, 2008), 57–67 (58); Verhulst, 'Dating Pochade', 153–55; Emilie Morin, *Beckett's Political Imagination* (Cambridge: Cambridge University Press, 2017), 184–237.
[54] Verhulst, *Beckett's Radio Plays*, forthcoming.
[55] Gabriel, 'Acoustic Scenery', 26.

bourgeois theatre in favour of a much more radical as well as innovative use of sound,[56] as exemplified by Marinetti's own *5 sintesi radiofoniche*.[57] Other Futurists, including Balilla Pratella, Guido Sommi-Picenardi or Italo Bertaglio, were all employed by the state broadcaster. This shows the close connectedness between Italy's avant-garde and its fledgling Fascist regime, whereas in Germany the Nazi party had purged the airwaves of it. True as this may be, Angela Ida De Benedictis stresses that 'these Futurist experiments produced no developments or follow-ups and tended to be viewed as little more than passing divertissements'.[58] Similarly, Massimo Ragnedda confirms that 'aside from modernist technology, the radio was little studied by the Futurists'.[59] Seen as a welcome opportunity at first, it soon became clear that 'the restrictions imposed by a political bureaucracy [...] affected radio institutions in ways that did not accord Futurism the chance to contribute to the new medium in the manner that Marinetti was keen to do'.[60] As Ragnedda concludes, 'in totalitarian Italy, as in totalitarian Germany, the radio was used as a vehicle for propaganda and cultural hegemony', but he crucially nuances that 'radio was not as powerful in Fascist Italy as in Nazi Germany'.[61]

Mussolini was slow to realize the medium's political potential and never used it as astutely as Hitler, Göring or Goebbels had. One reason is that the technological infrastructure was often plagued by malfunctions, and fewer people owned radio sets than in France, England or Germany, often limited to schools or public buildings and rarely out in the countryside. This made the printing press a far more effective instrument of state control, one that Mussolini was familiar with from his time as a journalist for the socialist newspaper *Avanti!* He did become 'a true superstar of Italian radio, playing with his high-pitched tones', and he even insisted that 'announcers reading his words on air had voices resembling his own',[62] but this still left ample

---

[56] Kahn and Whitehead, *Wireless Imagination*, 265–8.
[57] Angela Ida De Benedictis, 'Not Just Words, Not Just Music: Some Remarks about the Development of a Radio Art and Radio Drama in Italy', *Word, Sound and Music in Radio Drama*, ed. Jarmila Mildorf and Pim Verhulst (Leiden and Boston: Brill, 2023), 102–29 (105–6).
[58] Ibid., 106.
[59] Massimo Ragnedda, 'Radio Broadcasting in Fascist Italy: Between Censorship, Total Control, Jazz and Futurism', in *Broadcasting in the Modernist Era*, ed. Matthew Feldman, Erik Tonning and Henry Mead (London: Bloomsbury, 2014), 195–211 (208).
[60] Margaret Fisher, 'Futurism and Radio', in *Futurism and the Technological Imagination*, ed. Günter Berghaus (Amsterdam: Rodopi, 2009), 239–62 (229).
[61] Ragnedda, 'Radio Broadcasting', 196.
[62] Ibid., 197.

room for broadcasts other than popular or patriotic songs, Italian opera, news and programs on (military) history. Ranging from jazz and tango music to the occasional Jewish composer, they show that state 'control never reached the level of Nazi Germany'.[63] This leads Ragnedda to a rather ironic conclusion: 'The development of Italian radio under the Fascist regime in the beginning occurred almost entirely *despite* Mussolini's failure to realize its potential as a vehicle for propaganda.'[64] Or, more forcefully put by De Benedictis: 'Considered as little more than a plaything, Italian radio in the twenties and thirties was characterised by an amateur and unsystematic approach, which came nowhere near to exploiting its true potential'[65] – on either the political or the artistic level.

This state of affairs changed dramatically after the war. In addition to the Studio di Fonologia Musicale di Milano della RAI, co-founded by Luciano Berio and Bruno Maderna in 1954 – thus predating the BBC's Radiophonic Workshop by several years – in 1948 the state broadcaster also launched the annual Italia Prize or Prix Italia, an international competition open to the best radiophonic productions of the year in an ever-expanding range of categories. Part of Italy's reconciliatory post-war efforts, the prize encouraged global collaboration by capitalizing on radio's ability to connect people and transcend national borders, whereas previously the medium had mostly been deployed to divide and conquer. Germany took a few more years to reconnect with its pre-war experimental legacy, through the rise of the *Neues Hörspiel* (New Radio Play) of the 1960s, but as early as 1950 it had set up the *Hörspielpreis der Kriegsblinden* (War Blinded Audio Play Prize), a major national recognition awarded to the best radio play broadcast in the past year written in the German language. The name was chosen in honour of blinded war victims, who designed the sculpture that winners were presented with. As such, the award recognized the deplorable fate of broadcasting in the hands of totalitarian regimes, but also the aesthetic affiliation between the medium's lack of visuals and the victims' loss of sight. German radio stations translated and aired numerous productions from all over Europe – not least the UK – and vice versa. Beckett, too, benefited from these relations and had several of his radio plays aired in Germany. An example is *Embers* (*Aschenglut*), which McWhinnie guest-directed with Lothar Tim for Sudwestfunk (SWF) at their Baden-Baden studios in 1959.[66] Italy, as the official host of the Italia Prize, had become a crucial meeting place for these professional exchanges.

---

[63] Ibid., 205.
[64] Ibid., 201; emphasis added.
[65] De Benedictis, 'Not Just Words', 104.
[66] Beckett, *Letters: Volume III*, 248–9n10.

Biography: Sorrento and the Italia Prize

As is perhaps appropriate for a radio play that gives Dante prime of place, *All That Fall* was the BBC's official submission for the Italia Prize in 1957, yet it did not come out on top. The winner of that year, which counted 33 entries, was *Of This We Live, Of That We Die*, written by Herbert Heisenrich and produced by German radio station ARD. Beckett's second radio play, *Embers*, was submitted as the BBC's entry for 1959. While it is often believed to have won the award, Clas Zilliacus[67] and later James Knowlson[68] have clarified that it actually received the smaller and somewhat less prestigious RAI Prize – the Prix Italia that year went to John Reeves' *The Last Summer of Childhood*, produced by the Canadian Broadcasting Corporation (CBC). At first sight, this outcome is surprising, considering the popularity and success of *All That Fall* compared to the rather controversial reputation of *Embers*. It caused internal divisions within the BBC between McWhinnie and Bray, on the one hand, and Head of Drama Val Gielgud, on the other, because the radio play was considered too difficult, too gloomy and too sexually explicit as well as blasphemous, unmitigated by comedy.[69] This is apparent from the documents surviving at the BBC Written Archives and Beckett's extensive correspondence with Bray about the matter,[70] as well as the fact that the radio broadcast was censored.[71] However, if we take into account the cultural politics behind the Italia Prize, the nomination made perfect sense.

It quickly evolved into one of the most prestigious awards for radio programmes, selected by an international jury from entries all over the world. In 1953, when the number of submissions rose steadily, a second prize was created, offered and selected by the RAI itself. These two awards fulfilled entirely different functions. Whereas the Italia Prize was in theory instigated

---

[67] Clas Zilliacus, *Beckett and Broadcasting: A Study of the Works of Samuel Beckett for and in Radio and Television* (Åbo: Åbo Akademi, 1976), 79.
[68] Knowlson, *Damned to Fame*, 446, 790n4.
[69] Kate Whitehead, *The BBC Third Programme: A Literary History* (Oxford: Clarendon Press, 1989), 140.
[70] See Pim Verhulst, 'The BBC as "Commissioner" of Beckett's Radio Plays', in *Beckett and BBC Radio: A Reassessment*, ed. David Addyman, Matthew Feldman and Erik Tonning (London and New York: Palgrave Macmillan, 2017), 81–102.
[71] See S. E. Gontarski, 'Bowdlerizing Beckett: The BBC *Embers*', *Journal of Beckett Studies* 9, no. 1 (1999): 127–32; Pim Verhulst, 'A "healthy honest-to-God out-of-the-door life-loving deflowering": The (Self-)Censorship of Beckett's Radio Drama on the BBC Third Programme', *Samuel Beckett Today / Aujourd'hui* 34, no. 1 (2022), 134–47.

to promote 'a genuine radio art',[72] in practice it had a very 'conservative tendency' so that 'any radio drama made with electroacoustic means would always be dubbed "daring" or "audacious" and, in general, works that were more in line with a presumed popular taste would always be preferred'.[73] From this point of view, it is easy to see why *All That Fall* did not win the prize, incorporating elements of *musique concrète* and *acousmatics*, developed by the foremost exprimenter of French radio, Pierre Schaeffer, with whom McWhinnie went to study before taking on Beckett's radio play.[74] Then again, it was not experimental enough to win the RAI Prize, operating in the shadows of the more prestigious and lucrative Italia Prize to fulfil the 'innovative tendencies' its forebear was originally supposed to foster.[75]

Embers is radical in how it exploits radio as a 'blind' medium. It entirely revolves around the notion that, because the audience cannot see (only hear), they have no way of discerning what is real from what is merely imagined by Henry on the beach. When he points this out to his blind father, dead and conjured up in his son's imagination, listeners are placed in the same position as the old man, dependent on Henry's unreliable perception of his surroundings, relayed through an audibly distorted sensory apparatus:

> That sound you hear is the sea. [*Pause. Louder.*] I say that sound you hear is the sea, we are sitting on the strand. [*Pause. Louder.*] I mention it because the sound is so strange, so unlike the sound of the sea, that if you didn't see what it was you wouldn't know what it was.[76]

Self-consciously punning on the homophones 'see' and 'sea', *Embers* uses sound effects and a highly fragmentary, associative plot to continuously throw the listener off. Competition was stiff that year, with a record high of 45 entries, so the fact that *Embers* won the RAI Prize testifies to its avant-garde qualities. The Italia Prize had a more celebratory or promotional role, an image that did not sit at all well with Beckett or his work.

---

[72] Angela Ida De Benedictis, 'Between Art and Promotion: The Prix Italia, Its Historical Context and Aims in the First Fifty Years 1949–1998', *Radio Art and Music: Culture, Aesthetics, Politics*, ed. Jarmila Mildorf and Pim Verhulst (Lanham: Lexington Books, 2020), 85–98 (93).
[73] Ibid., 89.
[74] Louis Niebur, *Special Sound: The Creation and Legacy of the BBC Radiophonic Workshop* (Oxford: Oxford University Press, 2010), 36.
[75] De Benedictis, 'Between Art and Promotion', 90.
[76] Beckett, *All That Fall*, 35.

He seemed blissfully unaware of the distinction between the awards, if the recording of a short speech he gave at the ceremony in Sorrento is anything to go by:

> It is a great honour for me to have been awarded the Italia Prize for my radio play *Embers*. I do not ordinarily write for radio, but I think that it is a medium which has not been fully exploited and that there are great possibilities for writers in this form of expression.[77]

Beckett had let himself be persuaded to accompany McWhinnie on a trip to Italy for the occasion, the somewhat stammered or uneasy tone of his speech betraying the remorse he felt about the decision. He still sounded optimistic in his lettercard to Bray of 13 September 1959, boasting about the prospect of 'a delicious night' at a restaurant called 'Papavero', McWhinnie adding in his PS: 'Are avoiding contact with any form of radio life for as long as possible. So far so good.'[78] A week later, on 21 September, Beckett looked back on the whole affair as a 'grim jamboree' to Thomas MacGreevy, expressing similar sentiments in correspondence with Mary Hutchinson and, again, Bray, the latter being the most explicit:

> Apart from the hours spent with Donald away from the mob, Sorrento was grim and I hated it. [...] I'm sorry I went, I simply can't deal with these occasions and there will never be another. Everyone was very nice but I'm not and there it is. Excursion to Capri ile, Jesus. Donald stayed on for his holiday [...], I lost my bag between here and Paris or rather Alitalia did, haven't recovered it yet. Tell you all about it next week, more about it, what hasn't been lost in the haze mercifully.[79]

Meeting Robert Farren, Irish Radio's Controller of Programmes, was 'small consolation', as Beckett told MacGreevy, but the public relations side of the journey's second leg had clearly been too draining for him, dreading more of the same upon his return: 'Paris and people again next week. They'll have me in a monastery in the end.'[80] So, having at last made his way out of the *Inferno* that was Sorrento, thanks to the expert guidance of McWhinnie, who acted as a Virgil to Beckett's Dante, he found himself suspended in the *Purgatorio* of

---

[77] Beckett, *Letters: Volume III*, 245–6n1. The audio recording of this interview is available at https://www.youtube.com/watch?v=2AMWFsrcW-w.
[78] Verhulst, *Beckett's Radio Plays*, forthcoming.
[79] Ibid.
[80] Beckett, *Letters: Volume III*, 244.

Naples airport, with no assurance that Paris would offer the blissful relief of *Paradiso*. Some two years later, Beckett still vividly recalled the unpleasantness of his experience. Attending the premiere of composer Marcel Mihalovici's opera adaptation of *Krapp's Last Tape* in Bielefeld, Germany, Beckett wrote about the event to Bray on 1 March 1961: 'All has gone as well as such things can I suppose, no comparison anyway with the Sorrento inferno.'[81]

Beckett's Italian 'fiasco' and its long aftermath may also have left a trace in his last radio play, *Cascando*. It was written in French over the next couple of months, after he completed *Words and Music* for the BBC and put aside a false start that later became known as *Esquisse radiophonique* (*Rough for Radio I*). In one of the early typescripts of *Cascando*, the Opener – Ouvreur in French – emerges as an author figure tired of explaining his work to others, who assume he has it all in his head and therefore must be an authority. After crossing out 'On me dit, C'est dans ta tête. On m'écrit, C'est dans ta tête. On me téléphone, C'est dans ta tête', Beckett generalizes this comment to: 'On dit, C'est dans sa tête' (BDMP12, FT2, 01r). Particularly the phone calls and letters evoke critical or journalistic pressure for authorial validation of the kind that Beckett would have been exposed to in Italy. Opener used to counter these requests by trying to shut them up – in the deleted 'leur clouait le bec' (04r) – but he no longer protests. He is content to repeat that there is nothing in his head, and he no longer answers any calls; he just opens and closes the two audio channels of Voice and Music. In the first manuscript, the outside world has given up: 'On a renoncé' (FM1, 04r). In the second typescript, Opener has managed to shake his oppressors – 'On s'est sauvé'– with Beckett adding and then crossing out 'Plus de rats' (FT2, 04r). This erasure brings to mind the invective 'Crritic' in *Waiting for Godot*, which Vladimir thinks is worse than '[s]ewer-rat'.[82] Much like Opener tries to flee his critics, so the protagonist of *Cascando* – Woburn, Maunu in French – attempts to elude the voice that narrates him, in what becomes a witty metafictional game of cat and mouse for radio. As soon as Opener resumes his story, Woburn is able to slip away, but whenever the narrative pauses, Opener catches up to him again. Eventually, after sheltering in sheds and travelling at night past 'boreen' and 'giant aspens' while burying his face in the 'same old coat',[83] the protagonist takes first to the dunes and the sand, then to the sea in a skiff, hoping at long last to find some peace of mind.

---

[81] Ibid., 401.
[82] Samuel Beckett, *Waiting for Godot*, pref. Mary Bryden (London: Faber and Faber, 2010), 71.
[83] Beckett, *All That Fall*, 86.

This final scene closely resembles the ending of *Malone Dies*, where Lemuel, joined by the philanthropist Lady Pedal, takes Macmann and his fellow 'Johnny Goddams' on an 'outing to the islands'.[84] The 'group Lemuel' rides a 'wagonette' from the Saint John of God Hospital on the top of the hill in Blackrock down a 'sudden descent, long and steep' that sends them 'plunging towards the sea'.[85] In the boat, they observe 'a land receding, another approaching, big and little islands'.[86] The reference here is to an Irish setting, namely Dalkey Island and its surrounding islets, just off the east coast between Dublin up north and Killiney Strand with Whiterock down south. A typical embarkation point in those days would have been the small stone pier of Coliemore Harbour near Sorrento Point. This name derives from the supposed likeness of Killiney Bay's vista to that of the Bay of Naples, reinforced in the nineteenth century with the construction of Sorrento Park and Sorrento Terrace, which made the stately row of houses and their panoramic view coveted by celebrities including U2's Bono, or film directors Neil Jordan and Jim Sheridan.[87] Connected to the Vico Road and the Vico Bathing Place on Hawk Cliff, past the cul-de-sac of Sorrento Street and Coliemore Road, the area also links up with 'Work in Progress' by way of Beckett's essay 'Dante… Bruno. Vico.. Joyce'. Indeed, through a 'commodius vicus of recirculation', as per the opening and closing lines of *Finnegans Wake*, Beckett's last play for radio comes full circle, too. *Cascando* takes us back to 'Howth Castle and Environs',[88] that is, the Irish setting of *All That Fall* and *Embers*, yet now carrying Italian reverberations as well, having picked up even more cultural sediment 'a long the / riverrun'.[89]

Compared to the island in *Malone Dies*, which could easily be pinpointed geographically, like the 'islands' in the boat scene at the close of the story 'The End',[90] they assume a much more abstract quality in *Cascando*. Written almost 15 years later, the radio play could additionally be read in light of Beckett's gruelling Sorrento experience. There, he had a celebrity status foisted upon him by accepting the RAI Prize and giving interviews in front of the media – a small taste of what was to come after he won the Nobel Prize in 1969. Italy is a peninsula, of course, not a true island like Ireland,

---

[84] Samuel Beckett, *Malone Dies*, ed. Peter Boxall (London: Faber and Faber, 2010), 111.
[85] Ibid., 115.
[86] Ibid., 116.
[87] I am grateful to Feargal Whelan for sharing his expertise on Dublin with me.
[88] James Joyce, *Finnegans Wake* (London: Faber and Faber, 1971), 3.
[89] Ibid., 628, 3.
[90] Samuel Beckett, *The Expelled, The Calmative, The End & First Love*, ed. Christopher Ricks (London: Faber and Faber, 2009), 57.

but Sorrento and Capri share with Dublin and Dalkey a comparable separation of mainland and sea. In *Cascando*, however, the offshore island curiously loses the appeal it had as a potential safe haven in *Malone Dies*. In the novel, 'nobody lives' on Dalkey, except 'druidi'[91] – another Celtic-Irish reference. Capri, by contrast, was teeming with crowds of journalists and tourists in the full blaze of summer. In this sense, it is worthy of note that Woburn steers clear of the island – 'island gone –' and makes for the 'open sea' instead. With the 'land gone' and his back turned to the lights on the shore as well as those in the sky, face down in the boat, the waters hold him in abeyance, 'in the dark … elsewhere … always elsewhere'.[92] This 'dark' serves as a vague remnant of how Beckett originally conceptualized radio by way of Dante's *Inferno*. The 'elsewhere', in turn, highlights that the medium fulfilled an important function in his aesthetics of delocalization, a process whereby multiple geographies, through a dynamic of 'vaguening',[93] 'undoing'[94] or 'abstraction',[95] increasingly overlap, mix and merge into a cosmopolitan, global space. This encompasses Ireland, France and Germany, as critics have long recognized,[96] but also Italy, as this chapter has aimed to show.

Bibliography

Alighieri, Dante. *Divina Commedia*, edited by Enrico Bianchi. Florence: Salani, 1933.

———. *The Vision; or Hell, Purgatory, and Paradise*, translated by Henry Francis Cary. London and New York: Frederick Warne and Co., 1889.

———. *The Divine Comedy*, translated by Robin Kirkpatrick. London: Penguin, 2012.

Atik, Anne. *How It Was: A Memoir of Samuel Beckett*. London: Faber and Faber, 2001.

---

[91] Beckett, *Malone Dies*, 117.
[92] Beckett, *All That Fall*, 91.
[93] See Rosemary Pountney, *Theatre of Shadows: Samuel Beckett's Drama 1956–76, from 'All That Fall' to 'Footfalls' with Commentaries on the Latest Plays* (Gerrards Cross: Colin Smythe, 1988).
[94] See S. E. Gontarski, *The Intent of Undoing in Samuel Beckett's Dramatic Texts* (Bloomington: Indiana University Press, 1985).
[95] See Erik Tonning, *Samuel Beckett's Abstract Drama: Works for Stage and Screen 1962–1985* (Bern: Peter Lang).
[96] See Emilie Morin, ' "But to Hell with all this Fucking Scenery": Ireland in Translation in Samuel Beckett's *Molloy* and *Malone Meurt / Malone Dies*', in *Global Ireland: Irish Literatures for the New Millennium*, ed. Ondrej Pilný and Clare Wallace (Prague: Litteraria Pragensia, 2005), 222–34; Leslie Hill, 'The Trilogy Translated', *Beckett's Fiction: In Different Words* (Cambridge: Cambridge University Press, 1990), 40–58; Dirk Van Hulle and Pim Verhulst, 'Shifting Cultural Affinities in *Molloy*: A Genetic Bilingual Approach', *Samuel Beckett as World Literature*, ed. Thirthankar Chakraborty and Juan Luis Toribio Vazquez (London: Bloomsbury, 2020), 29–43.

Baker, Jo. *A Country Road, A Tree*. New York: Vintage, 2016.
Beckett, Samuel. *Dream of Fair to Middling Women*, edited by Eoin O'Brien. Dublin: Black Cat Press, 1992.
———. *La dernière bande suivi de Cendres*. Paris: Les Éditions de Minuit, 2007.
———. *All That Fall and Other Plays for Radio and Screen*, preface by Everett Frost. London: Faber and Faber, 2009a.
———. *Molloy*, edited by Shane Weller. London: Faber and Faber, 2009b.
———. *Murphy*, edited by J. C. C. Mays. London: Faber and Faber, 2009c.
———. *The Letters of Samuel Beckett, Volume I: 1929–1940*, edited by Martha Dow Fehsenfeld and Lois More Overbeck. Cambridge: Cambridge University Press, 2009d.
———. *Malone Dies*, edited by Peter Boxall. London: Faber and Faber, 2010a.
———. *Texts for Nothing and Other Shorter Prose, 1950–1976*, edited by Mark Nixon. London: Faber and Faber, 2010b.
———. *Waiting for Godot*, preface by Mary Bryden. London: Faber and Faber, 2010c.
———. *The Letters of Samuel Beckett, Volume III: 1957–1965*, edited by George Craig, Martha Dow Fehsenfeld, Dan Gunn and Lois More Overbeck. Cambridge: Cambridge University Press, 2014.
Brecht, Bertolt. 'The Radio as a Communications Apparatus'. In *Bertolt Brecht on Film and Radio*, edited and translated by Marc Silberman. London: Bloomsbury, 2015. 41–6.
Caselli, Daniela. '"The Florentia Edition in the Ignoble Salani Collection": A Textual Comparison'. *Journal of Beckett Studies*, vol. 9, no. 2 (2000): 1–20.
———. 'The Promise of Dante in the Beckett Manuscripts'. *Samuel Beckett Today/Aujourd'hui*, vol. 16, no. 1 (2006): 237–57.
Cory, Mark E. 'Soundplay: The Polyphonous Tradition of German Radio Art'. In *Wireless Imagination: Sound, Radio, and the Avant-Garde*, edited by Douglas Kahn and Gregory Whitehead. Cambridge: MIT Press, 1992. 331–71.
De Benedictis, Angela Ida. 'Between Art and Promotion: The Prix Italia, Its Historical Context and Aims in the First Fifty Years 1949–1998'. In *Radio Art and Music: Culture, Aesthetics, Politics*, edited by Jarmila Mildorf and Pim Verhulst. Lanham: Lexington Books, 2020. 85–98.
———. 'Not Just Words, Not Just Music: Some Remarks about the Development of a Radio Art and Radio Drama in Italy'. In *Word, Sound and Music in Radio Drama*, edited by Jarmila Mildorf and Pim Verhulst. Leiden and Boston: Brill, 2023. 102–29.
Fisher, Margaret. 'Futurism and Radio'. In *Futurism and the Technological Imagination*, edited by Günter Berghaus. Amsterdam: Rodopi, 2009. 239–62.
Frost, Everett and Jane Maxwell. 'TCD MS 10963: Dante, *The Divine Comedy*, Part I'. *Samuel Beckett Today/Aujourd'hui*, vol. 16 (2006): 39–49.
Gabriel, John. 'From Acoustic Scenery to Sonic Dramaturgy: Music in Radio-Specific Drama of Weimar Republic Germany'. In *Word, Sound and Music in Radio Drama*, edited by Jarmila Mildorf and Pim Verhulst. Leiden and Boston: Brill, 2023. 19–44.
Gontarski, S. E. *The Intent of Undoing in Samuel Beckett's Dramatic Texts*. Bloomington: Indiana University Press, 1985.
———. 'Bowdlerizing Beckett: The BBC *Embers*'. *Journal of Beckett Studies*, vol. 9, no. 1 (1999): 127–32.
Hartel, Gaby. 'Emerging Out of a Silent Void: Some Reverberations of Rudolf Arnheim's Radio Theory in Beckett's Radio Pieces'. *Journal of Beckett Studies*, vol. 19, no. 2 (2010): 218–27.
Hill, Leslie. 'The Trilogy Translated'. In *Beckett's Fiction: In Different Words*. Cambridge: Cambridge University Press, 1990. 40–58.

Joyce, James. *Finnegans Wake*. London: Faber and Faber, 1971.
Knowlson, James. *Damned to Fame: The Life of Samuel Beckett*. London: Bloomsbury, 1996.
Morin, Emilie. ' "But to Hell with all this Fucking Scenery": Ireland in Translation in Samuel Beckett's *Molloy* and *Malone Meurt / Malone Dies*'. In *Global Ireland: Irish Literatures for the New Millennium*, edited by Ondrej Pilný and Clare Wallace. Prague: Litteraria Pragensia, 2005. 222–34.

———. *Beckett's Political Imagination*. Cambridge: Cambridge University Press, 2017.

Murphy, John L. 'Beckett's Purgatories'. In *Becket, Joyce and the Art of the Negative*, edited by Colleen Jaurretche. Amsterdam: Rodopi, 2005. 109–24.

Niebur, Louis. *Special Sound: The Creation and Legacy of the BBC Radiophonic Workshop*. Oxford: Oxford University Press, 2010.

Nixon, Mark. *Samuel Beckett's German Diaries 1936–1937*. London: Bloomsbury, 2011.

Pountney, Rosemary. *Theatre of Shadows: Samuel Beckett's Drama 1956–76, from 'All That Fall' to 'Footfalls' with Commentaries on the Latest Plays*. Gerrards Cross: Colin Smythe, 1988.

Ragnedda, Massimo. 'Radio Broadcasting in Fascist Italy: Between Censorship, Total Control, Jazz and Futurism'. In *Broadcasting in the Modernist Era*, edited by Matthew Feldman, Erik Tonning and Henry Mead. London: Bloomsbury, 2014. 195–211.

Robinson, Michael. 'From *Purgatory* to *Inferno*: Beckettt and Dante Revisited'. *Journal of Beckett Studies*, vol. 5 (1979): 69–82.

Salisbury, Laura. 'Gloria SMH and Beckett's Linguistic Encryptions'. In *The Edinburgh Companion to Samuel Beckett and the Arts*, edited by S. E. Gontarski. Edinburgh: Edinburgh University Press, 2014. 153–69.

Tonning, Erik. *Samuel Beckett's Abstract Drama: Works for Stage and Screen 1962–1985*. Bern: Peter Lang, 2007.

Uhlmann, Anthony. 'Withholding Assent: Beckett in Light of the Stoic Ethics'. In *Beckett and Ethics*, edited by Russell Smith. London: Continuum, 2008. 57–67.

Van Hulle, Dirk and Mark Nixon. *Samuel Beckett's Library*. Cambridge: Cambridge University Press, 2013.

——— and Pim Verhulst. 'Shifting Cultural Affinities in *Molloy*: A Genetic Bilingual Approach'. In *Samuel Beckett as World Literature*, edited by Thirthankar Chakraborty and Juan Luis Toribio Vazquez. London: Bloomsbury, 2020. 29–43.

———. ' "Learn by heart": Beckett's Schoolboy Copy of *Macbeth*'. *Journal of Beckett Studies*, vol. 31, no. 1 (2022): 135–50.

Verhulst, Pim. ' "Just howls from time to time": Dating *Pochade radiophonique*'. *Samuel Beckett Today / Aujourd'hui*, vol. 27 (2015), 143–58.

———. 'The BBC as "Commissioner" of Beckett's Radio Plays'. In *Beckett and BBC Radio: A Reassessment*, edited by David Addyman, Matthew Feldman and Erik Tonning. London and New York: Palgrave Macmillan, 2017. 81–102.

———. 'A "healthy honest-to-God out-of-the-door life-loving deflowering": The (Self-)Censorship of Beckett's Radio Drama on the BBC Third Programme'. *Samuel Beckett Today / Aujourd'hui*, vol. 34, no. 1 (2022), 134–47.

———. *The Making of Samuel Beckett's Radio Plays*. London and Brussels: Bloomsbury and University Press Antwerp, 2024, forthcoming.

Whitehead, Kate. *The BBC Third Programme: A Literary History*. Oxford: Clarendon Press, 1989.

Zilliacus, Clas. *Beckett and Broadcasting: A Study of the Works of Samuel Beckett for and in Radio and Television*. Åbo: Åbo Akademi, 1976.

Part Three
POETIC VOICES

Chapter 6

BECKETT THE TROUBADOUR

Mario Martino

Abstract

This paper will examine Beckett's lifelong interest in Romance literature and troubadour poetry, and its relation to Italy, beginning with the recalling of some features and lasting effects of his early love affairs with Ethna MacCarthy and Peggy Sinclair. Furthermore, troubadour lyric poetry will be examined as serving Beckett in his search for a poetic language for modernity, which therefore will be set also against the background of key figures of modernism, such as Ford Madox Ford, T. S. Eliot and Ezra Pound. References to Beckett's poetic work – which spans from the 1930 'Whoroscope' poem to 'What is the word', written shortly before his death – focus on the 1930 lyric collection of *Echo's Bones* and on how its themes and forms anticipate Beckett's succeeding works.

It will also be contented that the temporal gaps in the poetic output of a long and consistent poetic production are in fact filled through the diffusion and absorption of the lyric mode in Beckett's dramatic and novelistic production, with specific references to *Molloy* and the Dantean character of Sordello.

Keywords: Beckett; poetry; troubadour; *Echo's Bones*; modernism; Sordello; *Molloy*

Drawing on the seminal work on Beckett's poetry by Laurence Harvey,[1] this paper will examine Beckett's lifelong interest in troubadour poetry, emphasizing how that is, to some degree, also related to Italy. Such an argument will entail examining Beckett's interest in early Romance literature in conjunction with some key figures of modernism, against which his own stance is to be set and interpreted. Additionally, we will touch upon how his interest is manifested

---

[1] Lawrence Harvey, *Samuel Beckett: Poet and Critic* (Princeton: Princeton University Press, 1970).

not only in a consistent lyric production throughout his whole career but also in the lyric mode of his novelistic production, with specific references to *Molloy*.

Recalling some biographical details might help define Beckett's bend towards Romance culture, particularly to that of the Middle Ages. It is well known that Thomas Rudmose-Brown, his college teacher of French, was also an admirer of Provençal language and literature, and affiliated with Félibrige, an association that aimed to renew the memory and modern relevance of the old literature and even bring back in use the old language. Moreover, Beckett's second major subject at Trinity College, Italian (which at some early stage he intended to choose as his main line of studies), offers another direct link with Romance literature. In fact, Italian as a University subject meant, above all, Dante, and this implied references to Dante's precursors.

Beckett's poetic interest grew during his philological studies, which carried the possibility of an academic career, even if Beckett grew soon dubious about it. Indeed, contingent on his application for an academic position at Cape Town University in 1937, a letter of recommendation written for him by Rudmose-Brown stated that he was an expert in Provençal language. However, what was inextricably associated with Provençal as an academic subject was its intimately poetic appeal to the artist to be. Between 1930 and 1931, Beckett seems to have decisively turned away from the possibility of pursuing an academic career, leaving his job as a teacher at Trinity College (a great disappointment and shock, both for William, Beckett's father, and for Rudmose-Brown, and also a cause of deep remorse for Beckett himself, still felt some 50 years later).[2] He chose instead the life of uncertainties and anxieties which characterized his next years of *Wander* and *Lehrjahre*.

Other connections are also relevant: During his studies at Trinity College, Beckett's interest in Provençal language and literature merged with his love for a fellow student, the brilliant Ethna MacCarthy, one year his senior. For a while, she was a guide to Beckett in this field of studies, after which Beckett was able to reciprocate and help Ethna in her academic duties related to the subject.[3] Somehow, the troubadours and their language appear to have been for them what the 'libro ... galeotto' is for Paolo and Francesca in the Dantean Comedy, despite the fact that Beckett's love for Ethna was never fully reciprocated; not as much, at least, as to prevent her from choosing Beckett's friend, Con Leventhal, as her lover and husband. The troubled relationship Beckett had

---

[2] James Knowlson, *Damned to Fame: The Life of Samuel Beckett* (London: Bloomsbury, 1997), 157–58.

[3] See Letter to MacGreevy, 29 January 1936, in *The Letters of Samuel Beckett, Volume I: 1929–1940*, eds Martha Dow Fehsenfeld and Lois More Overbeck (Cambridge: Cambridge University Press, 2009), 306, 309–10.

with Ethna colours his perception of the ancient poets, who had extolled both sensual and spiritual love, the carnal as well the ideal figure of the beloved; and who often sang of love as elusive and unattainable, and therefore a source of suffering, of 'passion'.

It may be guessed that a second affair, with his cousin Peggy Sinclair, contributed not only to Beckett's strengthening his interest in that poetic world, as Ackerley and Gontarski write,[4] but also, possibly, to his finding his own early troubadour hero in Walther von der Vogelweide (1170–1230) – who was active in Austria and Germany around the end of the twelfth and at the beginning of thirteenth century – and therefore also, somehow, a nuanced voice of his own (in this respect, as a young man of letters wishing for recognition, Beckett distanced himself from the mainstream, modernist preference for other early Romance poets, such as Arnaut Daniel, Bertrand de Ventadorn and Bertrand de Born).

It might be worth considering that Beckett began studying the German language after, and because of, the Sinclairs' visit to Dublin in 1928, when he fell in love with Peggy. It was a different kind of love from that with Ethna, since she was more responsive to her cousin's attachment. Nonetheless, Peggy joined/merged with Ethna in the poet's imagination, in objectifying the crucial opposition that ran through the poems of the troubadours, between a carnal love and a spiritual one, between the profane and the sacred. Notably, that opposition is apparent in the different love relationships portrayed especially in *Dream of Fair to Middling Women*, with the sensual Smeraldina-Rima (a travesty of Peggy), as opposed to the more idealized Alba (a travesty of Ethna) who has even a troubadour subgenre as her proper name.

Despite the opposition, though, a similar unhappy and tragic pattern linking both love relationships was soon to emerge. In the first place, tragic was the fact that, following Ethna, during the Christmas holidays Beckett was spending in Kassel in 1929, Peggy broke up their relationship. Second, and most importantly, tragic was the premature death of beloved Peggy on the third of May 1933 (many years later, in May 1959, Ethna also died of throat cancer, resulting in a renewed shock of pain for Beckett). It was just two years after the break-up of their love relationship that, when again in Kassel to spend the Christmas season with the Sinclairs, Beckett saw his cousin sick, with hardly mistakable signs of tuberculosis, and therefore with an impending death sentence on her.

---

[4] Chris J. Ackerley and Stanley E. Gontarski, *The Grove Companion to Samuel Beckett* (New York: Grove Press, 2007), 591.

Whatever unfulfillments, separation anxieties and self-torments were in the ancient body of songs, they could not fail but to ring with a note of heightened truth and deep sadness to Beckett. This is shown in the collection *Echo's Bones and Other Precipitates*, in the poem that more explicitly refers to the Meistersinger Walther von der Vogelweide, that is, 'Da tagte es', in the subgenre of an 'alba'. Whether the title phrase is picked up from Vogelweide[5] or, as it has been also suggested by Mark Nixon,[6] from Heinrich von Morungen – in whose 'Tagelied' 'da tagte es' is a refrain (both derivations are plausible, since both poets are included *Robertson's History of German literature*[7]) – it is all the same notable the way in which Beckett intensifies the pain of the impending separation of the lovers, surprised and annoyed by daybreak. The 'separation as death' shifts, as Harvey suggests, from metaphorical to literal, becomes the 'separation of death'.[8] In this, Beckett's poetics of reduction, of going to the root of things, is at work, since any separation is presented just a 'surrogate goodbye'[9] encapsulating and announcing the ultimate farewell. Moreover, in the same poem, the feeling of love is also universalized, merging his love for Peggy and that for his father. Both had died in 1933, Peggy just one month before William,[10] and the poem followed almost immediately in early 1934.

But Beckett felt more sympathetic to Vogelweide than he did to von Morungen. To Vogelweide he familiarly refers – even in *Stirrings Still* (1987), his very last prose – as Walther,[11] making him a prototype for this late Beckettian protagonist who would, like him, sit on a rock, legs crossed. When he was in Kassel, he might have heard of, or perhaps visited, the nearby Wartburg castle, where, in 1207, the munificent Landgraf of Turingen, patronized a competition among the most renowned Meistersingers, with Vogelweide prominent among them all, together with Wolfram von Eschenbach. The memorable event is sung with epic strain in the so-called *Wartburgkrieg*, and in the castle itself there is a huge pictorial rendering the same gathering, in a late-Romantic taste

---

[5] From Vogelweide's poem 'Nemt, frowe, disen kranz' ('take, lady, this wreath'), and specifically the lines 'dô taget ez und muose ich wachen' ('it was dawn and I had to wake)'. See Harvey, *Beckett: Poet and Critic*, 84.

[6] Mark Nixon, *Samuel Beckett's German Diaries, 1936–1937* (London: Continuum, 2011), 63.

[7] Robertson's *History of German literature*, probably read in 1934. See Nixon, *German Diaries*, 63.

[8] Harvey, *Beckett: Poet and Critic*, 84.

[9] 'Da Tagte Es': 'redeem the surrogate goodbyes/The sheet astream in your hand …'. See *The Collected Poems of Samuel Beckett: A Critical Edition*, eds Seàn Lawlor and John Pilling (New York: Grove Press, 2014), 22.

[10] 3 May and 26 June 1933, respectively.

[11] Ruby Cohn, *A Beckett Canon* (Ann Arbor: The University of Michigan Press, 2001), 380, remarks that the name is in 'its German spelling'.

by K. T. von Piloty.[12] Be it as it may, a different and important iconographic source (a famous portrait of the poet in the *Codex Manesse*, 1300 circa, inspired by the autobiographical parts in the mainly political 'Imperial Tone' that Vogelweide wrote around the end of the twelfth and the beginning of the thirteenth centuries[13]), foregrounds the one key feature of Vogelweide to which Beckett was particularly responsive: the 'melancholy and ponderous atmosphere', as Nixon writes,[14] in which the poet rests[15]; to the point that the image, featuring the rock Vogelweide is sitting on, and therefore evoking a Belacqua of sorts,[16] almost becomes an allegory of melancholy itself.

As suggested, this German line of interest might have helped Beckett find a voice of his own in the literary context of his age. In fact, it is worthwhile remembering that a keen interest in the Romance Middle Ages was rather widespread among the most prominent modernists. Besides Joyce, several father figures come to mind, for all the relative distancing Beckett kept from them. Ezra Pound, T. S. Eliot and even W. B. Yeats were all, in fact, Beckett's precursors in this respect.

After the first scholarly flourish in Germany, France and Italy, mainly focused on the poets like Arnaut Daniel, Bertrand de Ventadorn or Sordello, which has been pointed out by Hugh Kenner,[17] with the expatriate Pound there lands on the European shores a scrutiny of the troubadours marked by strong and revitalizing American traits. In fact, such a looking back to the Romance past, by the poets mentioned, was part and parcel with the cosmopolitan ideals of the early decades of the twentieth century, and with the craving for an extended Western tradition,[18] as much in the dimension of space (sometimes going beyond Europe and the West), as in that of time. It was a definite break from the *fin de siècle* exoticism that had already directed its attention

---

[12] Karl Theodor von Piloty (1826–1886).
[13] See von Vogelweide's famous 'Spruch' 'Ich saz uf eime steine' ('I sat on a stone'): Ian G. Colvin, *'I Saw the World': Sixty Poems from Valther von der Vogelweide* (London: Hyperion, 1978), 49.
[14] Nixon, *German Diaries*, 74.
[15] Walther von der Vogelweide – portrait of the Minnesinger (medieval German courtly love poet). Illustration from the *Codex Manesse*, around 1300. c. 1170–1230.
[16] Nixon, *German Diaries*, 74.
[17] Hugh Kenner, *The Pound Era* (Berkeley: University of California Press, 1971), 78.
[18] Pound is even ready to find in the old literature (and in Dante, with his defense of the vernacular) a back-up in the affirmation of his own Americanness against the normative English and the 'policing of authority'. See Daniel Katz, 'Ezra Pound's Provincial Provence: Arnaut Daniel, Gavin Douglas, and the Vulgar Tongue', *Modern Language Quarterly*, 73:2 (June 2012), 178.

to the troubadours.[19] Pound approached the subject with the classic tools that Beckett would later use, among which were Jean Baptiste Beck's *La music des troubadours*,[20] and Frédéric Mistral's *Lou tresor d'ou Félibrige*, that is a *Provençal-French Dictionary* and Thesaurus.[21] Actually, he began his poetic apprenticeship in 1905 by translating the 'Belangal Alba' (written in medieval Latin with insertions in Provençal), together with other Provençal poems, and 'introduced himself to the world as a twentieth-century troubadour in his youthful collection *A Lume Spento* (1908)' as Massimo Bacigalupo writes.[22] In 1910, he published *The Spirit of Romance*, the second chapter of which was entitled 'il miglior fabbro',[23] where Arnaut Daniel was acknowledged as the best of the troubadours.[24]

And yet Pound had still to learn a lesson which Beckett, apparently, was able to self-teach. As Kenner remarks, when in 1911 the American visited Ford Madox Ford, in Giessen, to present his senior with his volume of *Canzoni* – of which the initial six were all in Provençal form – he had the following caveat:

> Delve ages long in the works of Bertrand de Born; [...] let us do anything in the world that will widen our perceptions. We are the heirs of all the ages. But, in the end, I feel fairly assured that the purpose of all these present travails is the right appreciations of such facets of our own day, as God will let us perceive.[25]

This caveat was actually innate in T. S. Eliot who, needless to recall, strikingly embeds troubadour poetry in the living texture of modern poetry. Even with the title of his second poetic collection, be it via Dante, he actually addresses the reader in Provençal, with Arnaut's words: *Ara vos prec*.[26]

---

[19] On the sympathies of Irish intellectuals for Félibrige, and the affinities between the Pre-Raphaelite Movement and Félibrige, see Beatrice Laurent, 'The Irish Troubadour of the Provençal Félibrige: William Charles Bonaparte-Wyse', 105–118, in *Provence and the British Literary Imagination* (Milano: Di/segni 2013), eds Clare Davison, Béatrice Laurent, Caroline Patey, and Nathalie Vanfasse.

[20] Jean Beck, *La Musique des Troubadours* (Paris: Laurens, 1910).

[21] Frédéric Mistral, *Lou tresor d'ou Félibrige*, 1878–1886.

[22] Massimo Bacigalupo, 'Ezra the Troubadour', in *Provence and the British Literary Imagination*, 175–92.

[23] Ezra Pound, *The Spirit of Romance* (London: Dent, 1910), 22.

[24] Kenner, *The Pound Era*, 82.

[25] Kenner, *The Pound Era*, 81. On F. M. Ford and the troubadours, see also Christine Reynier, 'Mapping Ford Madox Ford's Provence in Provence', in *Provence and the British Literary Imagination*, 193–204.

[26] In the *Divina Commedia*, ed. Natalino Sapegno (Firenze: La Nuova Italia, 1956), Dante has Daniel utter his prayer in the language: 'Ara vos prec, per aqella valor/que vos guida al som de l'escalina,/ sovenha vos a temps de ma dolor' (*Purgatory*, XXVI, ll. 140–47). 'Sovegna vos' is quoted in *Ash Wednesday*, IV. (T. S. Eliot, *The Complete Poems and Plays* [London: Faber, 1969], 94). '*Ara Vos Prec*' was published by John Rodker at the Ovid Press, February 1920 (edition of 264 copies).

With *The Waste Land* (again, similarly, right from the opening epigraph), he pays homage to Pound using the same phrase 'il miglior fabbro', which heads the second chapter of *The Spirit of Romance*, thus adding layers of literary references to Dante's definition of Arnaut in the *Comedy*. With a hint of symmetry, and after the effect of a *finale*, towards the end of the same poem Eliot brings back the image of Arnaut, with the touching Dantean line on Arnaut reverting to his lone penitence: 'Poi s'ascose nel foco che gli affina'.[27]

Under such wide cultural pressures, Beckett also begins his literary career with poems to which he even referred, collectively and indifferently, as 'albas'.[28] His first collection, *Echo's Bones and Other Precipitates*, while bearing an original mark in mirroring, perhaps with irony, *Prufrock and Other Observations*, shows the strong inspirational power of the troubadours, albeit in highly obscure reinterpretations. Of the 13 poems in the collection, seven take their title from a troubadour subgenre, since there are two 'Albas', lamenting the approach of daylight and the need for separation of the clandestine lovers; three 'Serenas', where – for similar but opposing reasons – the fall of the evening is longed for; and two 'Enuegs', which are basically lists of afflictions, to which no one could have been more responsive than Beckett.

But the claim for a troubadour influence can also be made for the other poems. The first and last poems, for instance, explore the theme of art, which in itself was somehow characteristic of the troubadours.[29] Harvey is extremely perceptive in showing how the first poem of the collection, 'The Vulture', draws on 'Harzreise im Winter' ('Winter journey to the Harz mountains'), a famous and for Beckett haunting poem by Goethe, where a vulture is the symbol for art, and the poem therefore is about 'the artist on his Art'.[30] Beckett's lyric takes the image of the hovering vulture searching for prey from Goethe's poem and isolates it in title position, thus immediately shifting, from the 'The optimism, expansive joy and religious Mysticism of the original',[31] to violence, predation and destruction. However, the open intertextuality and artistic self-reflection the poem deals with make it worth considering that, in so doing, the poem works on the sharp contrast between the vulture

---

[27] Ibid., 75.
[28] In a letter to McGreevy, undated, 1931 (Ibid., 142) Beckett would refer to his quiet life punctuated with 'involuntary exonerations (Albas)' from more serious kind of academic work.
[29] The presence of such a theme is highlighted by the dense intertextuality of the collection, the very title of which draws on Ovidian mythical narratives. Knowlson observes that the poems are teeming with literary allusions (*Damned to Fame*, 223).
[30] Harvey, *Beckett: Poet and Critic*, 113.
[31] Ibid., 113.

and, say, the 'lauzeta' ('skylark') of Bertrand de Ventadorn[32] or the 'rosignol' (nightingale), both archetypal symbols of music and poetry.

The last lyric, 'Echo's Bones', duplicates the first part of the collection title. It concludes the whole collection on both a note of isolation in the poet's aimless walk and the artificiality of words and poems, all perceived, in a phrase recalling *The Tempest*, as 'muffled revels'.

As for the 'Sanies I' and 'Sanies II', the structure of the title is modelled on the 'albas', the 'serenas' and the 'enuegs', even if the title word itself is Latin, not Provençal. However, it becomes linguistically redefined by attraction, it would seem. They convey a sense of diseases in the body, of purulent wounds, so as to intensify the main expressive purport of the 'enuegs'. Moreover, 'Sanies I', after following the vagaries of the poet in a deadened urban context, finally evokes the image of Ethna ('I see main verb at last/ her whom alone in the accusative/I have dismounted to love')[33]: just a fleeting image, soon lost again, and so the poet urges himself on and away.

With a comprehensive, distanced look on them all, one might schematize: The 'albas' express a resistance to daylight; while the 'serenas' express an appreciation and desire for darkness. Thus, in the juxtaposition of opposites, the subverting of fundamental attributions of value to day and night takes place (it appears to be Dante in reverse, with a transmutation of values that goes back from the troubadours to the Cathar heresy, to Manicheism and gnostic ancient philosophy—to which Beckett was deeply attracted).[34] These two coupled subgenres are then matched by the 'enuegs', which list vexations (Latin 'inodium'); and the 'sanies', which carry on, listing vexations. In other words, the different troubadour subgenres, as taken up by Beckett, fit in a system condensing all experience in its essence. Titles are, therefore, abstractions, smoothing out all the 'demented particulars', as Celia's grandfather, Willoughby Kelly, would say.[35] Furthermore, the Roman numbers cannot but emphasize the repetitiveness and seriality of the poetic expression, its futility in saying one and the same thing, all over again: 'Enueg' I and II; 'Serena' I, II and III; 'Sanies' I and II. Clearly, the 'progression' announced by the cardinal numbers does not take place, so these

---

[32] From his famous song 'Can vei la lauzeta mover' (see *The Songs of Bernart de Ventadorn*, eds Stephen G. Nichols, John A. Galm and Bartlett A. Giamatti [Chapel Hill: University of North Carolina Press, 1965], 166–68), which also inspired Dante, *Paradise*, XX, ll. 73–76: 'Quale allodetta che 'n aere si spazia/Prima cantando, e poi tace contenta/ Dell'ultima dolcezza che la sazia' (Sapegno, ed., *La Divina Commedia*).

[33] Lawlor and Pilling eds, *The Collected Poems of Samuel Beckett*, 13.

[34] References to Manicheism and Gnosticism feature in *Murphy*. See Chris J. Ackerley, *Demented Particulars: The Annotated* Murphy (Edinburgh: Edinburgh University Press, 2010 [2004]), 113.

[35] Samuel Beckett, *Murphy* (London: Calder, 1963), 13.

hint, instead, at the 'repeat' one meets in plays to come, or at a like strategy in future titles shown in a play that is entitled simply 'Play', a film that is simply 'Film'; or in 'Rough for Theatre I' and 'Rough for Theatre II'; 'Rough for radio I' and 'Rough for radio II'; 'Act without words I' and 'Act without words II'.

Furthermore, one must be alert to recognize in Beckett a keen sense of form and organization in spite of the seemingly absolute, first-layer disorder of his imaginative utterances. Thus, dimly, perhaps, in *Echo's Bones*, there surfaces a structure that assigns the poems to four groups and relates them one another based on different but similar criteria: In other words, the 'albas' and 'serenas' are rather in opposition, while parallelism and specularity link the other two groups. However, this perception of distinctions in the four sub-groups goes together with an underlying feeling of uneasiness, anxiety and pain, which runs through the whole collection. The four groups, to put it differently, are therefore 'both one and many' to use a memorable phrase related to purgatorial shadows from a Dantean passage in *Four Quartets*.[36]

The question also arises how all of this is relevant in terms of and continues to be present in Beckett's *oeuvre*. In this respect, and to highlight the first, important feature – one that might be downplayed, given Beckett's identification as playwright, and subordinately, as narrator – Ackerley and Gontarski have made clear the continuity of Beckett's lyric production, with poems composed and collections published all along his literary career.[37] This is true in spite of what would appear as a long interruption between 1950 and 1975. Such a long *hiatus* of 25 years – which does not take into account the form of poems included in other genres[38] – simply suggests

---

[36] Eliot, *The Complete Poems and Plays*, 193.

[37] Ackerley and Gontarski, *The Grove Companion*. *Whoroscope*, the poem Beckett wrote on 15 June 1930 was his very first imaginative work to be published (exception made for the short prose of 'Assumption' (1929), and some translations and essays). After that, his lyric production goes from *Echo's Bones*, to the Poems in French 1937–1939, to the Poems in French 1946–1949, to the Poems in English 1974–1977, to the *Pseudo-Chamfort*, and, lastly, to the *Mirlitonnades* ('gloomy French doggerel'), written 1976–1978. Then, in symmetry with the beginning, the last imaginative work written by Beckett, in the Summer 1989, just a few months before his death, is again a poem: 'What is the word' (of which there had been a previous version in French, 'Comment dire', written at the Pasteur hospital in October 1988).

[38] Gabriele Frasca writes: 'la presunta sparizione della poesia propriamente detta fra la fine degli anni Quaranta e i primissimi anni Settanta, [...] cela in verità il diffondersi, per così dire, di una "metastasi poetica" nella lingua piegata a "narrare" o chiamata a fare scena' ('the supposed disappearance of poetry proper between the late 1940s and the very early years of the 1970s [...] conceals in truth the spread, as it were, of a "poetic metastasis" in the language bent to "narration" or called upon to become theatre'). See Gabriele Frasca, *Samuel Beckett: Le poesie* (Torino: Einaudi, 1999), XL.

that the lyric mode has migrated to other literary genres, the narrative and the dramatic, so there is no interruption in a fundamental continuity. Hints to such a migration might perhaps be inscribed and anticipated in some of the well-known statements Beckett gives of his famous vision of 1945, when he was visiting his mother in Ireland, soon after the end of the Second World War. If, as Knowlson writes in relation to it, 'in speaking of his own revelation, Beckett tended to focus on the recognition of his own stupidity',[39] other authorial phrasings on what had been going on would suggest that moving towards an intrinsically lyric quality of the language was simultaneously part of the crisis and worked towards a new direction in his poetics ('*Molloy* and the others came to me the day I became aware of my own folly. Only then did I begin to write the things *I feel*' [emphasis added]).[40]

The awareness of a previous 'folly', the decision to write 'the things I feel', links also with the concurrent determination to engage in 'the battle of the soliloquy').[41] Thus, with *Molloy*, the first of the narrative dramatic monologues of the *Trilogy*, albeit in a peculiarly dialogic tone of intimacy between the speaker and the reader – or between the speaker and his own double, resulting from a split personality – we begin to hear just one voice and one conscience that mediates everything and everyone, in a style that craves for the intensity of the lyric form.

It is no coincidence – it could be assumed – that from the very first pages of this novel one meets a troubadour again, as an archetype for the main character. Indeed, introducing himself at the beginning of the eponymous novel, right from the start of his journey, Molloy compares himself to two other characters, acknowledging his confusion on the matter, Belacqua or Sordello, in a new reference to Italy. It is a well-known passage:

> I was perched higher than the road's highest point, and flattened, what is more against a rock, the same colour as myself, that is grey. The rock, he probably

---

[39] Knowlson, *Damned to Fame*, 352.
[40] Gabriel D'Aubarède, 'Interviews with Samuel Beckett' (1961), in *Samuel Beckett: The Critical Heritage*, eds Lawrence Graver and Raymond Federman (London: Routledge, 1969), 217.
[41] 'Certes il fallait de la force pour rester avec Camier, comme il en fallait pour rester avec Mercier, mais moins qu'il n'en fallait pour la bataille du soliloque' (131) ['Admittedly strength was needed for to stay with Camier, no less than for to stay with Mercier, but less than for the horrors of soliloquy. 78]' (Cohn, *A Beckett Canon* [Ann Arbor: The University of Michigan Press, 2001] 136). Gabriele Frasca, besides remarking that, from a certain point of view, 'l'opera beckettiana successiva alla "rivelazione" […] è interamente poetica' ('Beckett's work subsequent to the "revelation" […] is entirely poetic' [Frasca, *Samuel Beckett: Le poesie*, XLII], writes that it is inscribed in that kind of '"dicibilità" già fortemente poetica che si è riscontrata nel balbettio monologico' [Ibid., XLVI]. (' "the utterable", already strongly poetic, found in the monologic babble').

saw. He gazed around as if to engrave the landmarks on his memory and must have seen the rock in the shadow of which I crouched like Belacqua, or Sordello, I forget.[42]

Because the basis of his comparison is the act of sitting near a rock, in the same position the Dantean Belacqua has in *Purgatory*, and since Belacqua has already been made the hero of *Dream of Fair to Middling Women* and of *More Pricks Than Kicks*, one is all too ready to solve Molloy's uncertainty in favour of the lutemaker and the confusion can be taken as just another index of the character's ageing and failing memory. However, here as elsewhere in Beckett, there is no dilemma to be solved once and for all and, so as not to miss nuances in the passage, it is preferable to stay open to possibilities.

No need to recall that, in general, Beckett's peculiar way of shaping characters has them shift into one another. Thus, Molloy's confusion prevents a definite identification with Belacqua or Sordello and rather suggests that he comprises, with their features merged, the one and the other, and that they might be devised as a collateral important pair, or pseudo-couple in the novel, like that of Molloy-Moran themselves, or the A and B Molloy is contemplating from afar.

Furthermore, there is some reason to provisionally privilege Sordello, instead, as a double of the protagonist, balancing the immediate claims for Belacqua. Sordello, of course, is much more charged with literary associations than Belacqua; it is enough to remember Browning's narrative poem with that title, or Rossetti's sonnet on the same; or Pound's initial *Cantos*, the *Draft of XVI Cantos*, published in 1924–25, where one finds a markedly prismatic figure of the Italian poet.

Sordello would then serve to highlight the artist in Molloy, had the latter not emerged as such from the opening paragraph of the novel, where we see him sitting in his room, writing and handing over his pages to an intermediary messenger for the dimly perceptible employer Youdi, who will send them back corrected and with his evaluations. Characteristically, they are both also vagrant artists: Molloy does not belong to any place, just like the Dantean Sordello, for whom 'loco certo non c'è posto'.[43]

---

[42] Samuel Beckett, *Molloy, Malone Dies, The Unnamable: A Trilogy* (New York: Alfred Knopf, 1997), 7.

[43] Dante, *Purgatory* (Canto VII, l. 40).

Moreover, by reflex, the focus on Sordello also brings to the foreground features in Belacqua that would otherwise be in the shadow, because not mentioned in the *Comedy*. In other words, while in the Dantean *Commedia* Belacqua, couched at the foot of Mount Purgatory, is expiating his sin of sloth, Beckett's image of Belacqua transcends the moral character of a sinner and results in a more complex image that partakes of the exegetical tradition of the *Comedy*: Beckett would have known the first commentators, like Benvenuto da Imola and the Anonimo Fiorentino, who, as Daniela Caselli writes, are both noted down in Toynbee's *Dictionary of Proper Names and notable matters in the works of Dante*.[44]

The commentators give more relevance to Belacqua the artisan and musician, features that also attracted Dante to the lutemaker. Indeed, one reads that he was seen 'squatting in the heart of his store, sculpting with great care and chiseling the heads and necks of lutes and zithers, or sustaining in the doorway the girds of eminent poets, or coming out into the street for a bit of song and dance'.[45]

On the other hand, the artist Sordello, also metonymically linked to Belacqua, since troubadours would use lutes to accompany their songs, has some other features both in opposition and in accord with those of the sinner Belacqua. In contrast, he is active and passionate, and a roaming person, moving from court to court; and yet he is likewise somewhat lazy, at least in point of honour, according to the characterization that Aimeric de Peguilhan gives of him.[46]

It would be also worthwhile to consider a different confusion in *Molloy* that occurs in the second half of the novel, a confusion that – given the diptych structure of this novel – can well match and interact with the one already considered. In fact, Moran, who at first looks like being in no doubt as to who Molloy is ('I remember the day I received the order to see about Molloy')[47] becomes soon uncertain as to his relation with himself ('For where Molloy could not be, nor Moran either for that matter, there

---

[44] Daniela Caselli, *Beckett's Dante: Intertextuality in the Fiction and Criticism* (Manchester: Manchester University Press, 2005), 38.
[45] Ibid., 38.
[46] Aimeric de Peguilhan was the most significant troubadour at the court of Azzo VI d'Este. There he wrote his famous complaints against the *joglaret novell* ('upstart little *joglars*'), 'Li fol e·ill put e ill fillol' (XXXII), among whom he sarcastically mentions Sordello. For the text of the sirventese, see Giorgio Barachini, 'Aimeric de Peguilhan. "Li fol e·ill put e ill fillol"', *Lecturae tropatorum 12*, 2019, http://www.lt.unina.it/, 51–85, accessed 4 July 2023, http://www.rialto.unina.it/AimPeg/10.32(Barachini).htm.
[47] Beckett, *Molloy, Malone Dies, The Unnamable*, 102.

Moran could bend over Molloy'),[48] and as to the name of his quest-object. In fact, he wonders about the ending part of the name which he is unable to recall precisely:

> What I heard – in my soul – I suppose, where the acoustics are so bad, was a first syllable, Mol, very clear, followed almost at once by a second, very thick, as though gobbled by the first, and which might have been oy as it might have been ose, or one, or even oc.[49]

Commenting on the four possible endings, Ackerly and Gontarski suggest that 'Moran's discussion and doubts are in a parody of the philological distinction between the southern and northern forms of old French, based on the word used for saying "yes", the distinction therefore made between a "langue d'oui" and a "langue d'oc"'.[50] Cleverly, that is, Beckett manages to connect again Molloy with medieval France, and also, specifically, by the latter variant, with the cradle of troubadour poetry. However, two names only are spelled in full and repeatedly in this passage: Molloy and Mollose, and Moran reflects that between those two 'the second seemed perhaps the more correct',[51] also adding that 'if I inclined towards "ose", it was doubtless that my mind had a weakness for this ending, whereas the others left it cold'.[52]

Molloy's partiality invites speculation. One might draw, for instance, on suggestions from the Greek language, by which Aldo Tagliaferri – discussing the 'iperdeterminazione' ('hyperdetermination') in Beckett's texts and tracing less obvious associations – argues that *molos* might point to 'pain', and *molobros* might point to a 'vagrant',[53] both basic and relevant concepts to the character. However, drawing instead on Ackerley and Gontarski's argument, a different suggestion would appear, activating connotative meanings within the frame of cultural associations that the two scholars provide: the basic consonantal sound (/s/) of the ending 'ose' might recall in alliteration Sordello, and refer to another important part of the medieval Romance geography, namely the region where 'yes' was not a 'oy' or 'oc', but a 'sì'; that phoneme would thus seem to discreetly corroborate earlier references to the Italian troubadour and his homeland.

---

[48] Ibid., 124.
[49] Ibid., 126.
[50] Ackerley and Gontarski, *The Grove Companion*, 463.
[51] Beckett, *Molloy, Malone Dies, The Unnamable*, 126.
[52] Ibid.
[53] Aldo Tagliaferri, *Beckett e l'iperdeterminazione letteraria* (Milano: Feltrinelli, 1967), 38.

Bibliography

Ackerley, Chris J. and Stanley E. Gontarski. *The Grove Companion to Samuel Beckett*. New York: Grove Press, 2007.

Ackerley, Chris J. *Demented Particulars: The Annotated Murphy*. Edinburgh: Edinburgh University Press, 2010 [2004].

Alighieri, Dante. *La divina commedia*, edited by Natalino Sapegno. Firenze: La Nuova Italia, 1976.

Bacigalupo, Massimo. 'Ezra the Troubadour'. In *Provence and the British Literary Imagination*, edited by Davison, Laurent, Patey, and Vanfasse, 175–92.

Barachini, Giorgio. 'Aimeric de Peguilhan. "Li fol e·ill put e ill fillol"'. *Lecturae tropatorum 12*, 2019, http://www.lt.unina.it/, 51–85. Accessed 4 July 2023. http://www.rialto.unina.it/AimPeg/10.32(Barachini).htm, [http://www.lt.unina.it/].

Beckett, Samuel. *Molloy, Malone Dies, the Unnamable: A Trilogy*. New York: Alfred Knopf, 1997.

———. *Murphy*. London: Calder, 1963.

Caselli, Daniela. *Beckett's Dante, Intertextuality in the Fiction and Criticism*. Manchester: Manchester University Press, 2005.

Cohn, Ruby. *A Beckett Canon*. Ann Arbor: The University of Michigan Press, 2001.

Colvin, Ian. *'I Saw the World': Sixty Poems from Valther von der Vogelweide*. London: Hyperion, 1978.

Davison, Clare, Laurent Béatrice, Patey Caroline, and Vanfasse Nathalie, eds. *Provence and the British Literary Imagination*. Milano: Di/segni, 2013.

Eliot, Thomas Stearns. *The Complete Poems and Plays*. London: Faber, 1969.

Fehsenfeld, Martha Dow and Lois More Overbeck, eds. *The Letters of Samuel Beckett, Volume I: 1929–1940*. Cambridge: Cambridge University Press, 2009.

Frasca, Gabriele. *Samuel Beckett: Le poesie*. Torino: Einaudi, 1999.

Graver, Lawrence and Raymond Federman, eds. *Samuel Beckett: The Critical Heritage*. London: Routledge, 1969.

Harvey, Lawrence. *Samuel Beckett: Poet and Critic*. Princeton: Princeton University Press, 1970.

Katz, Daniel. 'Ezra Pound's Provincial Provence: Arnaut Daniel, Gavin Douglas, and the Vulgar Tongue', *Modern Language Quarterly*, 73:2 (June 2012), 175–99.

Kenner, Hugh. *The Pound Era*. Berkeley: University of California Press, 1971.

Knowlson, James. *Damned to Fame: The Life of Samuel Beckett*. London: Bloomsbury, 1997.

Laurent, Béatrice. 'The Irish Troubadour of the Provençal Félibrige: William Charles Bonaparte-Wyse'. In *Provence and the British Literary Imagination*, edited by Davison, Laurent, Patey, and Vanfasse, 105–18.

Lawlor, Seàn and John Pilling, eds. *The Collected Poems of Samuel Beckett: A Critical Edition*. New York: Grove Press, 2014.

Nichols, Stephen G., John A. Galm, and Bartlett A. Giamatti, eds. *The Songs of Bernart de Ventadorn*. Chapel Hill: University of North Carolina Press, 1965.

Nixon, Mark. *Samuel Beckett's German Diaries, 1936–1937*. London: Continuum, 2011.

Pound, Ezra. *The Spirit of Romance*. London: Dent, 1910.

Reynier, Christine. 'Mapping Ford Madox Ford's Provence in Provence'. In *Provence and the British Literary Imagination*, edited by Davison, Laurent, Patey, and Vanfasse, 193–204.

Tagliaferri, Aldo. *Beckett e l'iperdeterminazione letteraria*. Milano: Feltrinelli, 1967.

Chapter 7

THE EMPTY HOUSE: *WATT'S* LEOPARDIAN TRACES

William Davies

Abstract

This chapter explores the ways in which Giacomo Leopardi's presence in the manuscripts of Beckett's war-time novel *Watt* draws the text's Big House pastiche into a pan-European, pessimistic-Romantic tradition sceptical of logic and reason as fundamentally positive human qualities. In doing so, this chapter examines how Beckett's invocation of Leopardi is vital to an underlying political parody in *Watt* and its manuscripts that takes stock of the troubling relationship between Enlightenment rationality and the barbarism of European fascism.

Keywords: Samuel Beckett; Giacomo Leopardi; W. B. Yeats; Second World War; pessimism; Enlightenment

Samuel Beckett's novel *Watt* had a turbulent genesis. Begun during the Second World War, the novel went through several phases of composition, from scattered notes to at least two stages of heavy revision of both plot and characters.[1] The *Watt* notebooks, held in the archives of the Harry Ransom Center at the University of Texas, Austin, evidence a writing process that both obsessed and frustrated its author.[2]

Before the familiar Watt and Mr Knott entered the story, Beckett's tale centred on an Irish Big House in decline and the trials and tribulations of its owner, James Quin, the last of a long line of aristocrats whose family

---

[1] For an overview of the novel's composition, see C. J. Ackerley, *Obscure Locks, Simple Keys: The Annotated Watt* (Tallahassee: Journal of Beckett Studies Books, 2005).

[2] *Watt* papers, Harry Ransom Center, University of Texas at Austin. The research for this chapter was supported by a visiting fellowship to the Harry Ransom Center.

have succumbed to various ailments and illnesses. Beckett's turn in *Watt* and its preceding manuscripts to an ironic revision of the Big House novel during the war has been convincingly argued by scholars as a form of historical negotiation that works through the obsessions with order and hierarchy shared (in very different forms) between European fascism and the Anglo-Irish Ascendency ideology of the 1920s and 1930s, particularly as formulated by W. B. Yeats.[3] In these readings, the 'comic attack on rationality' typically associated with *Watt* takes on subtle, interconnected political dimensions.[4]

Crucial to the satire of the Big House that runs through the manuscripts and into the published novel is the pervading sense of emptiness at the heart of seemingly urgent matters, whether it is Quin's family decline or Watt's desperate attempts to uncover the puzzles of the Knott household. This is at its starkest in the manuscripts, where Quin is described as one hounded by 'nothingness' in his life, a condition that seems to derive in part from his lack of family but also from his failed attempts to educate himself in European literature and philosophy. One of the few figures explicitly named from Quin's reading is the writer Giacomo Leopardi, whose pessimistic poetics does give Quin a sense of intellectual companionship, though provides him little in the way of relief.

This chapter explores how the invocation of Leopardi in the *Watt* manuscripts fits into Beckett's evolving relationship with the Italian writer and the pessimistic, counter-Enlightenment tradition he represents. In doing so, the chapter considers how such an invocation figures in the historical and political interconnections of Beckett's 'comic attack on rationality' in the *Watt* papers, from the composition context of the Second World War and barbaric reason of Nazism to Beckett's unsettled relationship with the politics of W. B. Yeats and the tradition of the Irish Big House.

---

[3] John Harrington, *The Irish Beckett* (Syracuse: Syracuse University Press, 1991); Patrick Bixby, *Samuel Beckett and the Postcolonial Novel* (Cambridge: Cambridge University Press, 2009); Seán Kennedy, 'Bid Us Sigh on from Day to Day: Beckett and the Irish Big House', in *The Edinburgh Companion to Samuel Beckett and the Arts*, ed. S. E. Gontarski (Edinburgh: Edinburgh University Press, 2014), 222–34. For Beckett and the Irish Big House in broader contexts, see W. J. McCormack, *From Burke to Beckett: Ascendancy, Tradition and Betrayal in Literary History* (Cork: Cork University Press, 1994) and Julian Moynahan, *Anglo-Irish: The Literary Imagination in a Hyphenated Culture*, (Princeton: Princeton University Press, 1995).

[4] Ackerley, *Obscure Locks, Simple Keys*, 13.

Quin's Empty House

The notion of Quin's nothingness is introduced in two and a half pages of a draft chapter aptly titled 'The Nothingness':

> The feeling of nothingness, born in Quin with the first beat of his heart, if not before, died in him with the last and not before. Between these dates it waned not, neither did it wax, but its strength at its beginning was as its strength at its end, and its strength at its middle as its strength at its beginning. The foetal soul is fullgrown.[5]

Malaise is a key theme of the early *Watt* drafts. Of what survives into typescripts from the initial notes, it is the feeling of nothingness in Quin that predominates: though 'free of disease' and the 'disorders to which old age is commonly a prey', Quin nevertheless 'felt tired and weak all day long', an affliction familiar since his 'twenty-first year'.[6] Already, Beckett bakes collapse into his potential narrative. His character is weary before he has even begun; progress seems unlikely.[7] Further still, Beckett puts centre stage a Big House master who is without family or children to carry on his line. Quin and his ancestors will fade, inevitably it seems, into the nothingness that has been there his whole life. In a short chapter draft preceding 'The Nothingness', the narrator recounts the deaths of Quin's siblings, a trauma which goes someway to explaining one dimension of the void Quin feels:

> James Quin. Eldest and sole surviving child of Alexander Quin, Master of Arts (Galway), Bachelor of Music (Kentucky), of Dublin, and of his wife Leda, née Swan, demi-mondaine, of Enniskillen, the other ten having died in infancy, boys and girls, one after the other, in order of seniority, to the no small regret of all concerned.
>
> The causes of death, beginning with the first and ending with the last, were as far as could be ascertained as follows: thrush, sausage poisoning, asphyxia, burns, rabies, scalds, summer diarrhoea, bubo, putrid sore throat and nodding convulsions.[8]

---

[5] *Watt* Typescripts, 55, quoted in William Davies, *Historicising Samuel Beckett's Post-Humanism*, PhD Thesis, 2018. https://centaur.reading.ac.uk/80000/. Subsequent TS quotations from this source.

[6] *Watt TS*, 35.

[7] For further discussion of *Watt* and the novel form, see my 'Narrating Disruption: Realist Fiction and the Politics of Form in *Watt*', in *Beckett beyond the Normal*, ed. Seán Kennedy (Edinburgh: Edinburgh University Press, 2020), 33–46.

[8] *Watt* TS, 41.

The net result, the narrator tells us, 'was that James, at the age of thirteen, found himself an orphan'.[9] With no children of his own, Quin has failed to secure the future of his lineage. In the end, whatever prestige and wealth accrued by his forebears, it was the vagaries of nature which dictated the family's fate.

It is difficult to ignore in the above description of Quin's parents the figure of W. B. Yeats and his poem 'Leda and the Swan' (1923). The reference to Yeats – one perhaps too blatant to survive into the final novel in any form – is unsurprising in the context of a Big House satire, though this allusion has so far gone with little comment in examinations of Beckett's negotiation with Yeats. For Yeats, the Big House was a key symbol of Anglo-Irish revival that he thought necessary to an ordered, safely hierarchical Irish society, a position against which Beckett is clearly reacting in *Watt*. He reached such conclusions before the war, at a time when, in Ireland in the 1920s and 1930s, an ambivalent but palpable nostalgia for the Big House was already suffusing Irish culture.[10] As Seán Kennedy observes, Beckett's relationship with the Big House tradition is unsettled, much as Ireland's remains now:

> the Big House appears to have a more complex hold on the Irish psyche, such that a majority of people seem grateful, now, for those that survived the conflagrations and, later, commodification in something approaching their original form. As symbols of colonial oppression they are difficult to ignore, but they have also persuaded the Irish of the continuing relevance of a complex and violent history [...] it is arguable that part of the drive behind *Watt*'s composition was [Beckett's] need to render the Big House tradition absurd as a way of distancing himself from a dangerous current of nostalgia circulating in Dublin the 1920s and 1930s.[11]

Further impulse for the parody in *Watt*, Kennedy argues, comes from how Yeats and other Ascendency fantasists viewed 'a restoration of the status of the Anglo-Irish as one aspect of a return to pre-democratic patterns of government in Europe generally'.[12] It seems that, during the chaos of the war,

---

[9] *Watt* TS, 43.
[10] For a useful summary of the cultural role of the Big House in the early twentieth century, including Yeats' views, see K. Sullivan's 'The Ecology of the Irish Big House, 1900–1950', in *A History of Irish Literature and the Environment*, ed. M. Sen (Cambridge: Cambridge University Press, 2022), 173–89.
[11] Kennedy, 'Bid Us Sigh on from Day to Day', 223.
[12] Ibid., 225.

Beckett felt compelled to probe the intellectual scaffolding behind this turn to rationalized forms of hierarchy, race and nationhood.

One form of the comedic dressing down of the Big House genre and its symbolic associations is the coy description of Quin's mother Leda as a 'demi-mondaine'. It is of course over-determined: it refers to both Quin's mother and the Leda of Yeats's poem, rendering the mother a far less staid maternal figure than might be hoped for by Big House traditionalists, while also suggesting for Leda an agency otherwise denied in the sexual assault narrative of Yeats' poem. Proust's Odette de Crécy and her marriage to Charles Swann is perhaps also an important touchstone here. 'Swan' thus becomes a signal to both Yeats' and Proust's works, an opposition that places Yeats' later preoccupations with social hierarchy against the transitioning between, and complication of, social classes that Proust makes central to Odette's characterization, all reinterpreted through the mother of a doomed Big House proprietor. Beckett's depiction of Leda as 'demi-mondaine' plays upon Yeats' particular interest in the role of Leda in the origins of the Trojan War, the end of the 'mythic' era and the beginning of the 'human'. After she is raped by Zeus, Leda births two eggs containing Clytemnestra and Helen. For Yeats, as outlined in *A Vision*, the assault of Leda signified the shift from the mythological to the human with the birth of the antithetical 'Love' and 'War'.[13] Symbolized by the 'sudden blow' of the 'brute blood of the air' upon the 'staggering girl',[14] the poem is a dramatic and violent imagining of Yeats' cycles of history, a process that proceeds regardless of those caught up in history's movements. Such a historical framework has affinities if not outright sympathies with the oppressive and violent impulses of fascism, as does Yeats' preoccupations with a return to order and hierarchy in Ireland through the resuscitation of the Ascendency class and its Big House estates. In recasting Leda 'née Swan' as a 'demi-mondaine', Beckett both provides her agency and subjects her symbolic potential to mockery, simultaneously lampooning a potentially decadent aristocracy and denying Yeats' own notion of history's crushing cycles symbolized by the rape that his poem depicts. Leda is restored to some manner of power over her body, but the result of

---

[13] 'I imagine the annunciation that founded Greece as made to Leda, remembering that they showed in a Spartan Temple, strung up to the roof as a holy relic, an unhatched egg of hers; and that from one of her eggs came Love and from the other War.' W. B. Yeats, *A Critical Edition of Yeats's A Vision* (Basingstoke: Palgrave Macmillan, 1978), 181.
[14] Yeats, 'Leda and the Swan', *The Collected Works of W.B. Yeats Volume I: The Poems*, ed. by Richard J. Finneran, 2nd ed. (London: Prentice Hall & IBD, 1997), 218.

aristocratic breeding is nevertheless a fruitless endeavour. In the Ur-*Watt*, Leda gives birth to neither 'love' nor 'war' but 'nothing'.

After the section on his family, Quin recalls that in his younger days, he engaged in a course of self-education in literature and philosophy, much as Beckett did. It is through this that he came to Leopardi:

> The prevailing sensation of Quin's life was one which he once had the extraordinary good fortune to find, if not expressed, at least suggested, in the works of that universally read and admired Italian humanist-poet, Count Leopardi, notably in his Night Song of the Wandering Shepherd of Asia and in his Desert Flower.
>
> This discovery, constituting the sole literary satisfaction of a long and patient life, fell within the period during which Quin devoted himself, with all the ardour of which he was capable, to a free and openminded consideration of the celebrated passages of the more celebrated works of the most celebrated authors, both British and foreign: a period which, after deduction of its numerous intermissions, cannot have fallen far short of eighteen calendar months.
>
> [...] [I]n the aforementioned works of the talented titled writer to whom allusion has been made [...] it was simply the sensation of being nothing, in the midst of an unbroken waste, under a cloudless sky, and no other.[15]

This is by no means the first instance that Beckett engages with Leopardi in his writing: he is notably invoked in the *Dante... Bruno. Vico.. Joyce* and *Proust* essays, as well as in *Dream of Fair to Middling Women* and *Molloy*. Leopardi is an interlocutor for Beckett at significant stages of his career: at the early moment where he assesses the possibilities of being a critical as well as creative writer; amid the turbulence and eventual failure of *Dream*; and the turning point of *Molloy* in which Beckett abandons an overtly referential aesthetic in favour of a more subtle approach. This appearance of the 'talented titled writer' in the *Watt* manuscripts, in a section heavily revised, marks the beginning of Beckett's course towards a far more experimental, formally self-conscious style of writing that is more sceptical of lineage and tradition. *Watt* is a novel preoccupied by lineage – be it Quin/Knott's ancestors and lack of future,

---

[15] *Watt* TS, 49, 53. The phrase 'Italian writer' is crossed out in favour of 'talented titled writer'. Both poems appear in Leopardi's *Canti*, of which a 1936 edition remains in Beckett's library. *BDMP*. Accessed 3 January 2023. https://www.beckettarchive.org/library/LEO-CAN.html.

Beckett's sense of the traditions he is working in and against, even where he locates the novel in his own body of work (its 'part in the series', as he put it)[16] – and the role of Leopardi in the novel is in part to allow Beckett to continue working through the ideas he wants to either inherit or cast off from his creative and intellectual predecessors.

Before going further, it is worth sketching the part Leopardi has played in our understanding of Beckett's aesthetic so far. Sustained attention to Leopardi's presence in Beckett's work is scant, yet the analysis already available in the critical literature – reinvigorated with confirmation of Leopardi's presence in Beckett's library at his death, there since he first read him at Trinity[17] – is indicative of the avenues Beckett's engagement with Leopardi opens for reflecting on his work and its position in wider cultural spheres. Roberta Cauchi-Santoro's study (2016) takes the central notion of 'desire' and traces the connections between Leopardi and Beckett's treatment of the theme, touching notably on the role Schopenhauer plays for Beckett and Leopardi's familiarity with wider trends in European Romanticism, particularly through the latter's reading of Edmund Burke on the sublime.[18] For Daniela Caselli, Leopardi is significant not just as a source of malleable ideas and quotations for Beckett to plunder but as a figure through whom we can better recognize how Beckett's texts position themselves in relation to the literary tradition 'by re-introducing "old" materials from the literary tradition into new circuits of meaning, moulding them to achieve new goals'; for Caselli, this results in a 'practice of subversion' by Beckett in which he is actively seeking to work 'within the system [of tradition]' while also negotiating his relationship to that tradition.[19] Caselli argues that the development of Beckett's engagement with Leopardi is representative of a wider change in his art:

> A progression can be observed in the intertextual modalities of appropriation of Leopardi by Beckett; in *Dante... Bruno. Vico.. Joyce* the brief quotation of Leopardi is used as a rhetorical device and highlights Beckett's early interest in Italian literature. In *Proust* Leopardi is quoted three times and considered as

---

[16] Qtd. in 'Preface', *Watt*, ed. C. J. Ackerley (London: Faber & Faber, 2009), vii.
[17] See Dirk Van Hulle and Mark Nixon, *Samuel Beckett's Library* (Cambridge: Cambridge University Press, 2013).
[18] Roberta Cauchi-Santoro, *Beyond the Suffering of Being: Desire in Giacomo Leopardi and Samuel Beckett* (Florence: Firenze University Press, 2016).
[19] Daniela Caselli, 'Beckett's Intertextual Modalities of Appropriation: the Case of Leopardi', *Journal of Beckett Studies* 6, Issue 1 (1996): 1–24, 1–2.

a representative figure of a tragic literary tradition of which Beckett considers himself a member. Leopardi was also the 'sage' who proposed the formula summarized by Beckett as the 'ablation of desire', which represented the goal towards which Belacqua, Murphy, and partially Watt struggled. In *Dream* Leopardi's poem [*A se stesso*] is diminished to the adjective 'gloomy' and it becomes a parodic instrument through which both Belacqua and the author of *Proust* are taunted by the narrator. On the intertextual level we observe this mocking, but on the thematic level the Leopardian concern with the 'ablation of desire' remains alive in Belacqua's aspiration to alienation. In *Molloy* the distance between Leopardi and Beckett is even greater: the reference [to Molloy as the 'incurious seeker'] is intratextual more than intertextual, and the ontological dimension of Leopardi's desire becomes simply sexual desire; but again, Molloy still aspires towards the suppression of all desires and tries to move in this direction through the progressive deterioration of his body.[20]

The parodic impulse towards Leopardi remains in the *Watt* manuscripts ('titled talented writer'), but his work and presence in the text nevertheless both encapsulate thematically the comedy of reason that *Watt* famously embodies and the knottier issue of the text's relationship to history and tradition.

Both poems by Leopardi noted in the *Watt* manuscripts appear in his book *Canti*, of which a 1936 edition remains in Beckett's library. 'Night Song of the Wandering Shepherd of Asia' is a traditional Romantic travelling poem in which the speaker addresses the moon over its course across the sky. The speaker compares the moon's journey to that of a 'Little old white-haired man, / weak, half-naked, barefoot'.[21] The speaker laments that:

> Man is born by labor,
> and birth itself means risking death.
> The first thing that he feels
> is pain and torment, and from the start
> mother and father
> seek to comfort him for being born.

---

[20] Caselli, 'Beckett's Intertextual Modalities of Appropriation', 14–15.

[21] 'Night Song', *Canti*, trans. Jonathan Galassi (New York: Farrar, Straus and Giroux, 2014). All references are to the e-book edition of the text. I quote the English translation since Beckett gives English titles in the *Watt* manuscripts.

The moon, a part of the indifferent nature that surrounds the speaker, cannot answer, leaving the shepherd to conclude that 'the day we're born is cause for mourning',[22] a theme we encounter across Beckett's oeuvre.

'Desert Flower', also translated as 'Wild Broom' or 'The Wild Flower of the Desert' ['La ginestra o il fiore del deserto'], also takes up the Romantic trope of a lone contemplative speaker. One of Leopardi's most significant works, the text is a long poetic essay on the importance of a pessimistic philosophical grounding for modern humanity and on reason's inability to reveal the sublime mysteries of nature.[23] Set in the shadow of Mount Vesuvius, the speaker sits atop 'the dry flank / of the terrifying mountain' using the vantage point to observe the 'grave and silent aspect' of Pompeii after it has been destroyed by the volcano's eruption.[24] For the speaker, the sight is emblematic of the naïve superiority that humanity believes it possesses:

>   Let him who loves to praise our state
>   come to these slopes and see how well our kind
> 40 is served by loving nature.
>   And he can also fairly judge
>   the power of the human race
>   [...]
>   Represented on these slopes you see
> 50 the magnificent, progressive destiny
>   of humankind.

Rejecting the anthropocentricism of the Enlightenment, the poem chastens humanity's self-satisfaction and sense of divinity. Instead, Leopardi turns to

---

[22] Having already suggested this in his short essay *Proust* by way of quoting Pedro Calderón de la Barca's 'ues el delito mayor / Del hombre es haber nacido' [For man's greatest crime is to have been born], this idea would remain with Beckett throughout his career and became one of his most publicly circulated statements after his interview in December 1969 with John Gruen in *Vogue* magazine.

[23] For Leopardi, the sublime encompassed his notion of 'desire' (a precursor of sorts to Schopenhauer's Will) and his idea of the 'illusions' by which humanity could encounter nature. As Roberta Cauchi-Santoro shows, Leopardi owned and had read Edmund Burke's work on the sublime in Italian translation, suggesting that he was at least familiar with, if not attuned to, the importance of the notion of the sublime in European Romanticism more broadly (22).

[24] 'Desert Flower', *Canti*, trans. Jonathan Galassi (New York: Farrar, Straus and Giroux, 2014). All references are to the e-book edition of the text.

nature, represented by the desert flower, as that from which humanity can learn; 'you, too, pliant broom', the poem concludes,

> you were never raised
> 310 by senseless pride up to the stars
> or above the desert, which for you
> was home and birthplace
> not by choice, but chance;
> no, far wiser and less fallible
> 315 than man is, you did not presume
> that either fate or you had made
> your fragile kind immortal.

Beyond humanity's metaphysical significance, the poem also focuses on the destructive potential of nature and the arrogance of humanity to think itself defiant and 'immortal'. This arrogance suffuses the forms of political violence that Beckett lived through, from the race politics of Nazism to Yeatsian visions of hierarchy and order: fantasies dedicated to a 'senseless pride' in 'home and birthplace'. Quin's identification with Leopardi is even more politically charged in this context, putting him on the right side of history even if it is a little too late for his nothingness to wane.[25]

Leopardi's pessimistic poetics rejects humanity's divine aspirations and its devotion to reason. This pessimism attracted Beckett in his youth; as he told A. J. Leventhal, 'Leopardi was a strong influence when I was young (his pessimism, not his patriotism!)'.[26] Beckett's attraction to Leopardi is much like his interest in Schopenhauer, who praised Leopardi as his contemporary in *The World as Will and Representation*.[27] Like Schopenhauer, Leopardi represented an important counter-Enlightenment thinker for Beckett, one who was interested in a philosophical pessimism that recognized the inherent suffering of the world and the primacy of nature. This is a Romantic impulse

---

[25] This characterization accords with Kennedy's argument that Beckett himself used the process of writing *Watt* to work through a feeling of complicity with the Big House tradition by way of his mother's family. See Kennedy (2014).

[26] *The Letters of Samuel Beckett II*, eds George Craig, Martha Dow Fehsenfeld, Dan Gunn and Lois More Overbeck (Cambridge: Cambridge University Press, 2011), 537.

[27] In *The World as Will and Representation*, Schopenhauer writes that 'everywhere his [Leopardi's] theme is the mockery and wretchedness of this existence. He presents it on every page of his works, yet in such a multiplicity of forms and applications, with such a wealth of imagery, that he never wearies us, but, on the contrary, has a diverting and stimulating effect.' Project Gutenberg edition. https://www.gutenberg.org/files/40868/40868-h/40868-h.html, Chapter XLVI, 401.

in the broad sense, but nature figures less as a source of transcendence or epiphany for Leopardi and more of destruction and terror. This tradition of pessimistic Romanticism does not straightforwardly map onto Beckett's work, but it nevertheless provides a further intellectual backdrop against which Beckett was working during the composition of *Watt*.[28]

Leopardi's counter-Enlightenment, Romantic position is most forcefully demonstrated in his response to war and terror. As Frank Rosengarten writes:

> Leopardi looked askance on the great overarching humanist principle of 'the dignity of man', which he found to be in blatant contradiction with the realities of human behaviour [...] it was because of his own extreme sensitivity to pain and insult, and his disgust at seeing the many ways in which tyranny and war were justified in the name of *Realpolitik*, or even defended as inherently good and reasonable, that he recoiled from abstract idealizations of human dignity.[29]

As Leopardi wrote in a notebook entry, gathered in the *Zibaldone*, he thought that one of the principal reasons for this discord between 'dignity' and the realities of suffering arose from cherishing rationality. Leopardi saw faith in reason and its centrality to progress as one of the greatest misunderstandings of the Enlightenment: 'there is no doubt that the progress of reason and the extinction of illusions produce barbarism, and an excessively enlightened population certainly does not become highly civilized'.[30]

This attitude to reason, one recognizable throughout *Watt* in its final form, is also echoed in the Romanticism of the poems Quin found particularly pertinent to his sense of existence. The novel Beckett had in mind at this stage is therefore operating within two contextual spheres: first, the Leopardian tradition of sceptical pessimism suspicious of reason; second, the historical context of the early decades of the twentieth century both in Ireland and on

---

[28] One of the chapters in the guide to Italian literature Beckett read while at university, *Disegno storico della letteratura italiana* by Raffaello Fornaciari, contains a chapter on 'Leopardi and Pessimism'. Though there are no reading traces in this chapter in an otherwise heavily annotated volume, Leopardi's name is underlined in the copy of Plumarcher's study of pessimism which Beckett also owned (*Beckett Digital Manuscript Project* 'Library' Module, eds. Dirk Van Hulle, Mark Nixon and Vincent Neyt, 2017, https://www.beckettarchive.org/library). For a discussion of the various ways that 'Romanticism' might be understood in terms of the pessimistic or the negative, see Eberhard Alsen, 'Introduction', in *The New Romanticism*, ed. Eberhard Alsen (London: Routledge, 2000), 5–7.

[29] Frank Rosengarten, *Giacomo Leopardi's Search for a Common Life through Poetry* (Madison, NJ: Fairleigh Dickinson University Press, 2012), 204.

[30] Leopardi, *Zibaldone*, ed. and trans. Michael Caesar et al. (Birmingham: Faroux, Straus and Giroux, 2013), 23–24.

the European continent in which various forms of barbarous thought were rationalized by certain members of the intellectual classes. Before the war, in a discussion on Schopenhauer with Thomas MacGreevy, Beckett used Leopardi to differentiate two traditions, one of which he commends and one which he rejects: '[Schopenhauer is] worth the examination of one who is interested in Leopardi & Proust rather than in Carducci & Barrès.'[31] Against a European poetics and philosophy of pessimism, Beckett compared Maurice Barrès, an anti-Semitic nationalist who endorsed a eugenic state policy predicated on racial hierarchies. Once France fell to the Nazis and was governed by occupying and Vichy forces, this intellectual realm became a political reality with frightening speed; this is the immediate context in which Beckett wrote *Watt*. There was perhaps some comfort in returning to the familiar space of the Big House while writing, but Beckett did not let it stay comfortable for long.

Though the published version of *Watt* loses the extended passages on Quin's existence, the attitude of Leopardi echoes throughout the published text's mockery of the unbounded rationalism adopted by Watt to engage with his experiences in the Knott household. Barbaric reason underpinned modern race ideology in Europe – that much was made apparent in Beckett's visit to Nazi Germany in the late 1930s – and Beckett was acutely aware of the different forms this could take, be it French nationalism (Barrès), Nazi ideology or the ongoing fantasies of the Ascendency in Ireland. Each of these contexts in some way provides *Watt* with its political charge. Before getting there, though, Beckett works through the more historically embedded life of Quin, whose affinities with Leopardi and sense of nothingness remain part of *Watt's* foundations.

Despite his studies and literary affinities, Quin's attempts to investigate or negate his dominant feeling are ultimately rendered of little consequence: 'it was simply the sensation of being nothing, in the midst of an unbroken waste, under a cloudless sky, and no other'.[32] Echoing the 'gloomy waste' so central to 'Wild Broom', the narrative positions Quin in a recognizably Leopardi-cum-Schopenhauer notion of an indifferent and crushing universe:

> The two forces that thus threatened to grind Quin's soul into its component atoms, were: on the one hand the sens [*sic*] of kinship with, on the other that of estrangement from, the All.[33]

---

[31] Letter to MacGreevy, July 1930, *The Letters of Samuel Beckett I*, eds Martha Dow Fehsenfeld and Lois More Overbeck (Cambridge: Cambridge University Press, 2009), 33.
[32] *Watt* TS, 53.
[33] *Watt* TS, 59.

Ensnared in the conception of a universe whose 'forces' of 'suffering' are 'without intermittence', Quin is ground down to dust. However, while Schopenhauer and Leopardi point to ways of enduring the suffering to which humanity is subjected, the futility with which Quin is beset is soon made apparent:

> In other words, Quin felt himself null, in order to continue in his being. Other descriptions than the above could be given of that which is above described. But the result would be the same.
> So much for the nothingness.[34]

Parody of both the intellectual and aristocratic classes of pre-war Europe is at play in the character of Quin, who is briefly an inspiring scholar seeking relief for the nothingness of his life (some authorial self-parody at work, undoubtedly). He is also a member of the declining class in Ireland who, intellectuals like Yeats reasoned, could be revived through anti-democratic and eugenic means. We do not need to look far to locate in the text's denunciation of Ascendency restoration the ideas also voiced by European fascists and other extreme right-wing groups, the Nazis above all, which used bogus race science to rationalize a politics of extermination. The irony of Quin is that his family have self-exterminated through mishap and illness; with them, their political clout and symbolism disappear into history. Scrutiny of eugenic reasoning lingers in *Watt* even after Quin disappears in the manuscripts, such as in the depiction of the tenants surrounding Mr Knott's house. These multiple layers are condensed, to use Seán Kennedy's term, allowing Beckett to engage with multiple historical and political strands at once in order to probe the deeper structural and intellectual systems at work. In constructing Quin/Mr Knott around a central 'nothingness' that is only briefly eased, though not cured, by the Romantic, counter-Enlightenment poetry of Leopardi, Beckett draws together both the rejection of the Anglo-Irish Ascendency ideals of lineage, hierarchy and cultural significance with a cultural heritage attuned to the implications of barbaric reason and its relationship to war and suffering. Amid the terrors of essentialized thinking which the war represented, Quin is, in his nothingness, ironically shored up against the very forces which brought Europe and the world to conflict. If the fascistic thinking of Nazism and late-Yeatsian rhetoric relies on the clear definition of identity within structures of power, Quin survives, at least until he is written out, by feeling 'himself null', fuelled by a Romantic, post-Leopardian nothingness that, whatever else his worth, allows him to 'continue in his being'.

---

[34] *Watt* TS, 59.

Bibliography

Ackerley, C. J. *Obscure Locks, Simple Keys: The Annotated Watt*. Tallahassee: Journal of Beckett Studies Books, 2005.

Alsen, Eberhard. 'Introduction'. In *The New Romanticism*, edited by Eberhard Alsen. London: Routledge, 2000. 1–27.

Beckett, Samuel. *The Letters of Samuel Beckett I*, edited by Martha Dow Fehsenfeld and Lois More Overbeck. Cambridge: Cambridge University Press, 2009.

———. *The Letters of Samuel Beckett II*, edited by George Craig, Martha Dow Fehsenfeld, Dan Gunn and Lois More Overbeck. Cambridge: Cambridge University Press, 2011.

———. *Watt*. London: Faber and Faber, 2009.

———. *Watt* Manuscripts and Typescripts, Harry Ransom Center, University of Texas at Austin. *Beckett Digital Manuscript Project*, Library Module, https://www.beckettarchive.org/library.

Bixby, Patrick. *Samuel Beckett and the Postcolonial Novel*. Cambridge: Cambridge University Press, 2009.

Caselli, Daniela. 'Beckett's Intertextual Modalities of Appropriation: The Case of Leopardi'. *Journal of Beckett Studies* 6, Issue 1 (1996): 1–24.

Cauchi-Santoro, Roberta. *Beyond the Suffering of Being: Desire in Giacomo Leopardi and Samuel Beckett*. Florence: Firenze University Press, 2016.

Davies, William. *Historicising Samuel Beckett's Post-Humanism*, PhD Thesis, 2018. https://centaur.reading.ac.uk/80000/

——— 'Narrating Disruption: Realist Fiction and the Politics of Form in *Watt*'. In *Beckett Beyond the Normal*, edited by Seán Kennedy, 33–46. Edinburgh: Edinburgh University Press, 2020.

Harrington, John. *The Irish Beckett*. Syracuse: Syracuse University Press, 1991.

Kennedy, Seán. 'Bid us Sigh on from Day to Day: Beckett and the Irish Big House'. In *The Edinburgh Companion to Samuel Beckett and the Arts*, edited by Stanley E. Gontarski, 222–34. Edinburgh: Edinburgh University Press, 2014.

Leopardi, Giacomo. Canti, translated by Jonathan Galassi. New York: Farrar, Straus and Giroux, 2014. E-book.

———. Zibaldone, edited and translated by Michael Caesar et al. Birmingham: Farrar, Straus and Giroux, 2013.

McCormack, W. J. *From Burke to Beckett: Ascendancy, Tradition and Betrayal in Literary History*. Cork: Cork University Press, 1994.

Mills Harper, George and Walter Kelly Hood, ed. *A Critical Edition of Yeats's A Vision*. Basingstoke: Palgrave Macmillan, 1978.

Moynahan, Julian. *Anglo-Irish: The Literary Imagination in a Hyphenated Culture*. Princeton: Princeton University Press, 1995.

Pritchard, William H., ed. *W. B. Yeats: A Critical Anthology*. London: Penguin, 1972.

Rosengarten, Frank. *Giacomo Leopardi's Search for a Common Life through Poetry*. Madison, NJ: Fairleigh Dickinson University Press, 2012.

Schopenhauer, Arthur. *The World as Will and Representation*. Project Gutenberg edition. https://www.gutenberg.org/files/40868/40868-h/40868-h.html.

Sullivan, K. 'The Ecology of the Irish Big House, 1900–1950'. In *A History of Irish Literature and the Environment*, edited by Malcolm Sen, 173–89. Cambridge: Cambridge University Press, 2022.

Van Hulle, Dirk and Mark Nixon. *Samuel Beckett's Library*. Cambridge: Cambridge University Press, 2013.

Yeats, W. B. *The Collected Works of W.B. Yeats Volume I: The Poems*, edited by Richard J. Finneran, 2nd edition. London: Prentice Hall & IBD, 1997.

Part Four

ECHOES. TRANSLATIONS, REVERBERATIONS

Chapter 8

BECKETT RESONATING IN ITALY: WHICH TEXT, WHOSE VOICE?

Rossana Sebellin

Abstract

This paper deals with the issue of translating a self-translated text, focusing on the Italian version of *Waiting for Godot* by Carlo Fruttero published by Einaudi. In the 1950s, the status of self-translator was still unclear both for the author, who was developing the habit after the success of his first play, and for Fruttero. This produced a situation somewhat confusing: Fruttero translated originally the French play, but several modifications were later introduced starting from the English version in new issues in collected volumes. This was never disclosed in the paratext. The result is that two different Einaudi versions of the Italian *Godot* are available in the market today, one strictly from the very first French edition by Minuit, the other occasionally integrating or modifying from the English version by Beckett, which had in the meantime come out.

Keywords: Beckett drama translation; self-translation; Italian translations; *Waiting for Godot* Italian translations

The aim of this chapter is to draw a picture of the translation of Beckett's drama into Italian. The working hypothesis is: is it time for new translations?

Before delving into the subject matter, it may be useful to mention that Beckett's studies in Italy are, so far, still quite fanned out in three relatively independent branches: English Studies since the late 1960s, French Studies and Comparative Literature Studies. In this maze of independent and largely self-referring scholarly debate was Beckett made known to the Italian public. It is relevant to keep this in mind because it bears on the kind of approach scholars, editors and publishers have had towards the epiphenomenon of Beckett's bilingual and self-translated drama.

This contribution will consider the translation of Beckett's drama in Italy, focusing in particular on *En attendant Godot/ Waiting for Godot*, but before attempting any description of the situation in its context, it is perhaps useful to outline a minimal theoretical framework in which to place the observation of the actual facts.

Although several scholars, among which myself, have written on the topic of Beckett's bilingualism and self-translation, and from multiple approaches, in relatively recent years, Chiara Montini has very effectively posed the problem of how to translate a self-translator. She deals with this in several studies, but I refer here to one article that appeared in Italy in 2013: 'Tradurre un testo autotradotto: *Mercier et/and/e Camier*'.[1]

Although Montini discusses here this specific case of self-translated text, one Rainier Grutman would label as 'delayed self-translation',[2] she (among others) investigates not only the theoretical problem but also the very pragmatic question of how to approach a self-translated text in a third language. French- and English-speaking readers and audiences encounter no such problems, and to some extent neither do German speakers, since translations into German were carried out with the constant contribution of the author, and they were therefore approved and sanctioned as the official German versions. The situation is very different in the case of the Italian language, where there are two possible source texts, and almost no supervision from Beckett. The usual approach dictates starting with the text that was written first, but even this approach may not be so easy in the case of an author like Beckett as some of his plays are what Grutman labels 'simultaneous translation'[3] (e.g. *Play/Comédie* and *Come and Go/ Va et vient*), therefore making it difficult even to establish chronological if not ontological order. At any rate, this does not qualify as an objective criterion. The second text, for example, could be considered an improvement on a first draft: so the second text should be chosen as the most updated and reliable. Or perhaps, the source language should be taken into consideration: translators working towards a Neo-Latin language should translate from the French version, and translators working towards a Germanic language from the English one, to promote lexical and syntactic consistency. Moreover, translations that are not self-translation can

---

[1] Chiara Montini, 'Tradurre un testo autotradotto: *Mercier et/and/e Camier*', in *Autotraduzione e riscrittura*, eds Andrea Ceccherelli, Gabriella Elina Imposti, Monica Perotto (Bologna: Bononia University Press, 2013), 141–51.

[2] Rainier Grutman, 'Beckett e oltre: autotraduzioni orizzontali e verticali', in *Autotraduzione e riscrittura*, eds Andrea Ceccherelli, Gabriella Elina Imposti, Monica Perotto (Bologna: Bononia University Press, 2013), 45–60 (48).

[3] Rainier Grutman, 'Self-translation', in *The Routledge Encyclopedia of Translation Studies* (Second Edition), eds Mona Baker and Gabriela Saldanha (London and New York: Routledge, 2009), 257–60 (259).

and of course do undergo an ageing process, especially when there are major shifts in perspective, language use and hermeneutics.

Back to Montini and the theoretical problems in the case she poses, translating a self-translator simplifies and at the same time complicates things for the translator. It simplifies some aspects because the second text can disambiguate certain passages and the solution the author has provided can help the translator. For Italian translators, for example, the French version of a text self-translated from English can help choices and avoid misinterpretations, since Italian and French, sharing a common Latin origin, show in many cases some lexical proximity. But translating a self-translated text is also a complicated business, as the translator has to constantly check and compare two texts that can present various degrees of discrepancies. If, as Umberto Eco wrote, translating is a negotiating process,[4] involving decision-making at literally every word, working with two texts means additional choices have to be considered, layering the text with a labyrinth of alternative options.

This in turn raises another theoretical question, long debated and infinitely debatable, which can only be mentioned here, namely the status and the concept of originality. Self-translation can be considered as a threat to the ontological and hermeneutical certainty of a text: any self-translated work has a duplicated original text, especially in the case of Beckett who in some cases composed the two versions at the same time (the previously mentioned 'simultaneous translations'[5]), the two texts influencing each other. In fact, the status of a fixed original, untouchable text is quite fluid in the author's mind too: in the case of *Krapp's Last Tape*, for example, while translating it into French, he decided a certain expression he had devised was a better option and in October 1958 asked Alan Schneider who was staging *Krapp's Last Tape* in the US to include a minor variation to the English text: 'wonderful woman though', in French becomes 'merveilleuse vieille cependant', and then Beckett decided he would change the English text for the American representation into 'wonderful old woman though'.[6]

When Montini approached the translation of *Mercier et / and Camier* into Italian (published by Einaudi in 2015), she was of course faced with two texts with macroscopic variations, the English version one-third shorter than the French one, extensively reduced in the process of self-translation. The French text,

---

[4] Umberto Eco, *Dire quasi la stessa cosa* (Milano: Bompiani, 2003). In particular, see chapter 4, 'Significato, interpretazione, negoziazione', 83–94.
[5] Rainier Grutman, 'Self-translation', 259.
[6] Maurice Harmon (ed.), *No Author Better Served: The Correspondence of Samuel Beckett and Alan Schneider* (Cambridge, Massachusetts and London, England: Harvard University Press, 1998), 49. (Letter dated 18 October 1958.)

written in the 1940s and published in 1970 by Minuit, was subsequently published also in English in 1974 by Calder and Boyars; Beckett had worked at the English translation intermittently since the late 1940s. To some extent, the previous translator of the novel into Italian (Luigi Buffarini) considered only one text and used the French. However, for what concerns *Murphy*, for example, the first translation in Italian by Franco Quadri (1962) was based on Beckett's translation into French carried out with Alfred Péron, and only in 2003 Gabriele Frasca translated the novel again from the English version (but with an eye on the French text as well, according to Montini). As mentioned above, conventions seem to imply that one should start from the first version of a text, but this convention can be challenged in the case of a self-translator, as – as we have seen – the second version can be deemed as an improvement on the first: this is particularly true with drama, where the *mise en scène* and productions often influence and modify the texts, as widely demonstrated by several studies. Beckett himself would instruct the Tophovens to consider the English version of *Fin de partie* when rendering it in German, as the two languages share a common origin. And even a canonical text as apparently stable as *Godot* was published in several variations, as Mary Bryden pointed out in her Preface to the Faber edition of 2010.

Montini proposes various solutions as to how a self-translator should be translated, some of them quite provocative, all thought-provoking:

- Translate the first text and ignore the second
- Translate the second and ignore the first
- Translate the first text and signal in footnotes the differences with the second one
- Translate the second text and signal in footnotes the differences from the first one
- Translate from both the first and the second texts, integrating the two originals
- Publish two different versions, one translated from the French and the other from the English text
- Publish two translations, each with the original version on the left page
- Publish two versions with their respective originals, thus having to display four texts simultaneously.

To these somewhat challenging ideas I would like to add yet another one, for the sake of completeness: publish a translated version with both the originals, in a trilingual edition.

I mention this possibility because in 1983 Giulio Einaudi – who had been virtually expelled from his own publishing company – was given a minor collection to direct, and he, together with Valerio Magrelli, created the series called *Scrittori tradotti da scrittori*, where they published several trilingual versions of texts, among which Beckett appears twice: with *Mal vu, mal dit* (n. 58 of the series), translated into Italian by Renzo Guidieri and edited by Nadia Fusini; and Joyce's *Anna Livia Plurabelle*, translated into French by Beckett and others and into Italian by Joyce and Nino Frank; in appendix, there is a further version translated by Luigi Schenoni. The volume has an introduction by Umberto Eco and was edited by Rosa Maria Bollettieri Bosinelli. The series was discontinued in 2000. The introduction to Joyce's volume by Eco gives a definition of what it is to be a self-translator:

> Ma quando il traduttore è l'autore [...] ecco che questo autore può tradurre cercando di rimanere fedele non al suo testo così come si è depositato nella lingua di origine, ma alla sua poetica, che avrebbe potuto dare origine (e di fatto la dà) a un altro testo che ne rappresenti la realizzazione inedita in altra lingua.[7]
>
> [But when the translator is also the author [...] this author can translate trying to remain faithful not so much to his/her own text as it has taken form in his/her original language, but rather to his/her poetics which could have produced (and which in fact does produce) another text which represents its original fulfilment in another language. (All translations from Italian, unless otherwise stated, are mine.)]

I have always found that this quote is particularly apt to be read together with the Proustian idea of writing as translation. So, after all, we are faced with the possibility of a duplicated original or with the idea that neither is original, and that – to quote Gabriele Frasca again

> è come se avessimo a che fare con due "testimoni" di un originale che non c'è [...]. È una bella questione [...] perché s'intravede, nell'originale che non c'è, una lingua che non c'è (*french? anglais? franglais?*). E bisogna, da traduttore terzo, imparare a frequentarla, questa lingua che non c'è.[8]
>
> [it is as if we had to do with two "testimonies" of a non-existent original [...]. It is an interesting question [...] because, in this non-existent original, one can catch a glimpse of a non-existent language (*French? Anglais? Franglais?*). And, as a third language translator, one needs to learn how to become familiar with this non-existent language.]

---

[7] Umberto Eco, 'Introduzione', in James Joyce, *Anna Livia Plurabelle*, Italian translation by James Joyce and Nino Frank (Torino: Einaudi, 1996), V–XXIX (XVII).

[8] Giancarlo Alfano (ed.), 'Traduzioni', in *Tegole dal cielo. L'"effetto Beckett" nella cultura italiana*, eds Giancarlo Alfano and Andrea Cortellessa (Roma: EDUP, 2006), 241–65 (258).

Beckett's *Waiting for Godot* Staged and Translated in Italy

Nothing of all the above-mentioned debate was evident for the first translators of Beckett's drama in Italy. Beckett's bilingualism was known and a source of interest for this Irish Parisian, but the self-translating habit was yet to become customary.

As widely argued, drama translation holds a peculiar space in the field of translation studies, as Bassnett points out in her seminal work on the subject: drama has to do with more than a literary language and has to consider other semiotic functions as well, and accordingly drama translations can stem from different impulses and have different aims: some texts are translated to be published and read, others to be staged. And in general, the status of dramatic texts has been debated in history and considered somewhat of less literary value compared to other genres, due to the fact their existence comes to life on the stage. This happened with Beckett's first text as well: the first translations of *Godot* were not published but were simply used for staging, testifying to the position of dramatic texts when it comes to their translation. Very soon, though, once the literary quality of Beckett's plays as well as Beckett's own literary fame became firmly established, it was clear a published translation was due and the rights were bought from one of the most prominent publishers in Italy: Einaudi, based in Turin.

The relationship between Beckett and Italy, from the point of view of first reactions to his dramatic work, was an ambiguous one. Initial reports from Paris on Italian journals were not particularly appreciative: a review in February 1953 by Marcel Le Duc, written for the periodical *Il Dramma*, reads: 'È una commedia tristissima, ricca di una profonda malinconia e fa stare in ansia per due ore. [...] una commedia molto probabilmente priva di estro, ma non di buone intenzioni; appena sgrossata, ma efficace, estremamente ben recitata [...] Non si direbbe (o parrebbe) ma questa commedia suscita perfino degli entusiasmi.'[9]

In spite of that Beckett was an immediate object of interest in Italy. The Paris production was invited to the Piccolo Teatro in Milan as early as 1953 as the Parisian *pièce* of the season. According to Franco Quadri, though, the Piccolo Teatro di Milano 'per nemesi storica diverrà, dopo quel battesimo,

---

[9] Marcel Le Duc, 'Il giallo tra le fauci. Parigi', *Il Dramma* 174 (Febbraio 1953): 44–46 (46). ('It is an extraordinarily sad comedy, full of a deep melancholy, and it makes one anxious for a couple of hours. [...] a comedy probably lacking in inspiration, but full of good intentions; just about roughed off, but effective and very well acted [...] One would not have said (or even thought) so, but the play has even kindled some enthusiastic reactions.')

il nemico ufficiale dello scrittore e un pesante ostacolo alla sua diffusione italiana',[10] all in the name of a supposed ideological, Manichean clash between 'razionalità contro irrazionalismo, Brecht contro Beckett'.[11] In fact, it is not until the fall of ideologies that Beckett could have an unreserved success and circulation in Italy, therefore in the late 1980s and especially after 1989.

The very first performance of *Godot* in Italian did not happen on stage, but on the Italian radio, as had happened in France: the more famous one was broadcast on 6 April 1955, Rai, directed and translated by Luciano Mondolfo; but there was a previous translation by Romeo Lucchese broadcast on 28 May 1954, directed by Piero Masserano Taricco, which, according to Domenico Scarpa, lasted 82 minutes.[12]

The first staging was in Rome, in November 1954 at the Teatro di via Vittoria, directed and translated by Mondolfo. The precise and documented reconstruction of Annamaria Cascetta places the production in the context of the 'fringe' group *I Gobbi*, which decided to stage the play: the company was mainly involved with cabaret productions and a variety of comedic types of performances. Because of that, they were so determined to establish this specific text as high-brow that they erased from the text everything likely to be funny or vulgar.[13] Therefore no cursing or offensive language, and a general taming of the Beckettian sharp language. The resulting paradox is that the elements of vaudeville and cabaret, ever so present in the text by Beckett, were ignored or reduced by a cabaret company which were in fact perfectly trained to make the most of the comic aspects and of the rhythm of Godot's speeches. Beckett was at any rate shunned by institutional, official theatres and quite loved and often performed by minor companies, which acted in smaller venues. At least at the very beginning.

The first Italian staging of *Fin de partie* was in September 1958 in Rome (directed by Andrea Camilleri) with the title *Il gioco è alla fine*, even though the original French production had been performed in Venice at the Biennale in 1958. With the same title, it was staged in Milan, in October 1959 (directed by Aldo Trionfo). In general, as many studies have shown, Italian productions very closely follow the first performances in France, Germany and the UK.

---

[10] Franco Quadri, 'Beckett in Italia', in *Le ceneri della commedia*, ed. Sergio Colomba (Roma: Bulzoni, 1997), 361–66 (361). ('[the Piccolo Teatro] in a sort of historical nemesis, after that baptism, has become the author's official enemy and a very substantial obstacle for its Italian circulation.')

[11] Ibid. ('rationality vs irrationalism, Brecht vs Beckett')

[12] Domenico Scarpa, 'Come Uno. Beckett & Borges, Fruttero & Lucentini', in *Tegole dal cielo. L'"effetto Beckett" nella cultura italiana*, 21–37 (26).

[13] Annamaria Cascetta, *Il tragico e l'umorismo. Studio sulla drammaturgia di Samuel Beckett* (Firenze: Le lettere, 2010). In particular, see the section 'La fortuna scenica italiana', 264–327.

Publication

For what concerns publication, Carlo Fruttero can be considered the mediator of Beckett's drama in Italy. A translator and later an author in his own right, Fruttero had moved to France in 1947 and began translating for Einaudi, having been co-opted by Italo Calvino. The well-established publishing company had been founded by Giulio Einaudi (son of the Italian President Luigi Einaudi) in 1933 with a strong, open anti-fascist aim and was based in Turin. The cultural and political ambition of the publishing company was immediately clear, and all the very young founders were at various times prosecuted: Giulio himself being sent first to prison and then exiled.

In the 1950s, Einaudi was flourishing and brimming with ideas (even if not always able to mediate efficiently between cultural penchant and financial wisdom) and had several different collections to implement. In 1953, Fruttero was asked to coordinate between the two directors of the new series about drama (*Collezione di teatro*), providing new international authors. In the appointing letter Luciano Foà wrote to him, it is clearly stated what the job Fruttero had to do was: 'Lei farà per noi revisioni di traduzioni e di bozze, lettura di libri [...], ricerche di biblioteca, *segnalazioni di novità estere*'[14] and more. As previously mentioned, Calvino himself had decided to appoint Fruttero for the position: 'Mi pare che sia una soluzione molto buona, che permetterà la ripresa della collana. Fruttero ha passione per il teatro, è aggiornato, è radiodrammaturgo, è pieno di qualità.'[15]

Fruttero appreciated Beckett's drama and instantly grasped its importance, as testified by his immediate solicitation to Einaudi to buy the rights to Beckett's work, and as further clarified in his preface to the first publication of *Waiting for Godot* in 1956, with his translation. At the beginning, Fruttero proposed a miscellaneous volume with plays by Beckett, Adamov and Ionesco. This idea did not encounter with Giulio Einaudi's approval (he would prefer three small volumes rather than a bulky one), and was also rejected by Beckett, who was absolutely against the idea of being published in a miscellany. That is most probably the reason why *Godot* only appeared in 1956, when the translation had been ready long before. Even Franco Lucentini had been involved in the publishing issues, as Lindon had threatened to withdraw

---

[14] Luciano Foà to Carlo Fruttero, 14 April 1953, quoted in Domenico Scarpa, 'Come uno', 24. Emphasis mine. ('You will do for us proofreading, translations revision, book reading, bibliographic research, recommendation of novelties from abroad')

[15] Italo Calvino to Gerardo Guerrieri, 14 November 1953, quoted in Domenico Scarpa, 'Come uno', 24. ('I think this is a very good solution, which may enable the series to flourish again. Fruttero is passionate about the theatre, keeps himself up to date, is a radio drama playwright, and is full of good qualities.')

the rights to Einaudi to give them to Garzanti if the volume was to be further delayed. Garzanti had obtained the rights for Beckett's prose and was trying to also acquire the ones for drama. Foà had sent a telegram to Lucentini and had rushed to Minuit in order to reassure Jérôme Lindon that Einaudi was finally going to come out with *Godot*, which appeared in June 1956. The slim volume had a preface by Fruttero where he mercilessly criticizes Beckett's prose (which he evidently had not been able to appreciate) but highly praises this play.

When Fruttero began translating Beckett, in many cases, there was only one text available to him, the French one. This was the case for *Godot* (even if by the time it was finally published in Italian the English version had been issued both in the USA by Grove Press, in 1954, and in the UK by Faber in 1956), and for *Endgame*. But later on, Beckett began attesting himself as a self-translator, even if the full extent of the implications connected to this fact were not completely grasped until much later by scholars and publishers. Fruttero's attitude towards Beckett's bilingualism (or 'equilingualism',[16] according to Frasca's definition) is quite casual if not indifferent: on several occasions he stated he used whatever was sent to Einaudi, regardless of the first language a play was written in. In other cases, though, he claims to have consulted both versions in order to carry out his own translation.

Fruttero, who in the course of his career found Beckett increasingly difficult to translate, also mentions that the self-translated second version was considered a help:

> Si vanno a controllare certe interiezioni, le sfumature di un'ingiuria, un *hélas* che di colpo sembra essenziale conservare in v.o.; e si passa a indagare come Beckett abbia tradotto se stesso dal francese in inglese e viceversa, che cosa abbia modificato emigrando da una tradizione, da una cultura all'altra, quali sfumature abbia dovuto precisare o abbandonare nel transito.[17]
>
> [One checks certain interjections, the nuances of an insult, a *hélas* which suddenly becomes necessary to preserve in the original French; and one then explores how Beckett translated himself from French into English and vice versa, what he modified migrating from a tradition and culture into another, what shades he had to clarify or abandon in transit.]

In an interview published in 2006, Fruttero relates how he stumbled upon Beckett by chance and how he had to consult the author about his own translation. For *Godot*, he sent the typescript and received a letter by Beckett

---

[16] Gabriele Frasca, 'Beckett & Beckett: il doppio come identità', in *Testo a fronte. Per il centenario di Samuel Beckett*, n. 35, 2006, edited by Andrea Inglese and Chiara Montini, 174–78, (177).

[17] Carlo Fruttero, 'Nel silenzio di Beckett', in *Samuel Beckett: Teatro completo*, ed. Paolo Bertinetti (Torino: Einaudi-Gallimard, 1994), xi–xv (xiv).

with all the alterations the author required: a couple of material mistakes, but mostly Beckett reintroduced lexical repetitions that Fruttero had not seen or appreciated for what they were and that Beckett, of course, wished to reinsert. From that episode onward, Fruttero claims that he would always consult Beckett, and he also went to visit him in Paris. On that specific occasion, Beckett asked him to read the translated lines aloud 'per sentire come suonassero, se fossero vicini alle sue intenzioni'.[18]

Gabriele Frasca in 2006 wrote that when he started translating Beckett and approached the author, Beckett was incredibly generous and kind with him, writing back and providing volumes Frasca was finding difficult to get hold of in Italy; he adds that at some point he started writing to him in Italian, 'lingua che Beckett conosceva benissimo, a sua detta meglio del tedesco [...] avrebbe del resto collaborato alle traduzioni delle sue opere in italiano, come fece con quelle tedesche dei Tophoven, se i nostri editori non l'avessero scoraggiato'.[19] So the small, unrecorded and virtually unrecognized collaboration between Fruttero and Beckett could have been much deeper and more effective.

This correspondence between Fruttero and Beckett is not among the letters which were published between 2009 and 2016. In fact, in the four volumes edited by George Craig, Martha Fehsenfeld, Dan Gurr and Lois Overbeck, Fruttero is barely mentioned and Beckett speaks quite disparagingly (and maybe slightly unfairly) about both the translations of *Godot*: the first, by Mondolfo, is defined as 'assez quelconque' ('pretty ordinary'),[20] and the second one by Fruttero labelled 'not a brilliant job, but faithful enough'.[21] Later on, Beckett also comments on Fruttero's preface to the Einaudi edition in 1956: 'Aspettando Godot [*sic*] is out from Einaudi with a foolish preface by the translator'.[22] Mondolfo's translation may be quite inadequate (Fruttero deemed it too literary, lacking the informal quality required by Godot's dialogues), while Fruttero was a man of theatre and had the sense of rhythm needed in a theatrical dialogue, especially one by Beckett.

---

[18] Giancarlo Alfano (ed.), 'Traduzioni', *Tegole dal cielo. L'"effetto Beckett" nella cultura italiana*, 242. ('To hear what they sounded like, if they were similar to his intentions.')

[19] Ibid., 255–56. ('a language Beckett knew very well, better than German according to him... he – on the other hand – would have worked on the translations of his writings into Italian, as he did with the German ones with the Tophovens, hadn't he been discouraged by our publishers.')

[20] Samuel Beckett to Jérôme Lindon, 14 October 1954, in *The Letters of Samuel Beckett*, eds George Craig, Martha Dow Fehsenfeld, Dan Gurr and Lois More Overbeck, vol. 2 (Cambridge: Cambridge University Press, 2011), 503–4.

[21] Samuel Beckett to Barney Rosset, 15 March 1956, in *The Letters of Samuel Beckett*, eds Craig, Fehsenfeld, Gurr and Overbeck, 608–9.

[22] Samuel Beckett to Nancy Cunard, 4 July 1956, in *The Letters of Samuel Beckett*, eds Craig, Fehsenfeld, Gurr and Overbeck, 631.

According to Gabriele Frasca, who translated Beckett's prose and poetry, the author's bilingualism was used as a shortcut by publishers to the point that 'tutte le opere teatrali beckettiane, per lo meno fino a *Play*, sono state tradotte dal francese, anche quando la prima stesura era in inglese'.[23]

The current situation for what concerns Beckett's dramatic works is as follows:

Carlo Fruttero translated *En attendant Godot* (1956), *Fin de partie* (1961), *Acte sans paroles I* (1961), *Acte sans paroles II* (1968), *All That Fall* (1961), *Krapp's Last Tape* (1968), *Embers* (1961), *Happy Days* (1961), *Words and Music* (1968), *Cascando* (1968), *Play* (1968), *Come and Go* (1968) and *Eh, Joe* (1968).

Carlo Fruttero and Franco Lucentini translated *That Time* (1976), *A Piece of Monologue* (1982), *Rockaby* (1982) and *Ohio Impromptu* (1982).

Floriana Bossi translated *Fragment de Théâtre 1* (1978), *Fragment de Théâtre 2* (1978), *Esquisse radiophonique* (1978), *Pochade radiophonique* (1978), *Breath* (1978), *Footfalls* (1978), *Ghost Trio* (1978), ... *but the clouds* ... (1978).

Camillo Pennati translated *The Old Tune* (1982), *Quoi où* (1982), *Nacht und Träume* (1982), *Catastrophe* (Fr) (1982), *Quad* (1982) and *The Old Tune* (1982).

John Francis Lane translated *Not I* (1974).

Maria Giovanna Andreolli translated *Film* (1982).

The Translation of *Godot*

When Fruttero started working on his translation (not when he finished, when he began), only one text was available to him: the French *Godot*. But in 1956, the English *Godot* had already been published and Beckett had already experienced wide international recognition. Fruttero translated from the French text, even though both the French and the English texts could have been available to him at the time. But, as already mentioned, Beckett's status as a bilingual, self-translating author was not well established neither with the author himself nor in his scholarly reputation.

The situation of the various editions is not as straightforward as it may appear and needs to be detailed. The first Einaudi translation (1956) closely followed the first Minuit edition issued in 1952. This Minuit edition was amended by Beckett after the staging of the play in early 1953, but the copyright edition in any Minuit publications is and remains 1952, even if the text has undergone some minor cuts. An edition of the text based on the first Minuit edition is the 1963 Collier-Macmillan edited by Germaine Brée and Eric Schoenfeld,

---

[23] Giancarlo Alfano (ed.), 'Traduzioni', *Tegole dal cielo. L'"effetto Beckett" nella cultura italiana*, 257. ('All dramatic works, at least up to *Play* were translated from the French even when the first version was in English.')

which still presents the excerpts later deleted from the official French edition. The first Italian translation was published in 1956 and, being based on the first Minuit edition, incorporates all the parts subsequently purged. In 1961, a collection of Beckett's drama was published by Einaudi including several texts[24] among which *Aspettando Godot*, but this version underwent numerous amendments and revisions that were never acknowledged by the publishing company (same copyright, same translator and never any mention of a revised translation): in the following pages, I will try to show what kind of changes were made and what text they are based on. I will also add that even the *Teatro completo*, published by the prestigious Einaudi-Gallimard in 1994, employed the text from the 1961 edition.

It is very clear from the first Italian edition (Einaudi 1956) that the English version was not taken into consideration and that only the first Minuit edition was the source of the translation. There are several indications which testify to the fact that Fruttero had only this first French text when he began working on his translation, which was concluded and ready much earlier than it actually came out, since the publication was delayed for the abovementioned internal conflicts within Einaudi. For the 1961 edition, though, it is evident that Fruttero used his own previous translation, therefore based on the French *Godot*, but that he possibly brought it up to date with the new French edition and that he also consulted the English text, the resulting Italian version a sort of collation between the two texts.

There are several differences between the two editions, too many to record them all. I will therefore concentrate on three main elements: proof that both Italian translations originate from the French text; proof that the second revised edition contains elements that are directly linked to the English text, and traces in the first translation that derive from the very first Minuit edition and have been deleted very early on, not appearing in any French Minuit edition after the first. I will navigate among the amendments that clearly stem from different

---

[24] There are several collections issued at intervals, which added texts sometimes as soon as they were published. I refer here to *Teatro*, issued in 1961, which included *Aspettando Godot; Finale di partita; Atto senza parole; Tutti quelli che cadono; L'ultimo nastro di Krapp; Ceneri; Atto senza parole 2; Giorni felici*; the following edition, issued in 1968, included additional texts: *Parole e musica; Commedia; Di' Joe; Respiro; Non io; Quella volta; Cascando* (in a revised edition according to Orlandini, see infra). The same texts were included in the 2002 *Teatro* collection by Einaudi (reissued in a different series in 2005). The 1994 Einaudi-Gallimard (*Teatro completo*) includes all Beckett's dramatic texts. The multiple editions, both as single texts and in collections, make it quite complex to reconstruct the situation with some precision. For a good reconstruction of Beckett's publications in Italy, see Lorenzo Orlandini, 'Bibliografia di Beckett in Italia', in *Tegole dal Cielo. La letteratura italiana nell'opera di Beckett*, edited by Gianfranco Alfano and Andrea Cortellessa (Roma: EDUP, 2006), 196–84.

source text: the first Minuit edition (reproduced in Collier-Macmillan) and the second Minuit edition, with cuts. For references to the Italian versions, I will use a 1956 Einaudi edition and a 1961 (2005) edition in the collection *Teatro*. I have also consulted the bilingual Grove Press edition. For the English texts, I will refer to the Faber text published in 2010.[25]

Always French First

As already stated, both Italian translations are based on the French text. Here are some examples of this instance.

In both Italian versions, we can find the excerpt about sleeping at Godot's in the straw, that was not originally translated by the author. Famously, an actor in Alan Schneider's company asked about it at the time of the US staging in the 1970s: in the letter dated 14 January 1971, Beckett provides the translation which does not appear in Faber editions (nor in the Grove Press bilingual edition) though it was reinstated in the collaboration with Asmus.[26]

In both Italian versions, when Vladimir exits suddenly and Pozzo is rather taken aback, there is this exchange derived from the French: 'Avrebbe dovuto trattenerlo. / Si è trattenuto da sé.' Einaudi 1956, 46 and 2005, 35. The English version is both more explicit and comic: 'He should have waited! / He would have burst' (Faber 32).

In both Italian translations, Estragon, requested his name, answers 'Catullo' (1956, 49; 2005, 37). As is well known, the English version has Adam as an answer.

Toponyms and *realia* are almost always taken from the French text, with the exception of the currency mentioned in the next paragraph. Lucky's monologue, for example, keeps all the French names and references: there is no attempt at reproducing the comic effect of both the originals changing place names for a domesticating effect and altering names to introduce puns in Italian. The mention of 'Bonnelly, a Roussilion' is in both 1956 and 2005 editions (74 and 62, respectively), comes from the French text (Minuit, 80) and is not present in the English one, where Vladimir forgets both the family name and the place.

At the beginning of Act Two, to mention a couple more examples, both Italian translations have the sentence where Vladimir has a linguistic doubt only in the French text: 'C'è mancato un pelo che non ci si impiccasse. (*Riflettendo*)

---

[25] From now on, in order to reduce the number of footnotes, I will indicate in brackets the editions I refer to, followed by page number. The editions are the one mentioned in the paragraph: Einaudi 1956, Einaudi 2005, Minuit 1952, Faber 2010 and Collier-Macmillan 1963.

[26] See Mary Bryden, 'Preface'. In Samuel Beckett, *Waiting for Godot* (London: Faber, 2010), vii–xviii (xiv).

Sì, giusto (*sillabando*) che-non-ci-si-impiccasse' (Einaudi 1956, 73, and 2005, 61). The English has a more direct sentence ('We nearly hanged ourselves from it', Faber 56). The linguistic doubt, a testimony of Beckett's sought-after linguistic uncertainty as a way of distancing himself from his native English, will also appear in later years in English, for example, in *Happy Days*, when Winnie wanders if the correct subject for hair is it or them.

Later on, on the same page, the landscape surrounding the characters is referred to as 'sables' in the French version (Minuit 79) and 'mud' in the English one. Both Italian editions have 'deserto', thus a reference to the sands of the French (Einaudi 1956, 74 and 2005, 62).

Sometimes French, Sometimes English: English Insertions in the French Background

Here are some examples of the various cases where the English text was interwoven with the French text in the Italian translation. The first indication of this attitude is evident from the first page of the two Italian versions: after Vladimir and Estragon meet at the beginning of Act One, the exchange is as follows:

Vladimiro: Sono contento di rivederti. Credevo fossi partito per sempre.	Vladimiro: Sono contento di rivederti. Ti credevo partito per sempre.
Estragone: Anch'io.	Estragone: Anch'io.
Vladimiro: Che si può fare per festeggiare questa riunione? (Einaudi 1956, 19)	Vladimiro: Di nuovo insieme, finalmente! Che si può fare per festeggiare questa riunione? (Einaudi 2005, 7)

The insertion ('Di nuovo insieme, finalmente!') is clearly from the English text: 'Together again at last!' (5), not present in the French text (see Minuit page 9).

On the following page, both Italian versions retain the reference to 1900 (present only in French), but when describing their appearance, Vladimir employs the expression 'Eravamo in gamba, allora' (Einaudi 1956, 20), which is a translation of 'On portait beau alors' (Minuit, 10). In the other version, we read 'Eravamo presentabili, allora', which derives from the adjective 'presentable' used in English (Faber 6).

On the same page, a few lines below, the cabaret banter about feeling pain has a modification of tenses deriving from the two versions: 'Hai male? [...] / se ho male! [...] / Hai avuto male? [...] Se ho avuto male!' (Einaudi 1956, 20), 'Fa male? [...] / se fa male! [...] / Fa male? [...] / Se fa male!' (Einaudi 2005, 8–9). Only the English Godot has all the exchange in the present tense and the repetition, the French has alternation present/present perfect and the variation in the repetition. The amendment in the translation appears to be due to the English text.

Following closely, there is a brief exchange in the 1956 Italian edition which is only present in the French text: it was deleted in the English self-translation and is not there in the 1961 (2005) Italian translation. 'La scuola laica? / Che ne so se era laica o non laica. / Stai confondendo col riformatorio' (Einaudi 1956, 22). A few lines later, the behaviour of Estragon's foot is described as 'Gonfia' (Einaudi 1956, 22) and 'Gonfia a vista d'occhio' (Einaudi 2005, 22). The first is a translation of 'Il enfle' (Minuit, 13), and the second of 'Swelling visibly' (Faber, 8).

In the exchange about the two thieves, which soon takes cabaret rhythm and nuances, the 2005 Einaudi edition integrates an excerpt derived from the English text which is not present in the French one: 'Ma no, stupido! Dalla morte. / Non avevi detto dall'inferno? / Dalla morte, dalla morte' (Einaudi 2005, 11).

A few lines later, when wondering about the appointment with Godot, Vladimir and Estragon in the first translation say: 'Ha detto sabato. [...] Mi pare. / Dopo il lavoro. / Devo aver preso nota' (Einaudi 1956, 25). In the second translation, we have: 'Ha detto sabato. [...] Mi pare. / Ti pare. / Devo aver preso nota' (Einaudi 2005, 13). It is clear that 'dopo il lavoro' is a translation of 'Après le turbin' (Minuit, 17), but the repetition of 'Ti pare' is taken from the English 'You think' (Faber, 11).

The beginning of the joke about the Englishman in the brothel is also changed from 'Dopo essersi ubriacato, un inglese si reca al bordello' (Einaudi 1956, 26) taken from the French ('Un Anglais s'étant enivré se rend au bordel', Minuit 19) to 'Un inglese che ha bevuto un po' più del solito' (Einaudi 2005, 15), which is a direct translation from the English ('An Englishman having drunk a little more than usual', Faber 12).

After the two tramps debate the suicide syllogism about who is to go first in order to both accomplish the deed avoiding an unsuccessful attempt for one of them, Estragon says 'Qui peut le plus peut le moins' (Minuit 21) which was translated as 'chi più può meno può' in 1956 (28), but after the English text was available ('If it hangs you it'll hang anything', Faber 14) it becomes 'Se impicca te, impicca chiunque' in the 2005 Einaudi edition (16), a direct translation from the English.

'Il signore ha per caso delle esigenze speciali?' (Einaudi 1956, 29) is clearly derived from the French text. Instead, 'Vostra Eminenza intende far valere le sue prerogative?' is a translation of the English version (Einaudi 2005, 17).

'E allora, è buona la tua carota? / Uno zuccherino. [...] È deliziosa la tua carota' (Einaudi 1956, 31) follow the French *Godot*. In the revised translation we find 'Com'è la carota? / È una carota. [...] Non dimenticherò mai questa carota' (Einaudi 2005, 19) which follow the English one.

'La mere brodait au tambour' (Minuit, 28) is translated as 'La madre ricamava' (Einaudi 1956, 33). The English version introduces a vulgarity (this instance contradicts Ruby Cohn's general idea that the French mainly introduces obscene language): 'The mother had the clap' (Faber, 19). The second Italian version follows this and has 'La madre aveva lo scolo' (Einaudi 2005, 22). In the next few lines, one of Pozzo's sentences is slightly different in the French and the English texts: the Italian translation follows the first in the 1956 Edition ('Della stessa specie di Pozzo! Di origine divina!', 34) and the English in the 1961 (2005) one ('Della stessa specie di Pozzo! Fatti a immagine e somiglianza di Dio', 22).

The reference to coins follows the French edition in the first translation ('un solo luigi' and 'cinque franchi', Einaudi 1956, 50–51), but after Beckett's change the reference in a reader-oriented translation into English, where only francs are mentioned, the Italian translation follows the same principle and the mention of the less known currency is substituted in both cases with the more commonly popular francs ('dieci franchi' and 'anche solo cinque', Einaudi 2005, 39).

When Pozzo is looking for his missing clock, he comments that 'C'est mon pépé qui me l'a donnée' (Minuit, 59). The English version has '"Twas my grandpa gave it to me!' (Faber, 43). The first Italian translation has 'Me l'ha regalato il mio papalino' (Einaudi 1956, 59): *papalino* a probable misspelling for *paparino*, the familiar, intimate way to refer to one's Father. The second Italian version has 'Un regalo del nonno', thus correcting the previous mistranslation: the French *pépé* means grandfather, therefore *nonno* (Einaudi 1961, 47).

In Act Two, which presents much fewer examples of variations in the Italian translations (mainly stylistic modifications to make the text more up to date linguistically), there is one difference which may derive from the English *Godot*: when Pozzo wants to know what place they are in, he mentions 'la Planche' (Minuit, 113) and 'the Board' in English (Faber, 83). The Italian versions have 'il Palco' (Einaudi 1956, 101) and 'la Tavola' (Einaudi 2005, 88), which seem to follow the French in the first case, and the English in the second.

Cuts and Ghosts

There are about 33 repartees in Act One and 51 in Act Two present in the first Minuit Edition which were subsequently deleted and are not present in any Minuit edition now. These lines, never included in the English text, are still there in the 1956 Einaudi edition of the play, but were expunged from the text of *Aspettando Godot* later included in the collections (from 1961 onwards) of Beckett's dramatic works. Grove Press' bilingual edition has no trace of the missing texts and does not mention the cuts.

The first cut occurs in Act One between the argument about why Lucky does not put down his luggage and the famous 'Nothing happens, nobody comes, nobody goes, it's awful' (Faber, 38). The 33 lines deal with the inability to remember what the characters were talking about and with a frenzy of metatheatrical references to the interruptions that occur constantly in the exchange. This excerpt can be found in the Collier-Macmillan 1963 edition (48–50).

In Act Two, there are seven cuts, scattered through the text and ranging in length from one line here and there to 20 repartees deleted in one single chunk (pages 88, 93, 96–97, 101–2, 104 of the Italian 1956 edition; pages 86, 90, 91, 95, 100–1, 103 of the Collier-Macmillan 1963 edition). The deletions are about repetitions, comments on actions just seen on stage, bickering among characters, mention of other people never seen on stage and so on. The most significant, in my opinion, is about why Pozzo has stopped crying for help: 'Ma non chiede più niente. / Perché ha perso ogni speranza' (Einaudi 1956, 93), a translation of 'Il ne demande plus rien. / C'est qu'il a perdu l'espoir' (Collier-Macmillan, 90). Possibly a too definitive judgement in a rather suspended situation. In fact, later on, Pozzo will in fact ask for help again. The two sentences are absent from both the Minuit edition and the English edition. The Italian translations have cut them from the 1961 edition onward.

Waiting for Godot: Conclusions

The comparison between these five versions (two French, two Italian and the English) shows clearly that the Italian translation was based on the French version but that in a second edition, a revised translation took into consideration the English text, also.

Fruttero's translations are generally very good, in spite of Beckett's opinion, but certainly the second version sounds even more natural and the dialogue is remarkably smooth, as the translator emended the language and updated it (even though only a few years had intervened between the first and second versions). As for other aspects of the translation, characters use the informal pronoun *tu* and the formal *lei* according to the situation, never the outdated, fascist-sounding *voi*.

As already stated, there is no translation of names in Lucky's monologue, therefore losing possible punning through assonance: the loss of references, literary and otherwise, may have been reduced and compensated by introducing a reference to Quasimodo at the end of Act Two, something Fruttero may have attempted in the first translation. 'Elles accouchent à cheval sur une tombe, le jour brille un instant, puis c'est la nuit à nouveau' (Minuit, 117) is rendered as 'They give birth astride of a grave, the light gleams an instant, then it's night once more' (Faber, 86). In Italian we read: 'Partoriscono a cavallo di una tomba, il giorno splende un istante, ed è subito notte' (Einaudi 1956, 105), 'Partoriscono a cavallo di una tomba, il giorno splende un istante, e poi è di nuovo la notte' (Einaudi 2005, 91). 'Ed è subito notte' is strongly reminiscent of the very famous 'Ed è subito sera', introducing a more resounding translation, with a direct quote from Quasimodo.[27]

From what I have analysed so far, I hope I have demonstrated that the second revised edition of the play in Italian integrates both original versions, French and English, with no attempt at any philological accuracy, thus depriving the Italian reader of any awareness as to the source text he is supposedly reading.

General Conclusions

I will briefly add that the same situation occurs with the translation of *Fin de partie / Endgame*: the first translation certainly employed the French version but subsequently integrated the English one in the collection. The situation is even more complicated than the one just illustrated for *Godot*, since the two versions of the translation (also by Fruttero) appear to have randomly referred to different source texts in the original and revised editions.[28]

According to Gabriele Frasca, even *All That Fall* was translated from the French, and in this case, the accusation is a heavy one because the French translation is not by Beckett, but by his friend Robert Pinget. It is true that at the very beginning, the hinny is translated as *il mulo / il bardotto* instead of *la mula*, as in the French translation, but later on the Italian text has 'è piena d'aria'[29] (feminine adjective) then back again to a male animal: 'smuoverlo', 'prendilo per la briglia', 'voltagli', 'dagli'[30]; the use of jelly in English, *bouse* in French, *marmellata* in Italian seems to suggest that the English version was used as the source text. There are more examples that support this hypothesis, but the issue needs further study.

For *Play*, on the contrary, I think the French version may have been used as main source text: the unusual *voi* in the confrontation between the two

---

[27] Salvatore Quasimodo, 'Ed è subito sera', in *Ed è subito sera*, Milano: Mondadori, 1942, rprt. February 1944, 119.

[28] For a reconstruction of this, see Rossana Sebellin, 'Il teatro di Beckett in Italia: tempo di ritradurre?', in *Ritradurre: forme, prospettive, strategie*, edited by Alessandro Amenta and Chiara Sinatra, *Kwartalnik Neofilologiczny*, LXIX, 2/2022, 268–81. https://journals.pan.pl/Content/123830/PDF/2022-02-KNEO-10-Sebellin.pdf.

[29] Samuel Beckett, *Tutti quelli che cadono*, in Id., *Teatro*, edited by Paolo Bertinetti and translated by Carlo Fruttero, Torino: Einaudi 2005, 155–94 (160).

[30] Ibid., 161.

women; the 'rilievi della signora'[31] where the French *reliefs* stands for leavings (as in the English original) and seems to suggest that the French text was used for the Italian translation; but the invented place names (Borgomalo and Villacenere[32]) seem to be a sort of translation of Ash and Snodland rather than Sept-Sorts et Signy Signet.

For what concerns *Happy Days*, it is difficult to establish which text was used for the Italian translation. According to Fruttero, the French version reached Einaudi but he asked to have the English text as well for comparison:

'For example, I first received *Happy Days* in French […], and I later had the English text sent over to me […] because I wished to see how he had worked on certain passages.'[33]

The case of *Not I* is even more peculiar: translated from the English version, not only because the translator John Francis Lane was British, but also because the translation was carried out before the French play was published. But in this specific case, where style and rhythm are the most important aspects of the play, it would probably have been a good idea to wait for the French version to come out and take it into account. Beckett, in fact, joined some units or split them in order to preserve a similar rhythm and the broken effect.[34] We are all familiar with the quote 'My work is a matter of fundamental sounds (no joke intended), made as fully as possible, and I take responsibility for nothing else',[35] but in the case of *Not I*, this is particularly true. Italian sentences and lexicon are generally longer than English, and more similar to French: in this case the French self-translation could provide a reliable guide.

On the whole, I do not think Fruttero or the other translators provided bad translations in general (even though there are some issues that need to be

---

[31] Samuel Beckett, *Commedia*, in Id. *Teatro*, edited by Paolo Bertinetti and translated by Carlo Fruttero (Torino: Einaudi 2005), 265–90 (274).

[32] Ibid., 276.

[33] Giancarlo Alfano (ed.), 'Traduzioni', *Tegole dal cielo. L'"effetto Beckett" nella cultura italiana*, 243. 'Per esempio *Happy Days* l'ho avuto prima nell'edizione francese […], e poi mi sono fatto spedire anche il testo inglese […] perché volevo vedere come lui avesse risolto certi passaggi'.

[34] See Rossana Sebellin, 'Bilingualism and Bi-textuality in Samuel Beckett's Double Texts', in *The Tragic Comedy of Samuel Beckett*, edited by Daniela Guardamagna and Rossana Sebellin (Bari: Laterza, 2009), 39–71. See also Rossana Sebellin 'Autotraduzione e traduzione allografa: il caso di *Not I / Non io / Pas moi* di Beckett. Stili a confronto', in *trame di letteratura comparata. Style and literary (Self-) Translation*, edited by Alessandra D'Atena and Rossana Sebellin, VI, 6, 2022, 149-163.

[35] Maurice Harmon (ed.), *No Author Better Served*, 24 (Letter dated 29 December 1957).

addressed, especially in the case of *Not I*). But it is certainly true that the situation appears quite unsystematic for what concerns the origin of the translated text and the choices involved. So, going back to my working hypothesis: the translations themselves, apart from some obvious corrections, may not be old, but it is certainly time for a new, more philologically accurate edition.[36]

Bibliography

Alfano, Gianfranco and Andrea Cortellessa (eds). *Tegole dal cielo. La letteratura italiana nell'opera di Samuel Beckett*. Roma: EDUP, 2006.

———. *Tegole dal cielo. L'"effetto Beckett" nella cultura italiana*. Roma: EDUP, 2006.

Beckett, Samuel. *Aspettando Godot*. Torino: Einaudi, 1956.

———. *Aspettando Godot*. In Id. *Teatro*. Edited by Paolo Bertinetti, Torino: Einaudi, 2002 (2005), 3–97.

———. *En attendant / Waiting for Godot: A Bilingual Edition*. New York: Grove Press, nd (1952, 1954).

———. *En attendant Godot*. Paris: Minuit, 1952.

———. *En attendant Godot*. Edited by Germaine Brée and Eric Schoenfeld. Toronto: Collier Macmillan Canada, 1963.

———. *Teatro*. Edited by Paolo Bertinetti, Torino: Einaudi, 2002 (2005).

———. *Teatro completo*. Edited by Paolo Bertinetti, Torino: Einaudi-Gallimard, 1994.

———. *Waiting for Godot*. London: Faber 2010 (with a Preface by Mary Bryden).

Cascetta, Annamaria. *Il tragico e l'umorismo: Studio sulla drammaturgia di Samuel Beckett*. Firenze: Le Lettere, 2000, 2010.

Colomba, Sergio. *Le ceneri della commedia*. Roma: Bulzoni, 1997.

Grutman, Rainier. 'Beckett e oltre: autotraduzioni orizzontali e verticali', in *Autotraduzione e riscrittura*, eds Andrea Ceccherelli, Gabriella Elina Imposti, and Monica Perotto, 45–60. Bologna: Bononia University Press, 2013.

———. 'Self-translation', in *The Routledge Encyclopedia of Translation Studies* (Second Edition), eds Mona Baker and Gabriela Saldanha, 257–60. London and New York: Routledge, 2009.

Harmon, Maurice (ed.). *No Author Better Served: The Correspondence of Samuel Beckett and Alan Schneider*. Cambridge, Massachusetts and London, England: Harvard University Press, 1998.

Sebellin, Rossana 'Autotraduzione e traduzione allografa: il caso di Not I / Non io / Pas moi di Beckett. Stili a confronto', in *trame di letteratura comparata. Style and literary (Self-) Translation*, eds Alessandra D'Atena and Rossana Sebellin, VI, 6, 149–163, 2022.

---

[36] As this chapter was undergoing editorial and publishing processes, Mondadori published a Meridiano devoted to Beckett (*Beckett. Romanzi, teatro e televisione*, 2023) edited by Gabriele Frasca, which contains prose and drama in new translations by Frasca himself. This upmarket, authoritative edition states very clearly which of the two versions written by Beckett is used as a source text for the Italian translation, thus addressing the issue here debated, so far neglected by publishers.

Chapter 9

BECKETT AFTER LANGUAGE

Mena Mitrano

This time around, for some reason, what strikes me about Augustine's description is how isolated the child appears, training its own mouth to form signs (something you might expect of a figure in a Beckett play) [...] Stanley Cavell
– 'The Argument of the Ordinary'.[1]

Abstract

The name 'Italian Theory' has come to refer to a transformative theoretical-critical turn, after poststructuralism, away from the sovereignty of language and towards the larger semantic horizon of life. The shift has determined a return to/of the conflict between language and the body. This article proposes that Samuel Beckett's play, *Not I* (1972), feeds such a renewed interest in the body's interference with the governing works of language. The discussion begins by approaching Beckett's text through Émile Benveniste's notions of subjectivity and enunciation, both ambiguously connected and traversed by a dynamic (and visionary) spatial-bodily dimension. Beckett's attunement to Benveniste, in turn, helps relocate the writer in the contemporary debate on the conflict between language and the body. *Not I* stands out because it is about a physical struggle against speech that suggests Beckett's own search for his own kind of living thought, a thought of 'movement and vitality', as he had phrased it in his early essay on predecessors, 'Dante ... Bruno. Vico.. Joyce.'

Keywords: Samuel Beckett; *Not I*; Émile Benveniste; body; language; Italian Theory

---

[1] Stanley Cavell, 'The Argument of the Ordinary', in Stanley Cavell, *Conditions Handsome and Unhandsome: The Constitution of Emersonian Perfectionism* (Chicago and London: The University of Chicago Press, 1990), 99.

The Scene of Instruction

Not I might be the exemplary Beckett play that Stanley Cavell has in mind in his reflection on the scene of language instruction in Augustine's *Confessions*. Written in 1972, it holds a special place in the Beckett canon: it is a linguistic play, about the possibility of speech. A spotlit mouth eight feet above the darkened stage speaks across from a compassionate auditor in a hooded djellaba, the traditional garment from North Africa.[2] The 'breathless, urgent, feverish, rhythmic' stream of words amplifies the momentous passage from silence to speech.[3] Mouth crosses to her new condition on an April morning, when she initially finds herself 'in the dark', able to hear only a 'buzzing' resembling a 'dull roar' within the skull and see a flickering beam without. Speech comes, trailing along a continuum of sound and light. She relates the event, and the sparse details of her story as a marginal social subject, in 'clipped phrases of three or four words, punctuated by ellipses and questions'.[4] The play revolves precisely on the scene of language instruction, rendering it as a problematic coming to speech that is never fully achieved. The protagonist, Mouth, is surprised at her 'lips moving'; she is surprised at the cheeks, the jaw, the tongue in the mouth; she appraises their movement as if for the first time or under a magnifying glass, marvelling at the bodily reality of speech, a fact that Beckett's script explicitly tarries on: 'the tongue in the mouth [...] all those bodily contorsions without which [...] no speech possible [...] and yet in the ordinary way [...] not felt at all [...] so intent one is [...] on what one is saying [...] the whole being [...] hanging on its words'.[5]

'[A]ll those bodily contorsions without which [...] no speech possible [...]': some stage productions enhance the play's distinctive focus on the apprehension of the irreducible corporeality of speech by doing away with the mysterious

---

[2] It is commonly assumed that Beckett saw the figure in Marocco in 1972. David Pattie, *The Complete Critical Guide to Samuel Beckett* (London and New York: Routledge, 2000), 43.
[3] Beckett quoted in Maurice Harmon, ed., *No Author Better Served: The Correspondence of Samuel Beckett and Alan Schneider* (Cambridge, MA: Harvard University Press, 1998), 283.
[4] Linda Ben-Zvi, *Samuel Beckett* (Boston: Twayne Publishers, 1986), 165.
[5] Samuel Beckett, *Not I*, in *The Complete Dramatic Works* (London: Faber & Faber, 1986), 373–83 (379). All page numbers in the text will be from this edition. I first happened on *Not I* in 2009 while doing research in the New York Public Library for the Performing Arts, where I watched a video of the New York première at the Lincoln Center in the fall of 1972. The play was directed by Alan Schneider, with Jessica Tandy in the role of Mouth, and it was included in the same program with *Krapps' Last Tape* and *Happy Days*, with Tandy's husband Hume Cronyn. My article draws heavily on the memory of that video.

auditor,[6] while in the play's video recording, the camera focuses tightly on a body part – Mouth. The removal of the auditor – the witness who might, even though silently, salute Mouth as a speaking subject, therefore as a social thing: a marginalized older woman to be pitied or empathized with – encourages all the more a reading of the play as a study of the notion of enunciation, in all its peculiarly ambiguous and disorienting entanglement with subjectivity. Beckett's Mouth, in fact, may be seen as the dramaturgical adaptation of the child's predicament in Augustine's scene of instruction, whereby, even as the speaker enunciates as he sees the adults do, he cannot experience himself as an I. Language is somewhere; his embodied self is somewhere else. Similarly, Mouth's birth to speech does not result in the simultaneous assumption of subjectivity. Even after her momentous crossing from silence to speech – an event that has attracted feminist readings – Mouth continues to experience her voice as external to her body: 'a voice she did not recognize'.[7] In compliance with Beckett's stage directions, which impose a 'vehement refusal' of the first person pronoun, Mouth never says 'I', the mark of subjectivity in language (Benveniste). Instead, she refers to herself as 'she', the third person pronoun which Benveniste has defined as a 'non-person', a syntactical representative or stand-in for the unique, embodied person.[8] Because it can be read simultaneously as a play about the impossibility of subjectivity – with the lack of 'a perceiving consciousness' that 'cannot claim her subjectivity'[9] – and the fundamentally alienating nature of language – 'If anyone can say I, then how can I be I?'[10] – *Not I* invites us to access the ambiguous, opaque relation between subjectivity and enunciation.

---

[6] In the 1975 Paris production of the play, Beckett omitted the auditor (Ben-Zvi, *Samuel Beckett*, 166).

[7] Beckett, *Not I*, 379. Written in the early 1970s, *Not I* echoes a central theme in the then-rising feminist thought, and that is precisely woman's birth to speech. The play lends itself perfectly to a feminist reading in which the woman is representative of a female subject traditionally excluded from language and symbolic expression. Linda Ben-Zvi, '*Not I*: Through a Tube Starkly', in *Women in Beckett: Performance and Critical Perspectives*, ed. Linda Ben-Zvi (Urbana and Chicago: University of Illinois Press, 1990), 242–48; Ann Wilson, '"Her Lips Moving": The Castrated Voice of Not I', in *Women in Beckett*, 190–200; Dina Sherzer, 'Portrait of a Woman: The Experience of Marginality in *Not I*,' in *Women in Beckett*, 201–7.

[8] Émile Benveniste, 'The Nature of Pronouns', in *Problems in General Linguistics*, trans. Mary Elizabeth Meek (Coral Gables, FL: University of Miami Press, 1971), 217–22 (221). For work that continues Benveniste's on the third person pronoun as a non-person, see Roberto Esposito, *Terza Persona* (Turin: Einaudi, 2007), especially chapter three, 127–40.

[9] Charles Lyons, *Samuel Beckett* (New York: Grove Press, 1983), 157.

[10] Alan Astro, *Understanding Samuel Beckett* (Columbia: University of South Carolina Press, 1990), 180.

Enunciation

The term 'enunciation' was first circulated by the linguist Émile Benveniste, the same thinker who discovered subjectivity in language. Subjectivity refers to the dialogic dispositive or I-You polarity of persons that, concealed in language, makes for the precondition of speech.[11] In the work of Benveniste, however, the line demarcating subjectivity and enunciation is rather thin. In his 1970 essay 'L'Appareil Formel de l' Énonciation', the term refers to '*the act itself of producing an utterance*, hence not the text of the utterance'.[12] He specified that this act 'refers to the fact of the speaker-agent (*locuteur*) mobilizing language individually for his or her own aims'.[13] Benveniste crucially defined enunciation as 'a process of appropriation': 'the speaker appropriates to himself the formal apparatus of language and enunciates his position as the subject (of what he enunciates), on the one hand, through specific indicators and, on the other hand, via other additional procedures'.[14] This individual act of appropriation 'inserts the speaker in his or her own discourse'.[15] Formulated in this way, enunciation seems to overlap with linguistic subjectivity, which in the essay on 'Subjectivity in Language' is similarly defined as a process of appropriation: 'Language is so organized that it permits each speaker to *appropriate to himself* an entire language by designating himself as I.'[16]

As a matter of fact, the focus on enunciation in the early 1970s seems to develop further the notion of subjectivity proposed in the 1958 essay on 'Subjectivity in Language',[17] this time with special attention to the ostensive pose that accompanies discourse as it is enunciated.[18] The unique person who, in Benveniste's subjectivity essay, designates herself as I, in the enunciation essay *appropriates* linguistic forms to show her position as subject: as someone present to herself at the same time that she shows herself as inserted in her

---

[11] Émile Benveniste, 'Subjectivity in Language', in *Problems in General Linguistics*.
[12] Ibid., 13.
[13] Émile Benveniste, 'L'Appareil Formel de l'Énonciation', *Langages 17* (March 1970): 13.
[14] Ibid., 14.
[15] Ibid.
[16] At this particular point in time, I am working with the Italian translation of Benveniste's essay 'La soggettività nel linguaggio', in *Problemi di Linguistica Generale*, trans. M. Vittoria Giuliani (Milan: Il Saggiatore, 1971), 310–19 (314). See the already cited English version in *Problems in General Linguistics*, trans. Mary Elizabeth Meek, 223–30.
[17] 'Subjectivity in Language' was first published in *Journal de psychologie* 55 (July–September 1958).
[18] Louis Marin and Lionel Duisit, 'The Iconic Text and the Theory of Enunciation: Luca Signorelli at Loreto (Circa 1479–1484)', *New Literary History* 14.3 (Spring 1983): 553–96 (559).

discourse.[19] When wondering about the kind of concrete questions elicited by the notion of enunciation, Marina Sbisà offers this example: an anchorman on the Italian TV reports on the speech of a foreign politician to the citizens of his country: we see 'the face that speaks' (*il volto che parla*), we hear the contents of the speech, in direct speech but in translation. The questions are the following: Who is the enunciator of what we hear? The politician? The anchorman? The translator? And who are the addressees of the enunciation (*enunciatari*): we as viewers? The citizens of the other country? Both?[20] Over time, such questions have encouraged the view that speech is polyphonic and that there is a plurality of enunciators, who might be in a relation of solidarity or of conflict among themselves, as well as a plurality of addressees (*enunciatari*).[21] But the point here is that, as long as enunciation is defined as the process through which someone appropriates (to himself/herself) the production of an utterance, becoming its subject,[22] it calls on us to witness a declaration of presence. Enunciation not only overlaps with the notion of linguistic subjectivity, which implies someone stepping forward as 'I', but also raises the question of the recognition of the subject by the receiver.

The kind of subjectivity recognition we are thinking about is not the same as what in linguistic pragmatics goes by the name of attitude, referring to a judgment issued by the receiver who may approve or refuse the speaker. There is a subjectivity recognition that 'may pre-exist and underlie the linguistic interaction itself', which remains largely understudied.[23] It is, however, a type of subjectivity recognition that we can see at play in Benveniste's concept of enunciation. If enunciation is about 'an act of appropriation' of language,[24] which, in Benveniste's formulation, inserts the speaker in his discourse (*L'énonciation est cette mise en fonctionnement de la langue par un acte individual d'utilisation*), this appropriation is simultaneously a crossing from system (structure) to individual speech, and to its acoustic materiality. The crossing is decided by the fact of the speaker positioning himself/herself as the subject of the production. In other words, the appropriation, as rendered in the thought of Benveniste, also indicates *the movement* in space of someone stepping forward and into that subject position.

---

[19] Benveniste writes: 'La presence du locuteur à son énonciation fait que chaque instance de discours constitute un centre de reference interne.' Benveniste, 'L'Appareil Formel de l'Énonciation', 13–18 (14).

[20] Marina Sbisà, *Linguaggio, Ragione, Interazione: Per una Teoria Pragmatica degli Atti Linguistici* (Bologna: Il Mulino, 1989), 263.

[21] Ibid.

[22] Ibid., 259.

[23] Ibid., 246–47.

[24] Thomas A. Sebeok, ed., *Encyclopedic Dictionary of Semiotics. Vol. 1* (Berlin/New York/Amsterdam: Mouton de Gruyter, 1986), 227.

There is a spatial layer to reckon with, and it has not escaped those who have defined enunciation after Benveniste. The entry for the term in the *Encyclopedic Dictionary of Semiotics* reads 'the phenomenon of enunciation remained for him [Benveniste] essentially an act of appropriation of language by a speaker which permits him to situate himself only in relationship to the world and no more'.[25] 'Situate' and 'relationship to the world' refer precisely to the spatial layer we are talking about.[26] Taking it into consideration has of course, over the past decades, expanded the study of language outside the confines of linguistics and opened up new theoretical perspectives.[27] Yet, the fact remains

---

[25] Ibid.

[26] As it will be inferred later, my argument about Benveniste's engagement of the notion of performance suggests that the enabling pose of the speaking subject is not so much about ontological being but about ontic reality. The enabling pose is not 'in relationship to the world and no more' but implies the regard of a witness.

As Marina Sbisà observed at the end of the 1980s, 'from a rigorously linguistic point of view, such an opening toward the non-verbal in the positing and construction of subjectivity might fall within the competences of a sociology of intersubjective relations' (Sbisà, *Linguaggio, Ragione, Interazione*, 260). After Benveniste, scholars have noted the ambiguity surrounding the concept.

[27] But the ambiguity has become an incentive, rather than an obstruction, to new productive inquiry. Thus, for example, it has caused Oswald Ducrot to introduce fine distinctions between empirical speaker and enunciator. Ducrot opposes the speaker understood as the subject of discourse to the enunciator of a discourse, that is to say, to the voice of someone that does not have the properties I recognize to the speaker but nevertheless 'speaks' in the sense that the enunciation conveys his or her point of view and attitude, even though it may not materially convey his or her words (Renzo Gubert and Luigi Tomasi, eds., *Teoria sociologica ed investigazione empirica. La tradizione della Scuola sociologica di Chicago e le prospettive della sociologia contemporanea* (Milan: Franco Angeli, 1996), 352). Intersecting Bakhtin's dialogism, Ducrot's research has helped to establish the view that speech is polyphonic. Yet, there is a different line of inquiry that more properly reflects the interdisciplinary opening indicated by Sbisà. In this line of inquiry, the ambiguity around enunciation first prompted Greimas and Courtes to pursue the hypothesis of 'a non-linguistic structure underlying linguistic communication' (Sebeok, *Encyclopedic Dictionary of Semiotics*, 226). Then, it expanded significantly to incorporate findings from the philosophy of language and semiotics. In his lead article to the 1970 special issue of *Langages*, 'Problèmes de L'énonciation', Todorov enthusiastically linked enunciation to the rise of a new idea of language as action, an idea imported from anthropological studies of non-Western societies and taken up by British philosopher of language J. L. Austin. Later on, Julia Kristeva, in 'The Phenomenological Subject of Enunciation', part of *Revolution in Poetic Language*, trans. Margaret Waller, introduced by Leon S. Roudiez (New York: Columbia University Press, 1984), 21–24, introduced within theoretical formalism a '"layer" of semiosis' which opened up linguistic inquiry to an ampler idea of the subject marked by a 'dialectical […] trans-linguistic "externality"' (21). Through this second line of inquiry, the questions around enunciation have been recirculated and have reached us through the conjoining of semiotics, psychoanalysis, and speech act theory.

that, in Benveniste, the relation to the world, implicit both in enunciation and in subjectivity, indicates a relation to language. Rather than being just any position in space, this relation suggests some kind of enabling, a frontal pose that exceeds the notion of speaker stance (pragmatics). Benveniste invites us to grasp the process of enunciation as the clean, unimpeded movement of a speaker-agent physically coming to stand in the midst of the heterogeneous torrent of speech, balancing herself in front of the world. It conveys the process that leads the speaker (*locuteur*) to what Beckett in *Not I* calls 'steady stream': '[...] and now this stream [...] steady stream [...] she who had never [...] practically speechless all her days [...] and now this stream [...] not catching the half of it [...]'.[28] As a process of appropriation, therefore, enunciation implies a preeminently kinetic apprehension of the speaker-agent *(showing herself as the subject of the production)*; it implies the elegant motion of a simultaneously corporeal and linguistic accomplishment, which is inbuilt in language. The markers of subjectivity, which in the reality of discourse, comprise the formal apparatus of enunciation – the first person pronoun, deixis, certain adverbs – do not simply signal an appropriation of language by the speaker but also the simultaneous assumption of a 'steady' pose which Benveniste saw as that marvellous opportunity offered to everyone by language only. Tracking the apparatus of enunciation, therefore, might entail envisioning another factor in the speaker's relation to language: the body standing, ready for the movement of speech. *Not I*, with its spotlight on the 'contorsions' of speech magnifies the almost muscular tension towards speech.

The Body in Space

The first person singular pronoun, despite its unique reference,[29] needs authentication by a witness. The compassionate witness originally included in the script on *Not I* is misleading. From this vantage point, Beckett's decision to eliminate the compassionate auditor in some stage productions is interesting. Better an audience who finds the play 'chilling', as director Alan Schneider reported to the playwright, since this kind of reaction focuses more tightly on the responsibility of authentication in the dynamics of reception.[30] The kinetic apprehension of subjectivity underscores the crucial role of the implied witness in the scene of utterance. Benveniste offers a full discussion of the implied witness in 'Analytical Philosophy and Language' (1963), his response to British

---

[28] Beckett, *Not I*, 379.
[29] Benveniste, 'The Nature of Pronouns', 218.
[30] Schneider to Beckett: 'I find it chilling', in Maurice Harmon, *No Author Better Served*, 280.

philosopher J. L. Austin on the topic of performative utterances. The linguist insists on the implied witness as the condition of validity of a performative utterance. In the process, he comes to understand the notion of subjectivity recognition through the notion of performance, deployed in a way that differs significantly from Austin's performatives.

At the start of the essay, Benveniste redefines the task of the linguist to include the study of 'the contexts in which [...] expressions are used to bring to light the implicit principle that governs them'.[31] At the time, this task was the domain of the British school of philosophy called analytical philosophy. Benveniste argues: 'But for linguists, at least for those who do not turn away from the problems of meaning and who consider that the content of the kind of expression is also their domain, such a programme is full of interest.'[32] Having first claimed the domain of meaning for the discipline of linguistics, he proceeds to revise the notion of performative utterance put forth by Austin. He now reminds his readers that in his 1958 essay on subjectivity he had discovered performatives before Austin did:

> while describing subjective forms of the linguistic utterance we gave a brief indication of the difference between *I swear* (a performative utterance in Austin's terminology), which is an action, and *he swears* (a constative) which is nothing but a description of a fact.[33]

At the time, Benveniste continues, 'the terms "performative" and "constative" had not yet appeared, but, nevertheless, that was the substance of their definition. Now the occasion presents itself to extend our views and make them more precise by confronting them with Austin's'.[34] What is at stake is the sense of 'performative' in the phrase 'performative speech acts'.

After identifying two areas in which performative utterances are produced, 'the area of acts of authority' and that of 'personal commitment',[35] he concludes that there are two defining traits to the performative utterance: first, 'a performative utterance has no reality except as it is authenticated as an *act*'[36]; second, a performative utterance 'has existence only as an act of authority'.[37]

---

[31] Émile Benveniste, 'Analytical Philosophy and Language', in *Problems in General Linguistics*, 232.
[32] Ibid.
[33] Ibid., 234.
[34] Ibid.
[35] Ibid., 235.
[36] Ibid., 236.
[37] Ibid.

Both traits, however, hinge on a common condition of validity, that is, that the authority of the speaker be recognized. Benveniste sees performative utterances as an example of the fundamental role of the implied witness in the recognition of the first person as he/she steps forward to enunciate her position as subject. The role of the implied witness in this process had been underestimated by Austin.

For Benveniste, the main condition of validity of a performative utterance is not, as Austin would have it, that it does something, but that the authority of the speaker be recognized:

> Now acts of authority are first and always utterances made by those to whom the right to utter them belongs. This condition of validity, related to the person making the utterance and to the circumstances of the utterance, must always be considered met when one deals with the performative.[38]

The way in which Benveniste understands the authority of the speaker here opens up a process of subjectivity recognition that will completely fade in the work of later scholars who rely on Austin to unpack the scene of utterance in terms of the discourse-power nexus. A prime example is, of course, Judith Butler. Here is her influential reworking of Austin's performatives:

> Implicated in a network of authorization and punishment, performatives tend to include legal sentences, baptisms, inaugurations, declarations of ownership, statements which not only perform an action but confer a binding power on the action performed.[39]

Butler's point is that performatives illustrate 'the power of discourse to produce that which it names'.[40] In other words, '[t]he performative is one domain in which power acts as discourse'.[41] Unlike Austin and his followers, Benveniste sees performative utterances as a concrete version of the same process of recognition which, in different degrees, underlies both the concept of subjectivity and enunciation. When working on these concepts, he had rendered the process in terms of space and movement. This is because for Benveniste, more than revealing a political network of domination, performative speech acts manifest the embodiment of the speaker; they

---

[38] Ibid.
[39] Judith Butler, *Bodies that Matter: On the Discursive Limits of 'Sex'* (London & New York: Routledge, 1993), 225.
[40] Ibid.
[41] Ibid.

testify to 'the traces of performative energy coursing through' the abstract notion of subjectivity.[42] Performative utterances underscore the uniqueness of the speaker and the unrepeatable quality of the utterance as a historical act. What interests us here is that Benveniste's engagement of the idea of performance thrusts into relief a different idea of subjectivity recognition:

> It [a performative utterance] cannot be produced except in special circumstances, at one and only one time, at a definite date and place. It does not have the value of description or prescription but, once again, of *performance*. This is why it is often accompanied by indications of date, of place, of names of people, witnesses, etc.; in short, it is an event because it *creates* the event.[43]

As used by Benveniste, 'performance' suggests a kinetic perception by the witness of the subject's pose, within a felicitous arrangement before the world. His criterion for the validity of a performative utterance comes from his 1958 subjectivity essay but also constitutes a new development. There is a marked emphasis on authority, in the sense of an almost ritualistic recognition of subjectivity within a spatial arrangement. This ritualistic recognition of the first person combines with an equally marked emphasis on the uniqueness of the performative utterance to evoke the theatrical sense in which Benveniste deploys 'performance' in his attempt to draw a distinction between himself and Austin.[44]

Unlike Austin, who associated performance with the power of language *to do* things, Benveniste understands performance in a more theatrical sense, not however in the sense of traditional theatre, but in a sense that is closer to performance *art* – as a certain, unrepeatable, self-referential arrangement of agents in space. Performance art emphasizes precisely unique and unrepeatable circumstances. The 'bodies of the performers are foregrounded or exhibited on their own terms' often in untheatrical settings.[45] He is less

---

[42] I am borrowing the expression from Richard Poirier, who used it to talk about Frank O'Hara's poetry in *Trying It Out in America* (New York: Farrar, Straus & Giroux, 1999).

[43] Benveniste, 'Analytical Philosophy and Language', 236.

[44] Benveniste's performative utterance belabours the I-you mutuality at the core of the 'Subjectivity in Language' essay. When I set himself up as a subject by referring to myself as I in my discourse, I also posits another person, one who, 'being, completely exterior to "me," becomes my echo to whom I say you and who says you to me' (Benveniste, 'Subjectivity in Language', 225). This mutuality is the rudimentary form of the implied witness that recognizes the authority of the speaker of the performative utterance.

[45] Tracy C. Davis and Postlewait, eds., *Theatricality* (Cambridge: Cambridge University Press, 2003), 25–26.

interested in asserting that performatives have the force of law and more in defining performatives as utterances that 'relate to the person of the speaker': 'Alongside acts of authority publishing decisions that have the force of law, there are utterances of pledges that relate to the person of the speaker: I swear [...], I promise [...], I make a vow, etc.'.[46] These utterances are 'historical and individual' acts which, similarly to performance art, foreground the dynamic, kinetic apprehension of the speaker by a witness.[47] He insists on the person of the speaker and on the fact that the witness is first of all called to recognize the enabling pose of subjectivity. Correcting Austin, he argues: 'Any verb of speaking, even the most common of all, the verb say, is capable of forming a performative utterance if the formula, *I say* [...]., uttered in the *appropriate conditions*, creates a new situation.'[48]

Just as in performance art the unique setting is functional to the recognition of the bodies of the performers, so in performative utterances, the appropriate conditions or unique arrangement in space are functional to the recognition of the embodied person saying 'I' and thereby setting himself up as the subject. The unrepeatable arrangement is 'the event that creates the event', that is, the authority of the speaker. The emphasis on the appropriate conditions opens the notion of authority to an almost ritualistic recognition of the speaker who *by* 'identifying himself as a unique person pronouncing I' comes into the pose of the subject.[49] As the linguistic and the theatrical meanings of *performance* blend, we are invited to unpack the scene of utterance as a slowed down ritual in which the unique reference of the first person must nevertheless come forward to be authenticated so that the speaker designating himself as 'I' can appear as if in 'a process of estrangement'[50] from a distance, in a deictic projection, held up for authentication in a solemn pose that is just as hypnotic as the music of Philip Glass.[51]

Benveniste's scene of recognition blazes the trail for the pulsing rhythm or repetitive buzzing that Beckett's Mouth hears in her brain all the time: 'for

---

[46] Benveniste, 'Analytical Philosophy and Language', 235.
[47] The full passage reads: 'Being an individual and historical act, a performative utterance cannot be repeated. Each reproduction is a new act performed by someone who is qualified. Otherwise, the reproduction of the performative utterance by someone else necessarily transforms it into a constative utterance' (Benveniste, 'Analytical Philosophy and Language', 236).
[48] My emphasis (Benveniste, 'Analytical Philosophy and Language', 236).
[49] Benveniste, 'The Nature of Pronouns', 220.
[50] Davis and Postlewait, *Theatricality*, 26.
[51] For a similar description of Glass's music, see Arlene Croce, 'Slowly Then the History of Them Comes Out', in *Writing in the Dark, Dancing in the New Yorker* (Gainesville, Tallahassee: University Press of Florida, 2000), 314–24, 316.

she could still hear the buzzing [...]'.[52] The buzzing cannot be defined ('so-called'): it's in the ear but it also transforms into a 'dull roar in the skull'.[53] Simultaneously: 'all the time this ray or beam [...] like moonbeam'.[54] Speech begins with a sentient someone trapped in the luminous pounding of uncertain sounds, whose trial is to be transformed from spectator to active participant.

To grasp the importance of this particular engagement of performance, it might be useful to compare Benveniste's response to Austin to Jacques Derrida's more celebrated reply to the British philosopher in 'Signature Event Context' (1971), where Derrida demolished Austin's difference between constative and performative utterances. The response was prompted by the following key passage from Austin:

> [A] performative utterance will, for example, be in a peculiar way hollow or void if said by an actor on the stage, or if introduced in a poem, or spoken in soliloquy. This applies in a similar manner to any and every utterance–a sea-change in special circumstances. Language in such circumstances is in special ways – intelligibly – used not seriously, but in ways parasitic upon its normal use – ways which fall under the doctrine of the etiolations of language. All this we are excluding from consideration.[55]

To which Derrida objected:

> Is not what Austin excludes as anomalous, exceptional, 'nonserious,' that is, citation (on stage, in a poem, or in soliloquy), the determined modification of a general citationality – or rather, a general iterability – without which there would not even be a 'successful performative'?[56]

Clearly, Derrida is invested in demolishing the difference between ordinary and theatrical speech. He initiates a hybridisation of the word 'performative' to refer both to a specific kind of utterance (which emblematically illustrates the thesis that language is a form of action) and to performance, in the sense of theatre or fictional representation. He derives from his critique of Austin's performatives a notion of performativity – also called citationality – that

---

[52] Beckett, 'Not I', 378.
[53] Ibid.
[54] Ibid.
[55] Austin qtd. in Eve K. Sedgwick and Andrew Parker, 'Introduction: Performativity and Performance', in *Performativity and Performance*, eds. Eve K. Sedgwick and Andrew Parker (London and New York: Routledge, 1995), 3.
[56] Derrida qtd. in Sedgwick and Parker, 'Introduction', 3–4.

is closer to repetition than to the kinaesthetic apprehension of the speaker-agent that I have been discussing so far. But Derrida's reading of Austin ironically voids the scene of utterance precisely of the performance element in which Benveniste had immersed it. Although it comes into being to dismantle the boundary between ordinary and theatrical speech set up by Austin, Derrida's version of performativity seems completely steeped in traditional scripted theatre, in which a text is repeated in recitation by many different actors.

Judging from his own response to Austin, Benveniste would agree with Derrida that it is wrong to exclude fictional or theatrical utterances as parasitic. In fact, that is not the point if we are trying to understand what a performative utterance is. As Benveniste specified, 'even a verb of speaking, *I say* [...], can produce a change' provided it is uttered by someone who is recognized as the authoritative subject in the appropriate situation. 'Appropriate situation' does not pit ordinary speech vs. theatre, or conversation vs. poem, as in Austin; rather, it underscores the recognition by the implied witness of the speaker as an authoritative subject. The concern of Benveniste remains the uniqueness of the I and of the utterance, which seem inseparable from a visual, kinetic apprehension by the implied witness of the person designating himself as 'I'. By contrast, Derrida is more invested in denying the coherence of the notion of a person. As a scholar of language, Benveniste is expected to know already what Beckett tried to stage, that is, that body and voice are not one and the same, that we experience our voice as other from our body. But Derrida's idea of citationality congeals the question of language in a vista of graphemes detached from meaning. Consequently, it departs from the fundamental problem of the transition from language to discourse (from which enunciation derives), and more importantly from a performative speaking subject in the sense of Benveniste, linked, that is, to the appropriate spatial arrangement for the linguistic and kinetic apprehension of an embodied someone who comes to language.

In the Austin–Derrida tradition, the sense of space and movement and the provocative gesture/action of the speaker inserting herself in her own discourse, so important in Benveniste, are sacrificed. The question of linguistic subjectivity is also lost, since the speaking subject is thought to participate in a metaphorics of presence that must be destroyed. From this viewpoint, the ambiguous relation between subjectivity and enunciation no longer makes sense.[57]

---

[57] The main difference between Derrida and Benveniste lies precisely in the theoretical use to which they put the linguistic performative. Recapping Derrida's reading of Austin, Andrew Parker and Eve Sedgwick recall that Derrida collapsed Austin's distinction between ordinary and theatrical speech and 'regarded both as structured by a generalized iterability, a pervasive theatricality common to stage and world alike' (Sedgwick and Parker, 'Introduction', 4).

After Language

The 'self-sufficiency of language' has been a key theme in Beckett's studies, so much so that in the recent past, the question has developed of an affinity between Beckett's work and poststructuralism.[58] As Anthony Uhlmann observed in the late 1990s, the problem in Beckett is that of being 'brought into consciousness through language', of being 'ply[ed]' with language by others.[59] Recently, however, the emergence of Italian Theory has called attention to the need to retell the poststructuralist story of the centrality of language. Philosopher Roberto Esposito reconstructs a line of reflection that is eccentric to poststructuralism, not because it rejects language, but because language is 'interrogated in its autonomous structure', and envisions a new theoretical turn that includes the linguistic turn within the broader paradigm of life.[60] What Esposito calls *pensiero vivente*, living thought, suggests 'the inadequacy of the linguistic horizon with regard to something that is irreducibly bodily', something that 'presses against [the] metaphorical and metonymical boundaries' of language.[61]

---

[58] Benjamin Keatinge writes that the work of Beckett is 'prescient of much poststructuralist thinking' (Benjamin Keatinge, 'Foreword', in Arthur Broomfield, *The Empty Too: Language and Philosophy in the Works of Samuel Beckett* (Cambridge: Cambridge Scholars Publisher, 2014) ix–xi, x).

[59] Anthony Uhlmann, 'The same and the other: Beckett's *The Unnamable*, Derrida and Levinas', in *Law Text Culture 3* (1997): 131. Uhlmann discusses Derrida and Beckett's common ground on the 'otherness of language': 'language is the relation *to/of* originary nonpresence and this non-presence moves symmetrically *(to/of)* between the same and the other. Language carries with it the trace of the other even where there is no phenomenon of the other.[…] As language can only describe through signifying rather than being, it cannot bring the same into true present being, only to a non-presence always at one remove from a "true presence" that can only ever be "sensed" (with this intuition itself constituting a sensation which is a phenomenon that can only signify).' Hence, the motif in Beckett (see *The Unnamable*) of not being 'caught', not being 'delivered' – the missing I or me. See Uhlmann, 'The same and the other', 127–47 (134).

[60] Roberto Esposito, *Pensiero Vivente: Origine e attualità della filosofia italiana* (Torino: Einaudi, 2010), 10. See also Giusi Strummiello, 'Tra biologizzazione dell'esistenza e storicizzazione della vita', *Ágalma* 38 (October 2019): 55–69.

[61] Esposito, *Pensiero Vivente*, 10. It is helpful to recall that the Beckett canon begins with an article that celebrates Joyce as the heir of Dante, Bruno and Vico. Beckett assimilates the modernist master to an axis of reflection which, with the addition of other thinkers (Machiavelli, most notably), suggests the search for a thought of 'movement and vitality', for a 'sensuous untidy art of intellection' (Samuel Beckett, 'Dante… Bruno. Vico.. Joyce', in *Disjecta: Miscellaneous Writings and a Dramatic Fragment*, ed. Ruby Cohn (London: John Calder, 1983), 33).

Italian Theory is only an example of the widespread contemporary need for retelling the story of language. The retelling is bound to impact Beckett Studies. As Dirk Van Hulle has observed, if the role of language was central in Beckett's criticism in the 1980s and 1990s, it has been reassessed recently, in step with the urge to move beyond 'language-centred poststructuralist criticism'.[62] *Not I* seems to be keyed well into this reassessment, and the reason for its attunement is that the play insists, as Italian Theory does, on the disjunction between body and speech.

Mouth, it would be helpful to recall, is the most demanding role in Beckett's theatrical repertoire as witnessed by the experience of the actresses. Both Jessica Tandy, who performed the first Mouth at the New York première, and Billie Whitelaw, who performed it at the Royal Court Theatre in London, emphasize the 'physical discomfort' involved in presenting the stage image.[63] In the case of Whitelaw, for example, she 'sat 10 feet high on a tall podium in a chair' and in James Knowlson's reconstruction, 'Her entire body was draped in black, so that it was not discernible in the darkness and only her mouth was illuminated by two spots from below, hidden by a screen from the audience; her body was strapped into the chair with a belt around her waist; her head was clamped firmly between two pieces of sponge rubber, so that her mouth could not move out of the spotlight, and the top part of her face was covered with black gauze with a black transparent strip for her eyes. And a bar was fixed […] to which the actress could cling and on to which she could direct her tension'.[64] Even though it presents itself as a play on speaking, *Not I* stands out because it is about the physical struggle against speech. It suggests how, to use Esposito's words, it is language that 'makes the body into a subject'.[65] Language entails, writes Felice Cimatti, 'the power to alter and control the body'[66]; it is 'essentially order, command, discipline': 'through language we enter society'.[67] The I must seize the word; yet, failure to do so is on display in Beckett's *Not I*.

---

[62] Connor qtd. in Dirk Van Hulle, 'Introduction: A Beckett Continuum', in *The New Cambridge Companion to Samuel Beckett* (Cambridge: Cambridge University Press, 2015), xxi.

[63] James Knowlson, *Damned to Fame: The Life of Samuel Beckett* (London: Bloomsbury, 1996), 596.

[64] Ibid., 597.

[65] Esposito, *Pensiero Vivente*, 15. 'E' il linguaggio che fa del corpo un soggetto.' For the modernist atmospheres of pensiero vivente, see Enrica Lisciani Petrini, 'La vita e le forme. Uno scorcio sul pensiero italiano primonovecentesco, e oltre', *Ágalma* 38 (October 2019): 35–44.

[66] Felice Cimatti, *La vita estrinseca. Dopo il linguaggio* (Napoli-Salerno: Orthotes, 2018), 17.

[67] Ibid., 19.

To close where we opened, with Stanley Cavell, what one discovers in Beckett, 'is not the failure of meaning (if that means the lack of meaning) but [...] our inability not to mean what we are given to mean'.[68] Here, Cavell refers to *Endgame*, but the discovery is assumed in *Not I*. When she speaks, Mouth is used by language, a fact illustrated by the physical trials of the actresses described above. If, as Cavell says, with reference to the major plays, 'the medium of Beckett's dialogues is repartee', the 'contest of wits', the taste/sound of victory and humiliation,[69] the monologue of *Not I* abandons all that to tarry in another zone. This is why, even though it is not a prayer, the play feels like a prayer: the invocation of a circular, recursive temporality – day after day, a day after another – a temporality of grace ('[...] tender mercies [...] new every morning') – countering the slicing of which language is capable.

Bibliography

Astro, Alan. *Understanding Samuel Beckett*. Columbia: University of South Carolina Press, 1990.

Beckett, Samuel. 'Dante... Bruno. Vico. Joyce'. In *Disjecta: Miscellaneous Writings and a Dramatic Fragment*, edited with a foreword by Ruby Cohn, 19–33. London: John Calder, 1983.

———. *Not I*. In *The Complete Dramatic Works*, 373–83. London: Faber & Faber, 1986.

Ben-Zvi, Linda. '*Not I*: Through a Tube Starkly'. In *Women in Beckett: Performance and Critical Perspectives*, edited by Linda Ben-Zvi, 242–48. Urbana and Chicago: University of Illinois Press, 1990.

———. *Samuel Beckett*. Boston: Twayne Publishers, 1986.

Benveniste, Émile. 'Analytical Philosophy and Language'. In *Problems in General Linguistics*, translated by Mary Elizabeth Meek, 231–38. Coral Gables, FL: University of Miami Press, 1971a.

———. 'L'Appareil Formel de l'Énonciation'. *Languages* 17 (March 1970): 13–18.

———. 'La soggettività nel linguaggio'. In *Problemi di Linguistica Generale*, translated by M. Vittoria Giuliani, 310–19. Milan: Il Saggiatore, 1971b.

———. 'Subjectivity in Language'. In *Problems in General Linguistics*, translated by Mary Elizabeth Meek, 223–30. Coral Gables, FL: University of Miami Press, 1971c.

———. 'The Nature of Pronouns'. In *Problems in General Linguistics*, translated by Mary Elizabeth Meek, 217–22. Coral Gables, FL: University of Miami Press, 1971d.

Butler, Judith. *Bodies that Matter: On the Discursive Limits of 'Sex'*. London & New York: Routledge, 1993.

Cavell, Stanley. 'Ending the Waiting Game'. In *Must We Mean What We Say?* 115–62. Cambridge, MA: Cambridge University Press, 2002.

Cimatti, Felice. *La vita estrinseca. Dopo il linguaggio*. Napoli-Salerno: Orthotes, 2018.

---

[68] Stanley Cavell, 'Ending the Waiting Game', in *Must We Mean What We Say?* (Cambridge: Cambridge University Press, 2002), 117.

[69] Ibid., 127.

Croce, Arlene. 'Slowly Then the History of Them Comes Out'. In *Writing in the Dark, Dancing in the New Yorker*, 314–24. Gainesville, Tallahassee: University Press of Florida, 2000.
Davis, Tracy C. and Thomas Postlewait, eds. *Theatricality*. Cambridge: Cambridge University Press, 2003.
Derrida, Jacques. 'Signature Event Context'. In *Limited Inc.*, translated by Samuel Weber, 1–23. Evanston, IL: Northwestern University Press, 1988.
Esposito, Roberto. *Pensiero Vivente: Origine e attualità della filosofia italiana*. Torino: Einaudi, 2010.
———. *Terza Persona. Politica della vita e filosofia dell'impersonale*. Torino: Einaudi, 2007.
Gubert, Renzo and Luigi Tomasi, eds. *Teoria sociologica ed investigazione empirica. La tradizione della Scuola sociologica di Chicago e le prospettive della sociologia contemporanea*. Milan: Franco Angeli, 1996.
Harmon, Maurice, ed. *No Author Better Served: The Correspondence of Samuel Beckett and Alan Schneider*. Cambridge, MA: Harvard University Press, 1998.
Keatinge, Benjamin. 'Foreword'. In *The Empty Too: Language and Philosophy in the Works of Samuel Beckett*, edited by Arthur Broomfield, ix–xi. Cambridge: Cambridge Scholars Publisher, 2014.
Knowlson, James. *Damned to Fame: The Life of Samuel Beckett*. London: Bloomsbury, 1996.
Kristeva, Julia. 'The Phenomenological Subject of Enunciation'. In *Revolution in Poetic Language*, translated by Margaret Waller, introduced by Leon S. Roudiez, 21–24. New York: Columbia University Press, 1984.
Lisciani-Petrini, Enrica. 'La vita e le forme. Uno scorcio sul pensiero italiano primonovecentesco, e oltre'. *Ágalma* 38 (October 2019): 35–44.
Lyons, Charles. *Samuel Beckett*. New York: Grove Press, 1983.
Marin, Louis and Lionel Duisit. 'The Iconic Text and the Theory of Enunciation: Luca Signorelli at Loreto (Circa 1479–1484)'. *New Literary History* 14.3 (Spring 1983): 553–96.
Pattie, David. *The Complete Critical Guide to Samuel Beckett*. London and New York: Routledge, 2000.
Porier, Richard. *Trying It Out In America: Literary and Other Performances*. New York: Farrar, Straus & Giroux, 1999.
Sbisà, Marina. *Linguaggio, Ragione, Interazione: Per una Teoria Pragmatica degli Atti Linguistici*. Bologna: Il Mulino, 1989.
Sebeok, Thomas A., ed. *Encyclopedic Dictionary of Semiotics. Vol. 1*. Berlin/New York/Amsterdam: Mouton de Gruyter, 1986.
Sedgwick, Eve K. and Andrew Parker. 'Introduction: Performativity and Performance'. In *Performativity and Performance*, edited by Eve K. Sedwick and Andrew Parker, 1–18. London and New York: Routledge, 1995.
Sherzer, Dina 'Portrait of a Woman: The Experience of Marginality in *Not I*'. In *Women in Beckett: Performance and Critical Perspectives*, edited by Linda Ben-Zvi, 201–7. Urbana and Chicago: University of Illinois Press, 1990.
Strummiello, Giusi. 'Tra biologizzazione dell'esistenza e storicizzazione della vita'. *Ágalma* 38 (October 2019): 55–69.
Uhlmann, Anthony. 'The Same and the Other: Beckett's *The Unnamable*, Derrida and Levinas'. *Law Text Culture* 3 (1997): 127–47.
Van Hulle, Dirk. 'Introduction: A Beckett Continuum'. In *The New Cambridge Companion to Samuel Beckett*, edited by Dirk Van Hulle. xvii–xxvi. Cambridge: Cambridge University Press, 2015, https://doi.org/10.1017/CCO9781139871525.
Wilson, Ann. '"Her Lips Moving": The Castrated Voice of Not I'. In *Women in Beckett: Performance and Critical Perspectives*, edited by Linda Ben-Zvi, 190–200. Urbana and Chicago: University of Illinois Press, 1990.